Designing with
Flash Memory

*The definitive guide to
designing flash memory
hardware and software
for components and
PCMCIA cards*

Designing with
Flash Memory

Brian Dipert & Markus Levy

The definitive guide to designing flash memory hardware and software for components and PCMCIA cards

Annabooks
San Diego

Designing with Flash Memory

BY

BRIAN DIPERT & MARKUS LEVY

PUBLISHED BY

Annabooks
11848 Bernardo Plaza Ct., Suite 110
San Diego, CA 92128
USA

619-673-0870

Printed in the United States of America

ISBN 0-929392-17-5
Second Printing April 1994

Acknowledgements

Both Brian and Markus would like to thank their colleagues at Intel Corporation. Knowingly (or unknowingly), their knowledge and expertise was a superb resource base for answers to questions we uncovered as we wrote. Special recognition goes out to Dave Cobb, Russ Eslick, Kurt Robinson, John Garney, Clark Thurlo, Peter Torelli, Steve Wells, Saul Zales, Greg Komoto, Larry Leszczynski, and John Williams; thanks, guys! Thanks also goes out to Wink Saville at Saville Associates, David Lawrence at Ventura Micro, and Amir Ban at M-Systems.

Several years of staffing the customer and sales force support hotline at Intel have also taught us what *not* to do when designing with flash memory (and also given us some great ideas we hadn't considered ourselves). To the salespersons and design engineers we've worked with; thanks for an inexhaustible list of topics for this book. We hope we've included answers for at least most of the questions you've asked us!

To our "partner in crime" Mary Ann Hooker (You Know), a big round of applause for the great graphics work and for putting up with us and our seemingly endless revisions. If it weren't for you, the figures would have looked like kindergarden crayon work!

Markus: "Words cannot express the thanks and love that I give to Danielle for all her support and for all the times she patiently listened to me say 'It's almost done'. Well it's finally done. Thank you to Jacob (although you can't read this yet) for being a great kid while your Dad worked, worked and worked."

Brian: "I give thanks to the Creator God, to my family back in Indiana (thanks for all your encouragement!) and to Lil, for patiently putting up with all those nights and weekends I spent looking at a computer monitor instead of at her. I hereby retire the notebook PC (at least for a while) and echo Markus' comment......it's finally done!".

The publisher and editor would like to extend his thanks to Marco Thompson and Gary Lorenc of Doctor Design, Inc. and to Ray Weiss of EDN who reviewed the book on a very tight schedule while it was still in three ring binder form. Thanks also to Rich Sjoberg who did the artwork for the cover.

Cover design by John P. Choisser, Annabooks.

Cover photo by Peter Menzel, Napa, California (707-255-3528). Peter caught this lightning bolt along with dozens of others one night in Tucson, Arizona. For more of Peter's work, see the *National Geographic* July 1993 issue. Peter has taken photos all over the world for *Geo, Life, Forbes, Stern, U.S. News & World Report, Smithsonian, The New York Times Magazine*, and many others. The glow at the bottom of this bolt is probably not the flash memory at the University of Arizona being re-programmed all at once. It is more likely the stadium, which puts out a pretty healthy glow of its own, lighting or no.

Contents

Figures

Tables

Foreword

Throughout the last five years, two major trends have shaped system usage of flash memory. Density has increased at the significant rate taken by a mainstream technology, and the cost has dropped below various traditional memories. Looking out over the coming years, these trends will continue and flash memory will alter the memory system architecture defined in the 70's and 80's.

Production volumes of the first 256-kbit flash memory started shipping in 1988. By 1992, multiple companies announced capability of 4 Mbit, 8 Mbit and even 16 Mbit densities. These densities, in a cost-effective, re-writable, non-volatile memory, provide designers with alternatives for sophisticated microprocessor-based designs. Rapid increases in the densities of flash memory, combined with the software upgrade assumption, have created "flash points" in many general computing systems.

Beyond code storage, designers have adopted flash memory for parameter and data storage. The amount of firmware or data storage and its usage in various applications has depended on the rapid decline in price points of the technology. In 1988, OEMs purchased 1 MByte of flash memory for $640. From that starting point, the price per megabyte has steadily dropped to $240 in '89, to $90 in '90-91, and to $30 in '92-93. This drop has enabled different classes of machines within an application family to adopt flash memory over time.

Another market dynamic helped accelerate the pace of "flash points" in 1993. OEMs who had adopted flash technology between '88 and '90 helped define the critical elements of the second generation flash product features. These products hit the market in 1991 and 1992. The features included erase blocking (symmetrical and asymmetrical for different applications), lockable "boot blocks," embedded write and erase algorithm automation, and ultra-low "power-down" functions. From this feature evolution, one can see another round of "flash points" in the areas of high volume PC BIOS and portable systems of all types.

Designers in 1991 and 1992 opened their imaginations and started defining new system features, capabilities and even new classes of systems. They broke with the traditional approaches of slicing the system memory budgets, as seen in the following examples. A notebook PC today may have only $15 of flash memory, relative to $100 of DRAM and $250 of hard disk. On the other hand, a Personal Digital Assistant may have $30 of resident flash memory, relative to $30 of SRAM, $20 multi-purpose PC card slot, and $0 for a hard disk. The PC card slot enables system expansion through flash memory and I/O cards.

Other applications that have started redistribution of the memory budget include data and telecommunication systems, printers, workstations, diskless terminals and POS terminals. These systems may balance kilobytes of fast cache SRAM, with megabytes of DRAM, and megabytes of either resident or removable flash memory. The flash memory in these applications improve network efficiencies or provide reliable local storage. In general, designers have recognized that the memory hierarchy established with the technologies available in the early 1970s, limits the system architecture in some way, thus creating additional "flash points". More will come over the coming years through the creativity of system designers allowed to dream.

Saul Zales
Components Marketing Manager
Intel Flash Cards and Components

Preface

Several years ago when the authors first began working at Intel, the flash memory industry was still in its infancy. This simple and relatively expensive (at that time) memory device was primarily being used as an EPROM or EEPROM replacement, but creative-minded people like Bruce McCormick (Intel's Director of Marketing for flash memory) and Dick Pashley (Intel's Flash Memory Divisional Manager) saw a great future for flash memory as a solid-state disk drive media and DRAM replacement. The evolving versatility of flash memory has allowed it to play a significant (and very interesting) role in optimizing the performance of many different applications.

Many articles, application notes and datasheets have been written to date on flash memory. However, this is the first comprehensive book on the subject. It combines the best of previously written literature and the latest information, along with the detailed, experienced knowledge of the authors, all in one binding.

Keeping up with the rapidly changing flash memory industry was a significant challenge. Although basic flash memory concepts often remained the same, in the course of the one year it took to write this book, many new technologies and devices were introduced and many new flash memory manufacturers entered the market. In some cases, it was very difficult to separate sensationalism and marketing "hype" from reality when deciding what to include and leave out. Given the pace of this industry, we'll probably soon begin work on the second edition........

By far the greatest challenge in writing *Designing with Flash Memory* was the sacrifice of (almost) every weekend, weeknight and vacation day so that we could provide you with this informative and enjoyable reference on flash memory (and return to our normal lives as soon as possible). Should you have any inputs on the book, whether positive or constructive (negative), feel free to contact the publisher at Annabooks. Happy Reading!

Brian and Markus
September 9, 1993

Chapter One: Introduction

Flash memory is the subject of this book; what it is, where it can be used (and why) and how it is integrated in system designs. At the time of this book's publishing, flash memory has been manufactured in volume for only five years, but in this short time frame it has achieved tremendous industry acceptance and rapid year-to-year volume shipment growth. As Figure 1.1 shows, business analysts predict a continuous and unabated growth throughout the forseeable future.

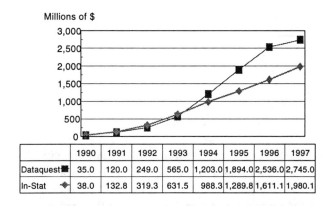

		1990	1991	1992	1993	1994	1995	1996	1997
Dataquest	■	35.0	120.0	249.0	565.0	1,203.0	1,894.0	2,536.0	2,745.0
In-Stat	◆	38.0	132.8	319.3	631.5	988.3	1,289.8	1,611.1	1,980.1

Figure 1.1: The Exploding Flash Memory Market

What's driving the interest in, and subsequently the success of, flash memory? Certainly its unique characteristics and capabilities, to be discussed throughout the book, represent part of the reason. However, flash memory is also relatively easy and economical to manufacture, and its cell architecture is comparatively simpler than other semiconductor memory approaches (see Figure 1.2).

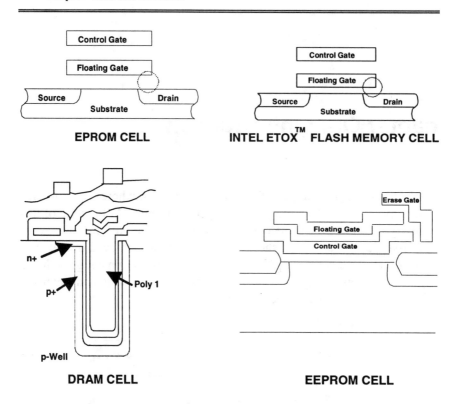

Figure 1.2: Flash Memory Cell Simplicity Enables Cost-Effective Manufacturing

Manufacturing ease, in combination with a simple cell architecture, contributes to lower cost and ultimately results in lower memory pricing. Just as enhanced features enable flash memory usage in more and more applications (as detailed in Table 1.1), pricing that crosses certain price points impels companies to begin using flash memory instead of the technologies they had previously used. Figure 1.3 shows industry predictions for flash memory pricing through the next several years.

LITHOGRAPHY	PACKAGING	DENSITY	$ PER MByte	# OF CYCLES	SPEED	APPLICATION
1.2 micron	DIP/PLCC	64 Kbit - 256 Kbit	$200	100	200 ns	Minimal-update, low-density code storage. Small lookup tables.
1.0 micron	TSOP	512Kbit - 2Mbit	$50-200	10,000	120 ns	High-density code storage. Data acquisition
0.8 micron	PSOP/TSOP/ Die	4Mbit - 8Mbit	$30-50	100,000	60 ns	High performance disk emulation Flash memory cards Resident flash arrays

Table 1.1: Flash Memory Evolution and Innovation
Broaden the Application Base

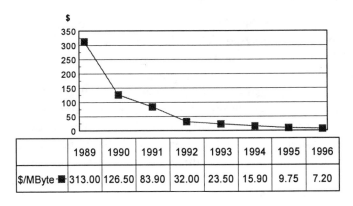

	1989	1990	1991	1992	1993	1994	1995	1996
$/MByte	313.00	126.50	83.90	32.00	23.50	15.90	9.75	7.20

Figure 1.3: Average Selling Price for 1 Mbyte of
Flash Memory Storage (Dataquest)

FLASH MEMORY COMPARED TO OTHER MEMORIES

A description of what flash memory is (and isn't), is most easily obtained by first defining the more established memory alternatives; ROM, RAM, EEPROM, and magnetic mass storage. By outlining flash memory characteristics in these terms, both its relative features, capabilities, and applications are most apparent.

ROM (Read-Only-Memory)

ROM is nonvolatile, but not in-system updateable. This memory family has several members (ROM, PROM, and EPROM), with varying degrees of flexibility of use differentiating them. ROM memories store permanent code and data that is required to initialize and operate a system and that must be accessible at relatively high speed (differentiating ROMs from magnetic disk drives, for example). Most ROM technologies employ a single transistor per cell and are therefore capable of high per-device memory densities.

RAM (Random-Access-Memory)

RAM is in-system updateable; rewriting of RAM contents is easily and quickly done by the system CPU. However, the affordable variety of RAM, dynamic RAM (DRAM), is volatile; memory contents do not retain their stored values when power is removed. DRAM stores temporary data and also shadows the contents of both ROM memory and magnetic mass storage during normal system operation for high-speed access. Another variety of RAM, battery-backed static RAM (SRAM), integrate a battery to retain stored data when system power is removed. These batteries are, of course, ultimately volatile and are also sensitive to temperature variations. In addition, SRAM is considerably more expensive than DRAM.

Each DRAM cell consists of a transistor and a capacitor that must be refreshed, or re-written occasionally due to leakage, to retain stored contents. DRAM today is the "technology driver", or lead product on a new manufacturing process, for many semiconductor companies. SRAM requires no periodic refresh and has faster access time, but trades off density and cost; SRAMs typically use between four and six transistors per cell, impacting attainable device densities and significantly increasing memory cost at a given density, relative to DRAM.

EEPROM (Electrically-Eraseable-Programmable-Read-Only-Memory)

EEPROM is a special kind of ROM that bears separate mention. It is in-system writeable on a byte-by-byte basis, like RAM, but it is also nonvolatile, like ROM. Writes to an EEPROM cell store or remove electron charge from areas of the cell transistor, resulting in a zero or one, respectively, when the cell is subsequently read. Per-byte alterability means that cell erase is part of rewrite. To speed this process, EEPROMs generate high internal voltage potentials (and subsequent high electric fields). This has the potentially unhappy consequence of impacting cell reliability through time, by causing cell oxide breakdown as the transistor is repeatedly re-written. EEPROM vendors often strive to extend memory lifetime via on-chip cell redundancy and error detection-correction logic. This added cell complexity, along with on-chip high voltage generation and considerable peripheral logic, limits per-device EEPROM density and increases cost for a given density, compared to other technologies.

Magnetic Mass Storage

Reference is made here to the resident hard disk drive and removable-media floppy disk drive. Magnetic mass storage is extremely dense, relatively inexpensive on a cost-per-megabyte basis (compared to semiconductor memory), and both nonvolatile and in-system updateable. However, its slow access time, due to platter seek, rotation delay, and inherent serial interface makes direct-read of code and data unrealistic. Instead, nonvolatile magnetic mass storage contents transfer to faster (but volatile) DRAM for CPU access. The fact that hard or floppy disk drives contain moving parts (the motor and heads) also suggests that they are potentially less rugged and more power-consuming than solid-state storage alternatives.

An Emerging Alternative: Flash Memory

Flash memory is the first significantly new memory technology to appear in almost 20 years, and yet in many ways it owes its heritage to its predecessors (specifically EPROM and EEPROM). Three distinct approaches exist today (which we'll discuss in detail a bit later), but regardless of their differences, several similarities emerge. Table 1.2 compares the fundamental features of flash memory with those of the other memory technologies discussed earlier.

	Nonvolatile	High Density	Low Power	One Transistor Per Cell	In-System Rewriteable	Fully Bit-Alterable	High Performance Read
Flash Memory	✓	✓	✓	✓	✓		✓
SRAM					✓	✓	✓
DRAM		✓			✓	✓	✓
EEPROM	✓		✓		✓	✓	✓
OTP/ EPROM	✓	✓	✓	✓			✓
ROM	✓	✓	✓	✓			✓
Hard Disk Drive	✓	✓			✓	✓	
Floppy Disk Drive	✓				✓	✓	

Table 1.2: Flash Memory Versatility Answers the Needs of Many Applications

Flash memory is inherently nonvolatile, with no refresh or battery requirements. This makes it a potential fit in applications that in the past used ROM, EEPROM, battery-backed RAM or magnetic mass storage. In-system updateability allows flash memory to match the requirements of designs that might have previously used RAM, EEPROM, or magnetic mass storage. Its simpler cell architecture (only one transistor) gives it significant density advantages over both EEPROM and SRAM, and compares favorably with densities achieved by ROM and DRAM on analogous manufacturing processes.

Finally, the combination of nonvolatility, upgradeability, and high density not only *enhances* designs that used other memory approaches in the past but also *enables* new designs and applications. Figure 1.4 shows that whereas more established memory technologies meet one (or several) of the ideal memory attributes, flash memory is the only approach to satisfy all three characteristics.

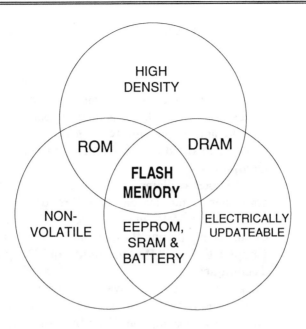

Figure 1.4: Flash Memory Satisfies Many Ideal Memory Attributes

A PREVIEW OF CHAPTERS TO FOLLOW

The remainder of this book will obviously cover the topic of flash memory in much more detail than the short discussion in this chapter! Using a modular structure, we have tried to organize the book so that you can quickly find the specific information you need.

Chapters and appendices are arranged as follows:

- **Chapter 2: Flash Memory Applications**
  This chapter gives insight into compelling uses for flash memory today, and a glimpse into future flash memory applications.
- **Chapter 3: Flash Memory Technologies**
  This chapter reviews the distinguishing characteristics of, and the technology behind, the dominant alternatives in today's flash memory market.

- **Chapter 4: Flash Memory Packaging Options and Update Alternatives**
This chapter shows the various packaging options available for both flash memory components and cards (and their relative strengths and shortcomings). It also discusses various flash memory update methods and their advantages and disadvantages.
- **Chapter 5: Hardware Interfacing to Flash Memory Components**
This chapter explains the integration of flash memory components into system hardware designs (covering both fundamentals and advanced techniques). It also discusses interpreting flash memory timing parameters.
- **Chapter 6: Power Requirements and Design Techniques**
This chapter clarifies various current and voltage specifications for flash memory, and discusses power and energy consumption of the flash memory subsystem in its various operating modes. 12V generation for flash memory program/erase is also covered here.
- **Chapter 7: Software Interfacing to Flash Memory**
This chapter covers first-generation manual and second-generation automated flash memory program/erase algorithms. It also offers suggestions on update routines and boot code kernals, and discusses advanced software techniques for multi-component flash memory arrays and cards.
- **Chapter 8: Special Hardware Interfacing Considerations for Memory Cards**
Although flash memory cards have similar properties to the devices within them, the hardware interfacing requirements are complicated by one significant factor: *removability*. In this chapter, we will discuss the PCMCIA signals as well as host implementations, including topics such as paging, buffering, and PCMCIA interface controller chips.

- **Chapter 9: Flash Memory File Systems**
  The biggest questions associated with solid-state drives made out of flash memory are: *What is a flash file system?*, and *Which one should I use?* The answers to these questions, and many more, lie within this chapter. It will give you the information needed to make an intelligent choice when evaluating the different flash file system solutions currently available.

- **Chapter 10: PCMCIA Software**
  This chapter delves into the various layers of software that connect removable PC cards to the applications that use them. Much of this section will discuss Socket Services, software that every system with a PCMCIA slot should include. We'll also review Card Services and flash card drivers.

- **Appendix A: Flash Memory Component Vendors**
- **Appendix B: Flash Memory Card/Drive Vendors**
- **Appendix C: Flash Memory Card/Component Programmers**
- **Appendix D: Component/Card Socket and Adapter Vendors**
- **Appendix E: 12V Converters**
- **Appendix F: Flash Memory Card Reader/Writers**
- **Appendix G: Flash File Systems**
- **Appendix H: PCMCIA and Software Vendors**
- **Appendix I: PCMCIA Compliance Testing Facilities**
- **Appendix J: PCMCIA Card Types**
- **Appendix K: Interface Controller Chip Register Functions and Vendors**
- **Appendix L: INT 21H Standard Disk-Related Functions**
- **Appendix M: Sample Flash File System Benchmarking Code**

Chapter Two: Flash Memory Applications

In Chapter One we answered a few basic questions about flash memory:

- *What* is it?
- *Why* use flash memory versus some other technology?

In this chapter, we'll continue this trend and take a stab at a few more fundamental questions:

- *Where* can flash memory be used (i.e., in what applications)?
- *When* do flash memory's features (in comparison to other memory alternatives) translate to system benefits?

Jumping ahead for a preview of upcoming topics, the remainder of this book will answer, in depth, the final questions of:

- *Who* is making it and how do the alternatives compare?
- *How* do I integrate flash memory in my design?

The potential applications for flash memory are numerous and varied. In some cases, flash memory *enhances* a design that had in the past used another type of memory. In other cases, flash memory is an *enabling* technology for designs and applications that, to a greater or lesser degree, never would have previously been possible. In either case, we'll group the large number of possible applications into a few broad categories for purposes of discussion, with specific comments where appropriate. Specifically, we'll cover the following areas:

- Data Accumulation
- Data/Lookup Table Storage
- Embedded Code Storage
- File Storage

Notice that in the previous paragraph we talked about the *potential* applications for flash memory. In many cases, flash memory is not the only memory approach that could be used in the system design. Both primary and secondary feature comparisons, as well as relative price analysis, will help determine the correct memory for your specific application.

In Chapter 1, we conducted a feature-by-feature comparison between flash memory and other solutions (ROM, RAM, EEPROM, magnetic media, etc.), while in Chapter 3 we'll compare and contrast the specific features of various flash memory approaches relative to each other. In this chapter, we'll translate memory *features* into application *benefits*. Drawing from the authors' personal experiences in dealing with customers, we'll give some insight into flash memory's comparative strengths and weaknesses as they relate to application needs, and into reasons why flash memory is (or isn't) a fit.

DATA ACCUMULATION

In this type of application, one or more flash memory components (or a flash memory card) are used to store information periodically collected from some type of external environment.

Medical Instrumentation

One example of data accumulation is medical instrumentation, where a variety of information about a patient (heart rate, brain activity, blood chemical concentration, etc.) is periodically sampled and stored. At some point (usually when the resident memory is full), the data is analyzed, often by downloading it to a master computer. The resident accumulated data is flushed, and subsequent sampling continues from this point.

Obviously, this type of system places a very high value on the stored information! Memory technologies used in the past included EEPROM and battery-backed RAM. Neither of these approaches will ever match the per-device density of flash memory, where density defines the amount of information that can be stored before filling the memory array. This type of application usually does not require the bit-alterability that RAM and EEPROM provide; so flash memory's lack of bit-eraseability may not be a drawback. Flash memory is inherently nonvolatile and does not rely on a limited-lifetime, temperature-sensitive battery to retain stored information. A high-density flash memory card provides the additional benefit of portability, if the data must be moved from the dedicated medical sensor to a computer for analysis.

Flight Recorders

Another system example of data accumulation is the "black box" flight recorder found on every commercial airplane today. If a plane crashes (a morbid scenario, we realize), the cockpit voice transcripts and stored accumulation of sensor data are used to reconstruct the events leading up to the accident and decipher its cause. Again, the value of the stored data is very high in such a system.

In the past, tape recorders and rotating magnetic storage were used in this application, but their poor temperature tolerance (and the fact that they have moving parts) were reliability limiters, compared to fully solid-state flash memory media[1]. A large array of EEPROM is cost-prohibitive compared to the flash memory alternative. Battery-backed SRAM is similarly density-disadvantaged, and battery reliability is questionable at temperature and shock extremes.

More Data Accumulation Examples

Additional data accumulation examples include point-of-sale terminals, where transaction information can be stored locally and batch-uploaded

---

[1] As a matter of fact, the FAA now prohibits the use of mechanical media.

to the server, minimizing network traffic and improving performance. Another example is handheld instrumentation, such as bar-code scanners or other portable data acquisition devices. A final data accumulation application example is remote sensing instrumentation, such as geological, geothermal, or weather data collection equipment.

Why Flash Memory for Data Acquisition?

Benefits of flash memory in data accumulation applications (compared to other memory alternatives) include its high density, inherent media ruggedness, reliability, and inherent nonvolatility. Flash memory's low power consumption also provides value in battery-operated designs.

Depending on the data sampling frequency, flash memory programming and erase performance may be critical in the design. In this case, software interleaving and background erase techniques (see Chapter 7 for more information), as well as careful selection of flash memories (see Chapter 3), will maximize write bandwidth. Carefully analyze the application cycling requirements when selecting a flash memory. When evaluating flash memory versus alternatives, assess whether RAM-like bit-alterability is needed, and whether this requirement can be worked around via software and alternate storage techniques.

DATA/LOOKUP TABLE STORAGE

In this type of application, the flash memory devices store large amounts of infrequently updated system data and/or lookup tables.

PBX Switcher

One specific data storage implementation is a telecommunications switcher. Your phone company's local exchange PBX switcher, for example, stores a large amount of information about each of its 10,000 (maximum) line subscribers, such as:

- Custom services that are enabled (call waiting, call forwarding, etc.) and additional information for these services (such as the phone number that incoming calls are forwarded to).

- The primary long distance service selected by the subscriber

In the past, ROMs/EPROMs were one memory technology commonly used to store this lookup table data. Every time a user changed his/her information profile, the switcher would have to be taken off-line while the ROMs were replaced: an expensive proposition that also required multiple redundant PBXs to prevent system downtime. Obviously, business and personal phone users would not tolerate the inability to make and receive calls while the PBX was being updated!

Another memory subsystem alternative consisted of a large array of RAM, backed up by an equivalent amount of magnetic storage (such as a hard drive). Besides the obvious cost of redundant memories (RAM and magnetic), any system glitch, reset, or power loss resulted in unacceptable system downtime as the PBX was re-initialized and data was copied from the hard drive back into the RAM array. Flash memory's combination of nonvolatility and updateability provides the in-system write capability lacking with EPROM, and eliminates the memory redundancy and long system recovery delay of RAM-HDD.

Laser Printers

Another example of a data storage application is the laser printer, which stores within itself the various fonts that it supports. These fonts have been historically placed in ROM or EPROM, where in-system update is not possible. You're in a sense stuck with the fonts that ship with your printer in a ROM/EPROM-based system. Given the ever-increasing explosion of new typefaces being used today, there's a very good chance that whenever you deviate from the standard limited set of Postscript or PCL fonts, those that you select will not be resident within the printer. In this case, the font information is downloaded along with the print job and temporarily stored in printer RAM, greatly slowing effective print performance.

Flash memory allows users to customize not only the specific fonts stored in the printer, but also to download and store custom graphics bitmaps (corporate logos), page templates and other information. Flash memory-based add-in font cartridges have been available for several years now, and are beginning to find their way directly onto system motherboards, especially in high-end network and color printers. The ability to easily customize resident fonts is a clear customer benefit and a differentiator in the increasingly-crowded laser printer market.

Why Flash Memory For Data/Lookup Table Storage?

Advantages of flash memory over alternatives in data/lookup table applications include its combination of in-system upgradeability and nonvolatility. High density is also often required by the system, and flash memory supports this need. Fast access time translates to quick data lookup and high system performance. Similar to the embedded code applications discussed next, you should evaluate not only component cost but also system cost through system lifetime (i.e., the likelihood of data updates) when choosing between flash memory and an alternative memory.

EMBEDDED CODE STORAGE

This is the traditional use for flash memory, replacing ROM or EPROM in storing the resident code (otherwise known as firmware) that runs a system. The vast majority of today's flash memory customers use it in this type of application. In fact, the term "flash memory" was coined specifically for its quick code update capability relative to EPROM.

PC BIOS

One very popular embedded code storage application is that of the personal computer basic input/output system (BIOS). The BIOS is the lowest level code interfacing the operating system to the specific hardware implementation. Acting as the glue that ties the two together (see Figure 2.1), it has a major role in the open system architecture of today's Intel-based computers. The BIOS allows the same operating system and graphical user interface (GUI) (for example MS-DOS^{TM} and Windows^{TM}) to run on both a low-end i386^{TM}SX system and the newest Pentium^{TM} microprocessor-based workstations.

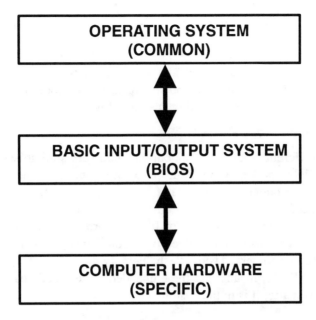

Figure 2.1: BIOS Glues Common Software to Unique Hardware

In the past, the BIOS was fairly well understood and easy to write, since systems themselves were relatively straightforward and standardized. However, today's computing world is vastly more complex. Listed below are some of the factors that have complicated the PC BIOS:

- More powerful and upgradeable CPUs
- Various local bus graphics standards
- Elaborate power management software
- PCMCIA expansion slots

As the creation of BIOS software grows more challenging, competitive pressures in parallel force ever-shorter time-to-market for new hardware designs. BIOS software creation therefore has become the gating item to product introduction, and consequently the probability of shipping systems with bugs is increasing. Flash memory (versus ROM or EPROM) allows easy, low-cost BIOS upgrade even after a system is in the user's hands. This is especially crucial in compact, hard-to-disassemble (and reassemble) computers. Flash memory also enables custom BIOS installation as systems are shipped; just-in-time manufacturing allows one hardware design to service multiple markets (price points, etc.). Finally, upgrade capability allows systems in the marketplace to be updated not only as BIOS bugs are discovered, but also as the BIOS is enhanced (power management code improvements being one example), strengthening customer loyalty.

Digital Cellular Phones

A totally different type of system, but one with very similar issues, is the digital cellular phone. Using Europe as just one example, the GSM digital cellular phone standard is not yet fixed, and is still being revised and enhanced. In the crowded, competitive cellular phone market, no manufacturer is willing to wait for full standardization before shipping products. Code instability and early obsolescence is therefore a big concern for customers. Using flash memory for code storage, versus ROM or EPROM, means that the embedded system code can be easily updated even after it is in the customer's hands.

Conceivably, upgrade could be as simple as the phone owner calling a toll-free phone number provided by the manufacturer. After a handshake is established, new code could be downloaded over the cellular link to the phone, whose embedded processor would control the update!

More Embedded Code Storage Applications

Other common examples of embedded code storage applications that can take advantage of flash memory capabilities include control software in laser printers and telecommunications bridgers/routers. Although these applications differ significantly, they have the same issues; a fairly expensive initial cost where the potential for code instability exists and/or where code upgrade is a key customer benefit and differentiator.

Why Flash Memory for Embedded Code Storage?

Flash memory's advantages for embedded code storage include its combination of nonvolatility and upgradeability. Fast access time increases system performance, eliminating the need to shadow code to faster RAM in many cases. High density also matches the growing software needs of today's complex designs. Low power consumption also benefits portable, battery-operated systems.

FILE STORAGE

The mechanical disk drive has traditionally (and economically) been the media chosen for mass file storage. HDDs have large capacity, low cost per byte, fairly high reliability, and acceptable performance. However, portable computing and industrial applications have placed new demands on these file storage devices. Industrial applications (being less cost sensitive) were the first to really use solid-state drives, having originally used battery-backed SRAM. During its short existence, flash memory has proven to be more reliable and certainly lower cost than SRAM. Even though this cost has not yet fallen quite low enough to ignite mass market acceptance of flash memory replacement of magnetic media, reasons for its use are becoming obvious.

Flash Memory Promotes Longer Battery Life

Long battery life is generally not possible with rotating motors, spin-up surges, and wasteful idle modes. Figure 2.2 depicts the energy consumption of various operating modes for file storage devices, contrasting the solid-state approach using flash memory and the mechanical disk drive.

Figure 2.2 clearly shows that the greatest amount of energy is wasted while the drive idles. To avoid constant spin-down and spin-up, the disk drive typically remains in the idle mode for at least 5 minutes after the last computer operation. An analogy can be drawn to the car waiting at the railroad crossing. How do you determine when to turn off the car's engine? For a short train, leave it on; for a long train, turn it off. A solid-state drive, especially one made with flash memory, can enter sleep mode almost instantly after the last access. Why? Because spin-up concerns do not exist. This yields significant energy improvements.

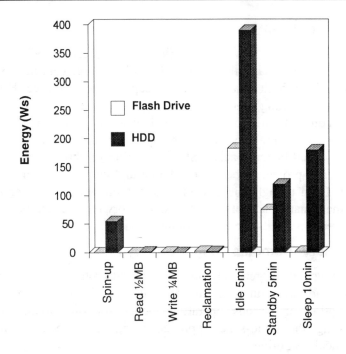

Figure 2.2: Energy Consumed During Various Acitivties

HDD Densities with FDD Interchange

Flash memory cards used for solid-state drives provide consumers with a removable mass storage device. Companies like Databook and Elan[2] have developed memory card reader/writers that look much like floppy drives, only with PCMCIA slots (Figure 2.3). Flash memory card users can therefore interchange information on a card between their portable computer and desktop workstation. High density flash memory cards avoids the cumbersome use of numerous floppy disks when transferring large amounts of data back and forth. Yes, it's true that flash memory cards are more expensive than floppy disks. But we're talking about portable computers that cannot afford the space for a floppy drive, nor

[2]Refer to the Appendix for a detailed listing.

are they willing to sacrifice the weight gain or the added energy consumption. Applications such as these will eventually push flash memory to the forefront, and as the PCMCIA slots on the latest generations of mobile computers show, this trend has already begun.

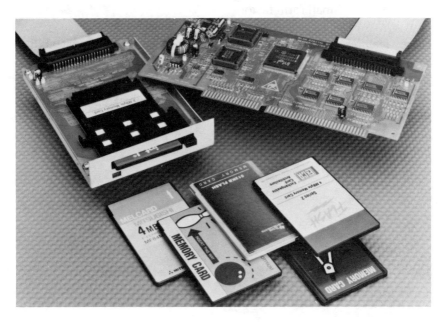

Figure 2.3: Elan Flash Memory Card Reader/Writer

SUMMARY

When evaluating flash memory versus an alternative memory solution, look beyond component-level (or card-level) cost and evaluate the total cost of the system, throughout its lifetime. Flash memory's strengths, exemplified in this chapter's applications, include:

- Full nonvolatility
- In-system program and erase
- Ruggedness
- Low power consumption
- Fast read/write
- High density
- Low cost
- Removability and portability
- Small form factor

These features, translated into system benefits like updateability, manufacturing ease, durability, light weight, small size, high performance, and shock resistance, are some of the reasons why flash memory is today often not the *other* memory evaluated for new designs, but the *only* memory choice!

Chapter Three: Flash Memory Technologies

From a very high-level perspective, Chapter 1 answered the question, "What is Flash Memory?" As a review, flash memory has the following primary characteristics:

- Nonvolatility (retains data stored to it when powered off), and
- In-System Updateability (stored data can be erased and replaced under system processor control)

As you can see, this is a pretty broad definition! Various semiconductor vendors have chosen unique and quite dissimilar silicon technology approaches to answer the above application requirements. Some flash memory approaches are *evolutionary*, based on existing memory types that are already nonvolatile and updateable. Other technologies choose a more *revolutionary* path.

This chapter will discuss in detail three flash memory technologies: NOR, EEPROM, and NAND. All three approaches meet the basic criteria for flash memory (nonvolatility and updateability). Where they differ, however, is in their secondary characteristics, some of which are listed below[3]:

- Read Performance
- Program/Erase Performance

---

[3]Chapter 2 discussed specific flash memory applications and indicated the highest priority features in each case.

- Number of Program/Erase Cycles Through Device Lifetime
- Power Supply Voltage Requirements
- Current Draw in Device Operating Modes
- Erase Block Size

When evaluating flash memory alternatives, do not overlook the manufacturing process complexity, and the size of the flash memory cell and periphery logic. Both factors translate into component cost, and ultimately to the price you pay for the component or flash-based subsystem from the manufacturer or distributor. Keep this in mind as you read about the "latest and greatest" flash memory technology unveilings. Creating something in the laboratory is one thing; consistently recreating it in high volume and with low cost in a manufacturing facility is entirely another matter!

As a framework for the following discussion, Figure 3.1 shows the 1992 relative market share for several flash memory semiconductor vendors. The anticipated demand for flash memory in the very near future is evident, and many semiconductor companies are gearing up to supply this market.

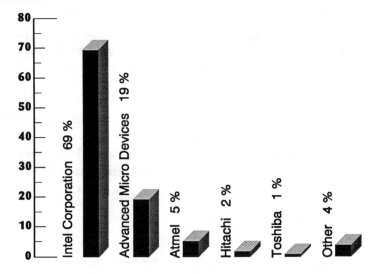

Figure 3.1: Dataquest 1992 Flash Memory Market Share (by company)

NOR FLASH MEMORY

(Examples: Intel Corporation, Advanced Micro Devices, Hitachi, Mitsubishi, NEC, SGS-Thompson, Fujitsu, Toshiba Corporation)

NOR flash memory was introduced by Intel Corporation in 1988, using the company's ETOX™ (EPROM Thin Oxide) process technology. Since that time, products based on similar technologies have been announced by several other semiconductor vendors. Figure 3.2 compares the ETOX flash memory cell with an EPROM (Erasable Programmable Read-Only Memory) cell. The similarity in this revolutionary approach is clear; NOR flash memory derives from an EPROM base. The key difference is in the silicon oxide thickness between the floating gate and substrate. This thinner oxide is the key to NOR flash memory operation; we'll see why in a moment.

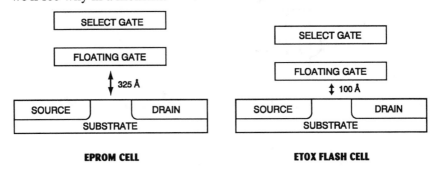

Figure 3.2:ETOX™ Flash Memory Cell Similarities Leverage EPROM Learning Curve

When shipped from the vendor, the default state of all cells in a NOR flash memory is one, corresponding to an *erased* condition. Figure 3.3 shows the voltages present on the cell when read. When erased, the floating gate of the flash memory cell does not block the cell from being turned on by the applied voltages on the select gate and drain. The resulting current is sensed at the transistor source, and translated to a one at the memory output pin.

Figure 3.4 shows a portion of a flash memory array and the interconnection of the various transistors. Device addresses enable specific wordlines and bitlines; in combination they select one transistor within the array per device output. This organization also explains the NOR name for this architecture; any "on" transistor (i.e., a selected, erased cell) in the chain results in the earlier-described current draw, sensed at the end of the chain and converted to an output one.

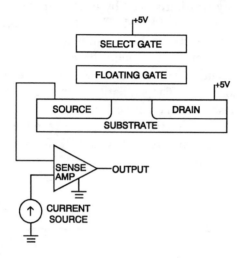

Figure 3.3: ETOX™ Flash Memory Cell Being Read

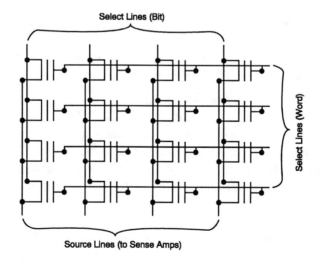

Figure 3.4: NOR Flash Memory Array Interconnect

Program

Changing a flash memory cell (or bit) to a zero is called *programming*.
NOR flash memory employs the same programming mechanism as
EPROM, namely hot electron injection. Figure 3.5 shows an ETOX
flash memory cell being programmed. As electrons travel from the
source to the drain through the substrate, the electric field generated by
high voltage on the select gate causes some of the highest energy
electrons to jump the gap and collect on the floating gate. What's the
result? Referring back to Figure 3.3, we see that the electrons now
present on the floating gate counteract the voltage on the select gate and
prevent the flash memory cell from turning on. No current flows from
drain to source, resulting in a zero on the memory output pin.

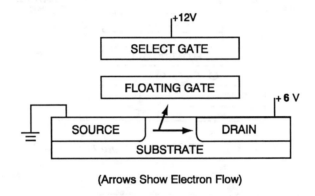

(Arrows Show Electron Flow)

Figure 3.5: ETOX™ Flash Memory Cell Being Programmed

NOR flash memory cells can be selectively programmed to zero. In other
words, programming is a *bit-level* operation. On a byte-wide flash
memory device, for example, one bit of a selected byte can be
programmed to zero, leaving the other seven bits at one. Later
programming of the same byte can change other bits to zero in the same
way. However, one key point to note about NOR flash memory (and
about other flash memory approaches, too) is that *programming only
changes ones to zeros.* Here lies a fundamental difference between flash
memory and other rewriteable memory technologies like RAM. To
change programmed zeros back into ones, we must use a different
mechanism, called erase.

Erase

EPROMs are erased by ultraviolet light. As shown in Figure 3.6, the extra energy generated by UV light enables electrons on the floating gate (put there by programming) to overcome the inherent semiconductor energy potential and return to the substrate. After erasure, an EPROM cell once again reads as a one. To allow UV light to shine on all EPROM cells on a device array, the package must include a built-in glass window. As manufacturing lithographies become smaller and smaller, it becomes harder and harder to ensure that UV light can reach all array cells. The window requirement also puts limits on how small the device package can become.

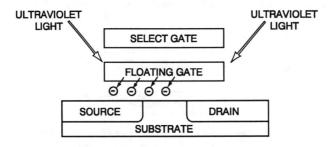

Figure 3.6: EPROM Cell Being UV Erased

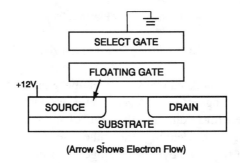

Figure 3.7: ETOX™ Flash Memory Cell Being Erased

Rather than using UV light, NOR flash memory cell erasure is accomplished electrically using a process called Fowler-Nordheim tunneling. Figure 3.7 shows the voltages on the flash memory cell during erase. The generated electric field pulls electrons from the floating gate. First generation *bulk-erasure* NOR flash memories erase all cells in the array at the same time. Second generation NOR devices erase in smaller blocks. Following the same train of thought, this is called *block erase*. Erase block size varies from flash memory vendor to vendor, and from device to device, based on the targeted applications.

Compared to EPROM, the array transistors in a flash memory need not be accessible to UV light exposure. This allows flash memory designers to run layers of interconnection over the cell versus around it, simplifying the design and minimizing the device die size. As an analogy, think of a multi-layer versus a single-layer printed circuit board. Also, flash memory does not require the window of an EPROM, allowing very small footprint (and less expensive) packaging[4].

Negative Gate Erase

Negative gate erase is similar but not identical to the conventional cell erase approach described earlier. Figure 3.8 shows the voltages on the flash memory cell during negative gate erase. Comparing this diagram with Figure 3.7, we see that although the voltages on the cells are different, the resultant voltage potential difference (and electric field) between gate and source is similar. Negative gate erase also uses Fowler-Nordheim tunneling to remove electrons from the floating gate.

Overerase

Removing too many electrons from the floating gate of a flash memory cell may theoretically result in an *overeased* condition (i.e., removing more electrons than were put there by a previous cell program). The effects of overerase are destructive to the flash memory device. Once overerased, a flash memory cell cannot be programmed again (within practical limits). Reads of this cell, as well as adjacent cells in the array, produce erratic and invalid results. Referring back to Figure 3.4, we see that an overerased cell, being "always on" even if not selected, overrides any valid data on the array transistor "chain". *Oops!*

---

[4]We'll see this again in Chapter 4.

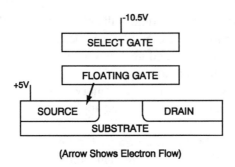

(Arrow Shows Electron Flow)

Figure 3.8: Negative Gate Erase

Fortunately, flash memory erase algorithms include built-in procedures to eliminate the potential for overerase[5]. First, cell erase (like cell programming) uses an iterative algorithm. Shown in simplified form in Figure 3.9, the built-in feedback loop ensures that the algorithm terminates and does not allow further removal of floating gate electrons once sufficient cell erase has been detected. Secondly, since all flash memory cells in a given device (or block within an device) are erased in parallel (and at approximately the same rate), preprogramming ensures that all cells are at a common initial programmed state. Without preprogramming, already-erased cells in the device or in a given erase block would be overerased while programmed cells were being erased.

Newer NOR flash memories control the erase algorithm internally, and automate both the erase preprogramming and iterative erase/verify steps. This dramatically simplifies system software algorithms and eliminates any potential for error. For more information, reference Chapter 7.

NOR Flash Memory Specifications

Table 3.1 provides a summary of NOR flash memory device characteristics, derived from data on Intel Corporation's latest-generation products. These specifications are indicative of the relative levels of performance possible today using NOR flash memory. However, exact

---

[5]If they are implemented *exactly* as published; a 'word to the wise' for system software programmers!

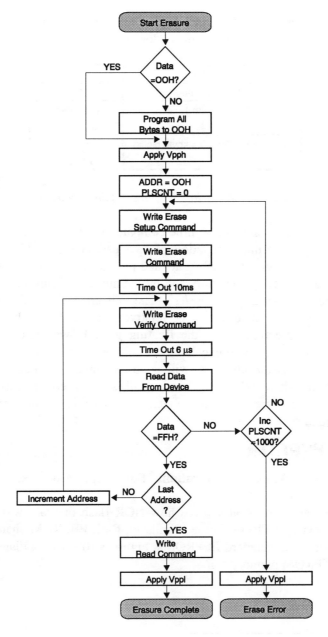

Figure 3.9: Iterative Basic Flash Memory Erase Algorithm

values will vary from device to device, from manufacturing process to manufacturing process, and from vendor to vendor[6].

Density	8 Mbit
Access Time	60 ns
Data Program Time	6 µs (min)
	9 µs (typ)
Block Erase Time (64 kbyte block)	0.3 sec (min)
	1.6 sec (typ)

Table 3.1: NOR Flash Memory Characteristics

Note the relatively slow erase time compared to read and program. Cell erase time is a primary function of two parameters; oxide thickness between floating gate and substrate, and internal erase voltage (it is also affected by device temperature, and by the number of times the cell has been erased previously, or *cycled*). The cell erase time of the ETOX processes is a direct result of the relatively low 12V and low current used to pull electrons from the floating gate. However, a low erase voltage also translates to excellent cell reliability and extended cycling performance. Later chapters will give examples of flash memory applications where cell erase time is (and is not) a concern, as well as discussing hardware and software techniques to hide the slow erase as a background system task.

FLASH EEPROM

(Examples: Atmel Corporation, Samsung, SunDisk, Catalyst Semiconductor)
The previous discussion showed how NOR flash memory was derived from an existing EPROM base. Similarly, flash EEPROM shares many similarities with standard EEPROMs. Figure 3.10 shows a diagram of a flash EEPROM memory cell.

---

[6]Consult vendor datasheets, application notes, and engineering reports for information on specific devices. Vendor contact information is in Appendix A.

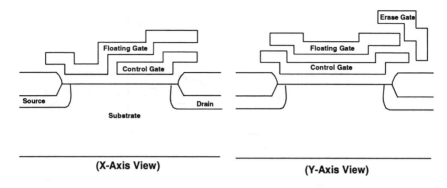

Figure 3.10: EEPROM-Based Flash Memory Cell

A standard EEPROM can be fully altered on a byte-by-byte basis. The byte erase operation is integrated in the write function, i.e., the byte is first erased and then reprogrammed with the desired data. A flash EEPROM, on the other hand, simplifies the silicon design by erasing on a block-level basis. When an EEPROM flash memory block is written, it is first erased and then programmed with data stored in an on-chip buffer.

Erase

Flash EEPROMs erase using Fowler-Nordheim tunneling, as do NOR flash memories. Most, however, use a separate erase gate per cell to collect electrons pulled off the floating gate. Regardless of the specific method, flash EEPROMs use much higher internally-generated voltages because of their greater oxide thickness compared to NOR flash, and to speed erase performance. Remember....erase is a built-in part of rewrite, not a separate operation as in the case of NOR flash. Figure 3.11 shows an EEPROM flash memory cell being erased.

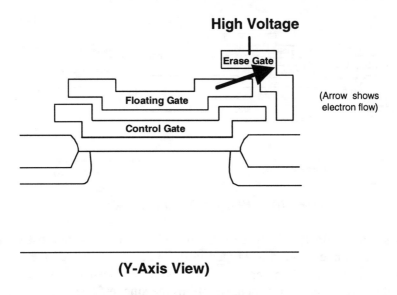

(Y-Axis View)

Figure 3.11: EEPROM-Based Flash Memory Cell Being Erased

Programming

Some flash EEPROMs program cells via hot electron injection. Most, however, use a reverse form of Fowler-Nordheim tunneling shown in Figure 3.12. The combination of voltages on the select gate and drain stores electrons on the floating gate, versus removing them, as seen with Fowler-Nordheim erasure. Again, high internal voltages are used for fastest programming performance.

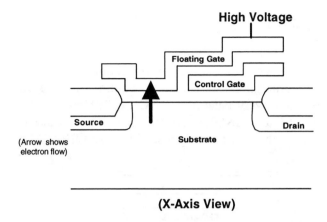

(X-Axis View)

Figure 3.12: EEPROM-Based Flash Memory Cell Being Programmed

Flash EEPROM Memory Specifications

Table 3.2 summarizes flash EEPROM memory characteristics[7]. Since erase is a built-in part of the flash EEPROM program algorithm, flash EEPROMs speed up the erase process time compared to NOR flash memory, primarily via the higher internal voltages on the EEPROM cell. However, over time this may potentially have a negative impact on cell reliability. As the EEPROM cell undergoes repeated erasure, the high electrical field can break down the thin oxide region, causing failure. Some EEPROM vendors have implemented redundant cell and internal error-correction schemes to combat this "Achilles Heel".

Density	1 Mbit
Access Time	90 ns
Data Program Time	150 µs

Table 3.2: EEPROM Flash Memory Characteristics

---

[7]Taken from Atmel Corporation documentation.

NAND FLASH MEMORY

(Example: Toshiba Corporation)

NAND flash memory is a relatively new technology approach pioneered by Toshiba Corporation. As shown in Figure 3.13, the NAND flash memory cell looks very much like a NOR cell! However, the periphery logic designed into NAND is very different, and the internal program and erase approaches most closely resemble flash EEPROM methods.

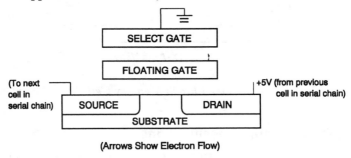

(Arrows Show Electron Flow)

Figure 3.13: NAND Flash Memory Cell Being Read

Like Figure 3.4, Figure 3.14 shows the interconnection of transistors in a NAND array. Data sensing along the chain is serial in nature, and the architecture reflects its name.

Program and Erase

NAND flash memory cells program and erase via reverse and forward Fowler-Nordheim tunneling, respectively. Figures 3.15 and 3.16 show the internal voltages on the cell in each case. Note that unlike flash EEPROM memory tunneling, NAND flash memory applies voltages to the substrate itself, in addition to the select gate.

NAND Flash Memory Specifications

Table 3.3 shows initial specifications for Toshiba's first NAND flash memory-based device. NAND flash memory primarily targets solid state disk drive replacement applications, and the feature set reflects this, with fine-resolution blocking and fast cell erase. However note the slow initial read access time due to serial data read, which may limit broad application usage. Some NAND devices include error detection and correction (EDAC) cells and associated EDAC logic.

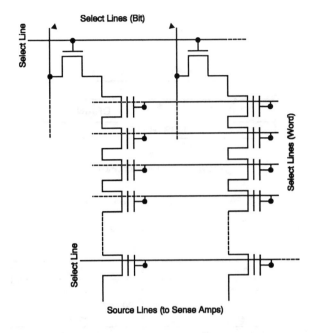

Figure 3.14: NAND Flash Memory Array Interconnect

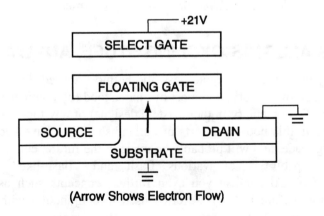

Figure 3.15: NAND Flash Memory Cell Being Programmed

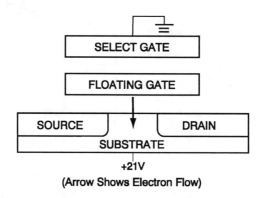

Figure 3.16: NAND Flash Memory Cell Being Erased

Density	4 Mbit
Access Time	15 µs (initial read) 80 ns (subsequent serial access)
Data Program Time	4 ms (min)
Block Erase Time (4 kbyte block)	6 ms

Table 3.3: NAND Flash Memory Characteristics

WHAT'S ALL THIS *CYCLING* STUFF, ANYWAY?

The subject of cycling is quite possibly the most abused (by companies supplying flash memory) and most misunderstood (by companies buying and using flash memory in their system designs) of any topic you'll find discussed in this book! All sorts of outlandish claims have been made, are being made, and will probably be made in the future, concerning the cycling capabilities of various flash and "flash-like" memory technologies. To confuse you even further, concepts such as MTBF (mean time before failure) are often used in conjunction with cycling specifications. Flash memory vendors often mean well (from a marketing perspective) when they include these numbers, but since an industry standard for the determination or calculation of MTBF doesn't exist, it is often subject to liberal interpretation and modification. Therefore, MTBF numbers for different flash memory devices and technologies cannot be directly compared without knowing the recipes that were used and the assumptions that were made when the measurements were taken.

We are going to explain cycling in its most fundamental definitions for you, and provide guidelines by which you can calculate your own MTBF numbers for your specific flash memory design and implementation. Our goal here is to cut through all the meaningless marketing hype and provide you with valid, useful information.

What is cycling? A cycling number is:

a)   The minimum number of times a flash memory device (or block within a device) can be erased and programmed in a reasonable amount of time without loss of device functionality, at

b)   A specified failure rate percentage, or FIT (failure-in-time) level.

Flash memory vendors often ignore the latter part of the above definition when publishing their cycling specifications. What good is it to know how many times you can erase an array of flash memory cells if you have no idea of the probability that some of the cells will fail before reaching this cycle count? A parallel can be drawn here with stereo equipment, where inflated claims are sometimes made of an amplifier's output power capability without mentioning how distorted the output signal was when this power was measured. What good is it to hear loud music if you can't understand it? (Of course, with some forms of popular modern music this could be seen as a positive!) Similarly, what good is it to be able to erase flash memory to an extended number of cycles if the media is essentially unusable when it reaches this cycle count? Clearly both parts of the cycling definition are valuable and useful information.

Failure Analysis

Before each flash memory device is shipped to a customer, it undergoes extensive testing to screen out known and detectable failure mechanisms both in the circuitry itself and in the manufacturing process on which the device was made. Even after this testing, it is known and accepted that a certain very small (hopefully!) number of devices will eventually fail, even when operated at all recommended specifications. Some sources of this failure, common to all flash memories as well as other memory technologies, are listed below:

- Package Integrity Failures
- Random Circuitry Failures
- Data Reliability Failures (i.e., programmed zeros turning back into ones)
- Program Failures (inability to change a one to a zero), and
- Erase Failures (inability to change a zero back to a one)

Reputable flash memory vendors spend a great deal of time and effort calculating and predicting their failure rates. Published reliability reports contain these predicted failure percentages, and are available for your inspection. We'll restrict the following discussion to the last two failures listed above, program and erase (or cycling) failures.

How and why does a flash memory cell fail due to cycling? Two different mechanisms combine here; one a more "destructive" phenomenon (oxide breakdown) and the other "non-destructive" in nature (electron trapup).

Oxide Breakdown

Notice the thin oxide region between the substrate and floating gate regions in Figure 3.10. As a flash memory cell is repeatedly erased and reprogrammed, the electrons move back and forth through the oxide region under an electric field. This stresses the oxide, and in its most severe form can result in oxide breakdown and a short circuit between oxide and substrate, rendering the cell non-functional. High quality oxide with low probability of defects, as well as a lowered electric field to minimize oxide stress, are ways that flash memory vendors can minimize the likelihood of oxide breakdown.

Electron Trapup

Recall that the earlier definition of cycling included the phrase "erased and programmed in a reasonable amount of time". This is key to the definition of electron trapup. As a flash memory cell accumulates higher and higher cycle counts, electrons become trapped in the oxide region, lowering electron mobility through the oxide and resulting in increased program and erase times. The program and erase algorithms must apply more pulses to program or erase the cell sufficiently to ensure data integrity and retention. Since the impact of electron trapup is simply a failure to program or erase within an allowed time and not a "hard" failure of the cell itself, we call it a "non-destructive" phenomenon.

Mean Time Before Failure

With cycling and failure rate data, and with a good understanding of how flash memory will be used in your system, you can calculate MTBF values for your specific design. As an example, we'll use the Intel 28F008SA 1 Mbyte FlashFile™ memory in a configuration of 20 chips (20 Mbytes total).

The Intel 28F008SA is rated for 100,000 cycles on each of its sixteen 64 kbyte blocks (independent of any other block). Data taken through 10,000 cycles shows no cycling failures, translating to a 0% cycling failure rate (pretty impressive!). Therefore, for this example we'll use the more stringent device failure rate of .01%, which encompasses *all* device failure mechanisms listed earlier in this chapter. The value 0.01% is the historic worst-case device failure rate seen with production-rated Intel flash memories, and the 28F008SA should perform at least this well (if not better).

A 0.01% failure rate (translating to 100 FITS or failures-in-time) means that fewer than 1 in 10,000 devices will fail after 10,000 cycles and 1,000 hours of operation. The scenario under which we'll calculate MTBF assumes that a 10 kbyte file is written to the 20 Mbyte array of flash memory every 10 minutes; a pretty rigorous set of assumptions if you think about it!

A flash-friendly file system could use a linked list structure to write multiple copies of a file and fill up clean flash memory, marking old versions of the file "dirty" but not erasing them immediately[8]. This significantly minimizes cycling of flash memory media. Therefore, given the file and flash memory array sizes, we can make the following calculations:

(20 Mbyte array) / (10 kbyte file) = 2,000 file writes can be done before an array erase is required
(2000 file writes/erase) x (10,000 cycles per 28F008SA block) = 20 x 10^6 file writes
(20 x 10^6 file writes) x (10 minutes/write) x (1 hr/60 minutes) = 3.33 x 10^6 hours MTBF

This means that our 20 Mbyte flash memory array has a Mean Time Between Failures of over 3 million hours, at a failure rate of 0.01%. Not bad, eh?

Extended Cycling-The Flash Memory Manufacturer's Options

Earlier when defining cycling, we inferred that the easiest way some flash memory vendors achieve extended cycling was by downplaying the negatives and accentuating the positives of their technology approaches. This, while true, is not the only means of reaching the extended cycling "Holy Grail"! Several other concrete tradeoffs have been made by various flash memory suppliers, both in technology and architecture, in pursuit of this goal.

Oxide breakdown can be eliminated by producing very high quality, uniform oxide for each flash memory cell. This is much more difficult than it might first appear, and in fact is probably the most complex problem that semiconductor vendors have struggled with as they attempt to ramp up their flash memory manufacturing capabilities. The oxide layer, at 100 Å thick, is made by laying down several layers of silicon *atoms*, no simple task. Remember, too, that for an 8 Mbit flash memory, not one cell but over *8 million* must be manufactured correctly to yield a functional device, and that potentially several hundred devices can be made from each 6" or 8" silicon wafer.

Another technology tradeoff can be made with respect to the internal electric field during program and erase, which is a function of the

---

[8]See Chapter 9 for more information.

magnitude of the internal voltages. A lower electric field lowers the stress on the oxide (a positive) but also slows program and erase times (a negative). Intel Corporation, with its ETOX flash memory approach, has made this choice, and has added device functionality to minimize the system performance impact of the resultant slow block erase time[9].

Where flash memories use higher internal voltages (flash EEPROM and NAND flash memories), added circuitry attempts to circumvent the impact of oxide breakdown and resultant cell damage. EEPROMs often use redundancy schemes which lower cycling failures at the expense of doubling cell size and adding complexity. Toshiba's NAND flash memory integrates error detection and correction (EDAC or ECC) directly on the silicon to mask the device impact of single cell failures. While potentially extending the cycling capability of the device, this approach adds complexity and die size to each device, and also impacts read performance.

Extended Cycling-What Can You Do?

What can you do to match the cycling requirements of your design to an appropriate flash memory architecture? First and foremost, fully analyze the cycling you truly require, and take all possible steps to minimize this cycling. A design that uses flash memory for embedded code storage may only be erased and reprogrammed ten times through its lifetime. On the other hand, a memory card used for file storage may have blocks of flash memory updated thousands or hundreds of thousands of times. Specifically with respect to file storage, Chapter 9 will explain how software companies have re-architected file storage beyond the hard drive paradigm to match the unique characteristics and capabilities of flash memory. These concepts, while possibly not directly applicable to your specific design, will provide examples of cycle minimization and management, linked list structures, and wear leveling.

In Chapter 7 we'll discuss the system software algorithms that initiate and control flash memory erase and program. In cases where erase failure has occurred due to non-destructive electron trapup, this chapter

---

[9]Upcoming chapters will discuss flash memory automation, the RY/$\overline{\text{BY}}$ output and erase suspend/resume capability.

will show you how to extend cycling by supplying the flash memory media with additional erase and program pulses.

Finally, it's your responsibility to understand the conditions under which various flash memory vendors have calculated their products' cycling capabilities, and to request additional information if needed. By correctly interpreting not only minimum cycling information but also the failure rates associated with this cycling, you can intelligently compare and choose among the many flash memory offerings in today's market, as they match the requirements of your design.

SUMMARY

The basic concept of the flash memory cell is relatively simple. Again referencing Figure 3.3 as an example, storing electrons on the floating gate changes the stored cell data from a one to a zero, and removing them changes it back to a one. The challenge for flash memory vendors has been to make flash memory:

- Simple, with the smallest possible cell and minimal periphery logic, translating to a small die size and lowest silicon cost,
- Manufacturable, with a technology development approach that can be easily and cheaply moved to the vendor's production line, and
- Feature-set-rich, with technologies and devices that answer the requirements of their target markets.

The flash memory market is still in its infancy. The system designer has a wide range of product offerings from multiple flash memory vendors to choose from, based on several unique technology approaches. In Chapter 2, we've already covered flash memory applications in detail, and discussed the features that are of highest importance in each case. In combination with the information from this chapter, you'll be able to choose the flash memory that makes the most sense for your design!

Chapter Four: Packaging Options and Update Alternatives

At first glance, the title of this chapter may appear to combine two unrelated topics. However, as is sometimes the case, things are not always as they first seem! A wide range of factors influence the choice of an appropriate component package, including board space, end system form factor, operating temperature range, manufacturing tolerances and available assembly techniques. Flash memory's electrical update capability has enabled small form factor packaging, originally impossible with some other memory technologies. In some applications, flash memory packaging is as crucial (or more so) to the design as are nonvolatility and updateability (PCMCIA memory cards being one example).

The selection of a package, in many cases, automatically determines which flash memory update methods are available during prototyping, when manufacturing the system and once it is in the customer's hands. Conversely, if a specific update technique must be supported, it can factor into the package chosen. Specifically, issues such as the requirement and ability to socket and (therefore) remove the flash memory can define which package is used in the design.

In this chapter, we'll cover the following package options:

- DIP (**D**ual **I**n-**L**ine **P**ackage)
- LCC (**L**eaded/**L**eadless **C**hip **C**arrier)
- SOJ (**S**mall **O**utline **J**-Lead **P**ackage)
- SOP (**S**mall **O**utline **P**ackage)
- TSOP (**T**hin **S**mall **O**utline **P**ackage)

- SIMM (Single In-Line Leadless Memory Module)
- PCMCIA (Personal Computer Memory Card International Association) Memory Cards

.........and, we'll explain the following flash memory update methods:

- Off-Board PROM Programming
- On-Board Update
- In-System Write

PACKAGING OPTIONS

Throughout time, component packages have increased in number and diversity to match the needs and capabilities of the devices themselves, and of the systems that use them. Packaging innovations have solved height, footprint, weight, leadcount, thermal, reliability, electrical and mechanical constraints, among others. A package does not necessarily add to the theoretical performance of the device, but an improperly designed package, acting as the flash memory's weak link, will severely impact this potential.

DIP (Dual In-Line Package)

This "grandparent" of device packages (Figure 4.1), has existed in essentially the same form factor for over two decades! Today's DIP packages are generally made of ceramic or plastic materials. Common package widths are 0.6" (frequently used in nonvolatile memories like flash memory or ROM) and 0.3" (for devices with smaller die sizes, like programmable logic). Package length depends on the number of pins used by the device. Pin-to-pin spacing is 0.100", often referred to as 100 mils.

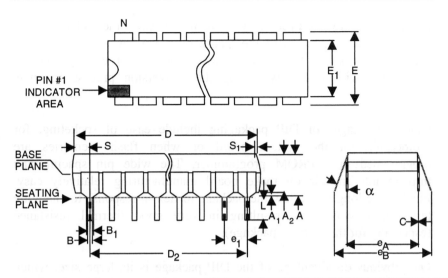

Family: Plastic Dual In-Line Package						
Symbol	Millimeters			Inches		
	Min	Max	Notes	Min	Max	Notes
α	0°	15°		0°	15°	
A		4.83			0.190	
A1	0.38			0.015		
A2	3.81		Typical	0.150		Typical
B	0.41	0.51		0.016	0.020	
B1	1.14	1.40		0.045	0.055	
C	0.20	0.30		0.008	0.012	
D	41.78	42.04		1.645	1.655	
D2	38.10		Reference	1.500		Reference
E	15.24	15.88		0.600	0.625	
E1	13.46	13.97		0.530	0.550	
e	2.54		Reference	4		Reference
eA	15.24		Reference	0.600		Reference
eB	15.24	17.78		0.600	0.700	
L	3.18	3.43		0.125	0.135	
N	32		600MIL	32		600MIL
S	1.78	2.03		0.070	0.080	
S1	1.14			0.045		
ISSUE	IWS 4/19/90					

Figure 4.1: DIP (Dual In-Line) Package Dimensions

When used for flash memory, backwards compatibility represents one of the biggest advantages of the DIP package. Specifically, DIP packaging is also commonly used for EPROM memories, since the wider package makes for easy inclusion of the quartz glass window for UV-erasure. Many DIP-packaged flash memories are closely (or exactly) pinout-compatible with EPROMs, easing the conversion process for new designs.

Other advantages of DIP packaging include ease of socketing, for prototyping on the system board or when flash memories are programmed in a PROM programmer. The wide pin spacing and through-hole installation make board manufacturing relatively easy. Finally, the long pins allow the package to flex in response to changing temperature conditions, resulting in very good thermal resistance (especially for the ceramic package).

One obvious disadvantage of the DIP package is its large size, which translates to excessive board area consumption and height above the board. When building a compact system, smaller packages should be considered. Since the electrically eraseable (vs. UV) flash memory does not require a window, this removes one key advantage of the DIP package. Reference Figure 4.2 for a size comparison between DIP and TSOP packaging on Intel's 28F001BX Boot Block flash memory. As new system designs accelerate the transition from traditional through-hole packaging to more compact surface-mount methods, the incremental manufacturing cost for any remaining DIP-like devices becomes excessive and, in many cases, unacceptable.

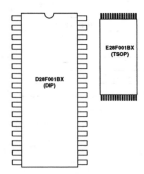

Figure 4.2: DIP / TSOP Package Comparison (Actual Size)

LCC (Leaded/Leadless Chip Carrier)

LCC was the first surface-mount option available to the market, and is today still one of the most popular packages. Although available as leadless and leaded versions, the leaded version (Figure 4.3) is most common for memories due to socketing and manufacturing simplicity. A common characteristic of leaded chip carrier is .050" lead spacing (50 mils), oriented in a J-lead configuration so that the ends of the leads curl underneath the package.

In the past, leaded LCC packages were manufactured either out of ceramic materials (so that a window could be added for EPROMs; this is also commonly called Cerquad), or various plastics. In the latter case, the package was called PLCC (for Plastic Leaded Chip Carrier), and resulted in one-time-programmable EPROMs, or OTP-ROMs. Again, since flash memory does not require the EPROM's window for erasure, plastic PLCC packaging dominates, except in the most severe temperature tolerance designs.

PLCC's key advantage over DIP is its more compact footprint and height, allowing board designers to squeeze more components into a given area. PLCC prototyping sockets are easily available from multiple vendors[10], and many PROM programmers support the PLCC package in addition to DIP.

---

[10]See the Appendix for more information

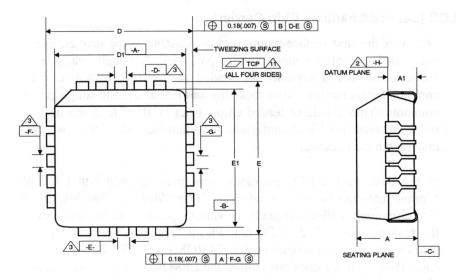

MM(INCH)

Family: Plastic Leaded Chip Carrier-Square				
Symbol	Millimeters		Inches	
	Min	Max	Min	Max
A	4.19	4.57	0.165	0.180
A1	2.29	3.05	0.090	0.120
D	12.3	12.6	0.485	0.495
D1	11.4	11.6	0.450	0.456
D2	9.91	10.9	0.390	0.430
E	12.3	12.6	0.485	0.495
E1	11.4	11.6	0.450	0.456
E2	9.91	10.9	0.390	0.430
N	28		28	
CP	0.00	0.10	0.000	0.004
TCP	0.00	0.10	0.000	0.004
LT	0.23	0.38	0.009	0.015
ISSUE	IWS 10/12/88			

Figure 4.3: LCC (Leaded Chip Carrier) Package Dimensions

One of PLCC's key disadvantages, however, is inherent in its lead configuration. To manufacture a surface-mount board, the components are placed on their sites and the board is exposed to a heat source which melts the solder onto the device leads. PLCC's J-lead configuration means that the portion of the lead attached to the system board is *under* the component package. This makes post-soldering lead inspection difficult or, depending on spacing between components, impossible. PLCC devices in many cases must also be carefully handled, packed in silicon gel or other moisture-absorbing material until attached to the board. Unless this is done, the plastic package can absorb moisture from the atmosphere (humidity-dependent), which turns to steam during the solder melt process and can crack the package or die inside. Thinner packages like TSOP (to be discussed shortly) do not tend to have this problem; their narrower thickness allows the steam to easily exit the package without damaging the device.

PLCC also has leads on all four sides, which precludes the system designer from running board traces directly under the package. This may be a concern in space-critical designs, where the only alternatives available are routing traces *around* the flash memory or using expensive multi-layer boards. Figure 4.4 shows trace routing comparisons between PLCC and PSOP packages. Finally, the square PLCC package is often unusable for high density flash memories, which tend to have narrow, long and rectangular die and therefore do not fit in the package interior.

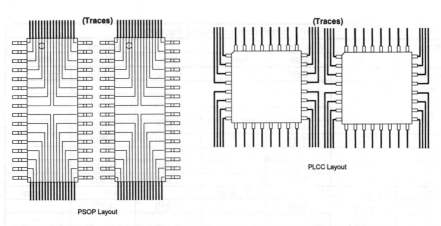

Figure 4.4: Trace Layout Comparison: PSOP vs. PLCC

SOJ (Small-Outline J-Lead)

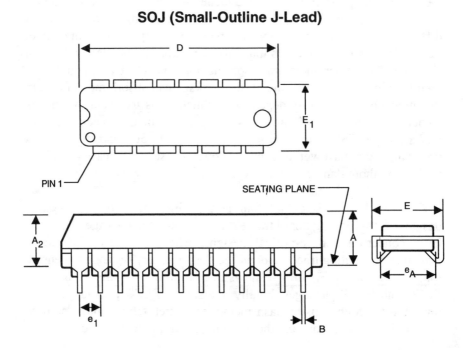

Family: Small Outline J-Lead Package						
Symbol	Millimeters			Inches		
	Min	Max	Notes	Min	Max	Notes
A	3.35	3.61		0.132	0.142	
A1						
A2	2.74	3.00		0.108	0.118	
A3						
B	0.38	0.51		0.015	0.020	
D	15.75	16.18		0.620	0.637	
D2						
E	8.38	8.64		0.330	0.340	
E1	7.49	7.75		0.295	0.305	
e1	1.27		Typical	0.050		Typical
eA	6.60	6.99		0.260	0.275	
eB						
L						
N	24			24		

Figure 4.5: Small Outline J-Lead (SOJ) Package Dimensions

This surface-mount package, shown in Figure 4.5, eliminates some, but not all, of the problems associated with the first-generation PLCC. It uses the same 0.050" (50 mil) lead spacing and J-lead configuration as PLCC, and therefore, inherits PLCC's post-soldering lead inspection difficulties. However, the rectangular package aids in trace routing and better matches the rectangular silicon die inside. SOJ packages, like PLCC, are fairly easy to socket for prototyping.

SOP (Small Outline Package)

SOP has all the advantages of SOJ (compared to PLCC), and in addition has a modified gullwing lead configuration (shown in Figure 4.6). Compared to SOJ or PLCC, this greatly improves the post-soldering lead inspection process, since leads extend beyond the package making them clearly visible at all times.

The main disadvantage of SOP today is restricted availability of sockets for prototyping. However, this is quickly changing as the package becomes more and more common. See the Appendix for more information on SOP prototype socket and socket adapter vendors.

TSOP (Thin Small Outline Package)

TSOP (Figure 4.7) represents the state of the art in surface mount packaging. TSOP is only slightly larger than the die inside the package, and is only 1.2 mm thick. Compared to bare die, TSOP provides full device functional and speed testing before the device is shipped from the flash memory manufacturer. Packaged nonvolatile memories are also easier to handle and more reliable than their bare die equivalents.

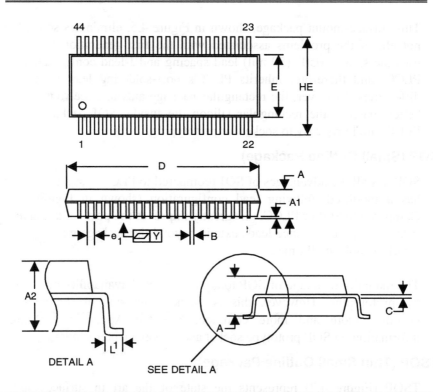

Family: Small Out-Line Package								
Symbol	Millimeters			Notes	Inches			Notes
	Min	Nom	Max		Min	Nom	Max	
A			2.80				0.110	
A1	0.13	0.225	0.35		0.005	0.009	0.013	
A2	2.17	2.3	2.45		0.085	0.091	0.097	
B	0.35	0.40	0.50		0.014	0.016	0.020	
C	0.13	0.150	0.20		0.005	0.006	0.008	
D		28.20	28.70			1.110	1.130	
E	13.10	13.30	13.50		0.516	0.524	0.531	
e1		1.27				0.050		
He	15.7	16.00	16.30		0.618	0.630	0.642	
L1	0.75	0.80	0.85		0.029	0.032	0.033	
N		44				44		
Y			0.10				0.004	
θ			8°				8°	
ISSUE								

Figure 4.6: Small Outline Package (SOP) Dimensions

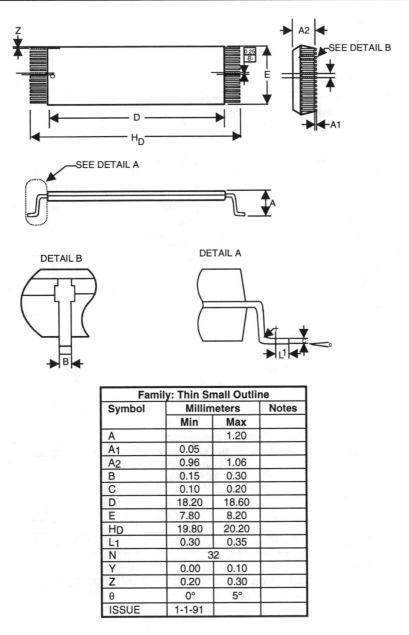

Figure 4.7: TSOP (Thin Small Outline Package) Dimensions

Several flash memory suppliers are offering TSOP-packaged devices in both standard and reverse pinout configurations, as demonstrated in Figure 4.8 with Intel's 28F008SA. This allows highest density-per-in^2 arrays of multiple flash memories. The resulting component layout and trace routing is called "serpentining". Figure 4.9 makes it clear where this name came from. Flash memory cards represent one example application that uses TSOP devices and the serpentine layout.

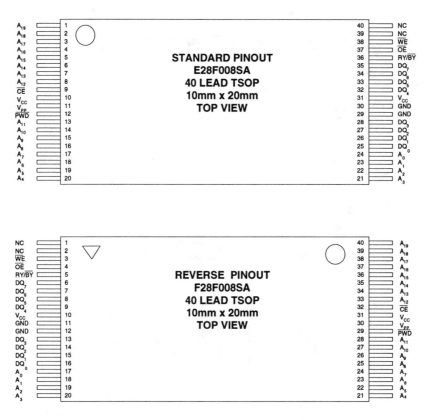

Figure 4.8: Standard and Reverse TSOP Packages

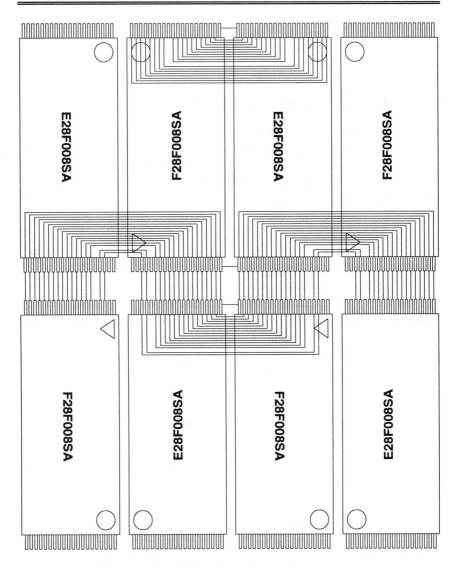

Figure 4.9: TSOP Serpentine Package Layout

The main hurdle to overcome with TSOP-packaged flash memories is the very narrow 0.020" (20 mil) lead spacing. TSOP devices are virtually impossible to socket by hand; pick-and-place equipment should be used. Fine-pitch automated soldering techniques are essential for high-yield TSOP board manufacturing. As with any new technology, the number of TSOP handling solutions today is sparse, but will increase with time as not only flash memory but other logic devices become available in this ultra-small package.

SIMM (Single In-Line Leadless Memory Module)

SIMMs are one way of combining multiple flash memory components on a single board. SIMMs offer the advantage of being an add-in module that enables system expandability. In comparison to a fixed array of flash memories on the system motherboard, SIMM modules can be inserted into any open connector, allowing the density per SIMM connector to be varied to match the specific needs of the system.

The package dimensions are fairly standardized across the industry for nonvolatile memories of all types (Figure 4.10). However, be careful! The actual SIMM pinout (what signals are on what pins) can vary from manufacturer to manufacturer. Not every SIMM will function in every SIMM connector, although they may all physically fit. As an example, Figure 4.11 shows the pinouts for SCM Microsystems' 1 and 2 Mbyte flash memory SIMMs.

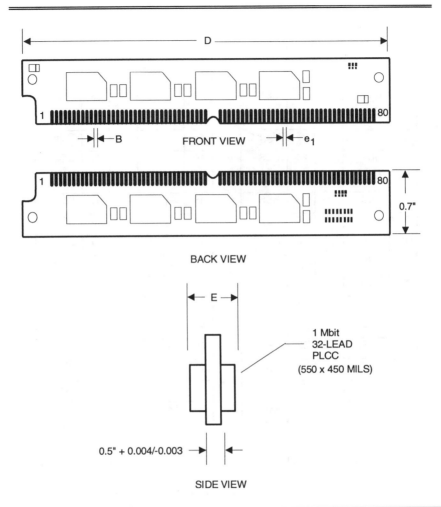

Figure 4.10: SIMM Package Dimensions

Family: Single In-Line Leadless Memory Module						
Symbol	Millimeters			Inches		
	Min	Max	Notes	Min	Max	Notes
B	1.04		Typical	0.041		Typical
C	1.19	1.37		0.047	0.054	
D	117.98	118.24		4.645	4.655	
E	8.38			0.33		
e^1	1.27		Typical	0.050		
N	80			80		Typical
ISSUE	IWS 9-19-90					

1	V_{SS}	21	CE3#	41	A_{11}	61	DQ_9
2	V_{CC}	22	CE2#	42	A_{10}	62	DQ_8
3	OE#	23	CE1#	43	A_9	63	DQ_7
4	WEH#	24	CE0#	44	A_8	64	DQ_6
5	WEL#	25	V_{SS}	45	A_7	65	DQ_5
6	NC	26	RES	46	A_6	66	DQ_4
7	RES	27	RES	47	A_5	67	DQ_3
8	RES	28	RES	48	A_4	68	DQ_2
9	RES	29	RES	49	A_3	69	DQ_1
10	RES	30	NC	50	A_2	70	DQ_0
11	RES	31	NC	51	A_1	71	V_{PP}
12	RES	32	NC	52	A_0	72	V_{CC}
13	RES	33	NC	53	RES	73	PD_1
14	RES	34	NC	54	V_{SS}	74	PD_2
15	RES	35	A_{17}	55	DQ_{15}	75	PD_3
16	RES	36	A_{16}	56	DQ_{14}	76	PD_4
17	NC	37	A_{15}	57	DQ_{13}	77	PD_5
18	NC	38	A_{14}	58	DQ_{12}	78	PD_6
19	NC	39	A_{13}	59	DQ_{11}	79	PD_7
20	NC	40	A_{12}	60	DQ_{10}	80	V_{SS}

Figure 4.11: SCM Microsystems Flash Memory SIMM Pinout

SIMMs provide relatively easy system upgradeability, but modules cannot be added or removed with the system powered up, and the system must usually be partially disassembled to access modules. The PCMCIA flash memory card, which we will discuss next, has this hot-socketing capability.

PCMCIA Flash Memory Cards

Memory cards of all types (RAM/ROM/EEPROM/Flash) have been around for many years. In most cases, each card manufacturer had their own custom physical connector dimensions and pinouts. This incompatibility limited the number of cards available per machine and made card interchange between machines very difficult if not impossible.

The original PCMCIA 1.0 specification (established in 1991) eliminated both of these problems by standardizing on a common 68-pin, 16-bit parallel, memory-only interface for cards with densities as high as 64 Mbytes. The Japanese equivalent of PCMCIA, JEIDA (Japan Electronics Industry Design Association), also standardized on the same 68-pin configuration, bus timings, interface voltages, etc. In 1992, PCMCIA introduced a second version of the specification (i.e., PCMCIA 2.0) which added I/O capability (e.g., modem, fax, lan) to the 68-pin socket by using reserved pins and multiplexing the functionality of some exisiting memory signals.

The advantages of PCMCIA-compatible flash memory cards include:

- They can be inserted and removed during host system operation, similar to a floppy disk. This is an important attribute when the flash memory card is used as the mass storage subsystem. (Hot insertion and removal also has the disadvantage of complicating the system software, as we'll explain in Chapter 10 on PCMCIA software.)
- Flash memory cards are also very rugged, with the components inside the card protected by the tough plastic or metal casing. The host system houses the male side of the connector interface, eliminating bent pins during card handling.
- The small size (no bigger than a credit card, and only slightly thicker) makes PCMCIA cards extremely portable.
- The parallel (versus serial) interface does add to the interface pincount, but allows not only file system mass storage in the card but also direct-execute code capability.

Although all PCMCIA cards incorporate the same 68-pin electrical interface, the physical dimensions of the package differs. The four types are:

*   Type 1 (Figure 4.12) - Measures 3.3 mm thick and accommodates memory cards only.
*   Type 2 (Figure 4.13) - Measuring 5mm thick, the thicker Type 2 card will often be used by some vendors in flash drives, as well as most I/O card products. A system's Type 2 slot is backwards compatible with Type 1 cards.
*   Type 3 - An even thicker (10.5mm), Type 3 card form factor, primarily designed for removable hard drives.
*   Type 4 - This card type, proposed to be 18mm thick, has not yet been ratified by PCMCIA. It will be used for high capacity magnetic media hard disk drives. Although Type 4 could be packed with flash memory devices to achieve very high densities, these densities would carry along with them a very high price tag!

For more information on the PCMCIA hardware, electrical and timing standards, reference Chapter 8.

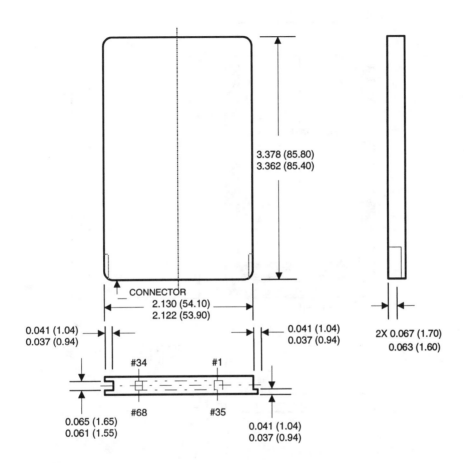

*Figure 4.12: PCMCIA / JEIDA Type 1 PC Card
Package Dimensions*

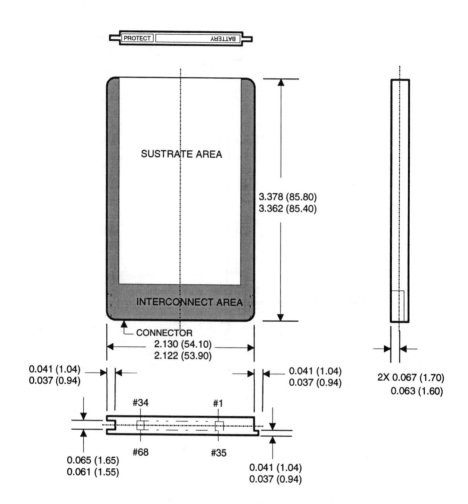

*Figure 4.13: PCMCIA / JEIDA Type 2 PC Card
Package Dimensions*

Flash Drives

Although this category doesn't exactly conform to the typical expectations of a package, it nevertheless plays a very significant role in flash utilization. A flash memory card requires system software and hardware resources to function as a solid-state drive; it interfaces directly to the system bus. Conversely, the flash drive plugs into a system via an IDE (or PCMCIA-ATA) interface and has all required software and hardware contained within. Table 4.1 compares some of the features of flash drives and flash memory cards.

FLASH DRIVE	FLASH MEMORY CARD
Attaches to the system via an IDE or PCMCIA-ATA interface	Direct system interface allows faster access and execute-in-place (XIP)
Completely integrated solution eliminates system overhead, provides O/S and hardware independence	Requires a system-operated flash file system and system hardware resources
Inherently higher cost due to additional hardware besides flash memory media (CPU, RAM, 12V converter, etc.)	Minimal parts count yields low cost

Table 4.1: The Key Differences between a Flash Drive and a PCMCIA Flash Memory Card

From a very simplistic view, Figure 4.14 compares the standard mechanical disk drive to a disk emulator or flash drive. Aside from the type of media chosen for storage, both drives look about the same in that they both have an IDE interface controller and a media controller.

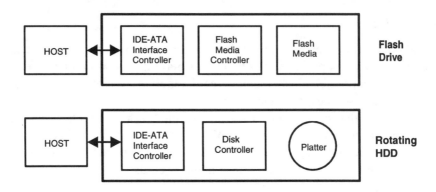

Figure 4.14: Mass Storage Architecture

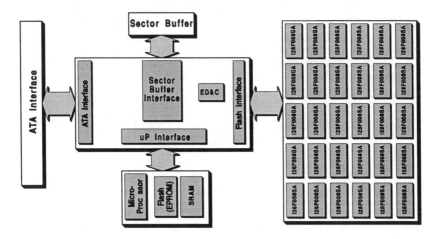

Figure 4.15: Flash Drive Architecture

Figure 4.15 shows a flash drive in more detail. Notice the various components contained within:

- Flash array - Notice how it is isolated from the system. The size of the array depends on the overall size and form factor of the flash drive, which will typically range from the 2.5" HDD form factor to PCMCIA Type II.

- Microprocessor - Handles everything from internal data movement to management of the flash memory media.
- Power converter - Some drives contain a built-in DC-DC converter so that the system only has to supply 5V. The internal generator takes care of providing 12V for the flash memory write and erase operations.
- Flash memory - Stores the code used by the processor for its activities.
- Interface controller - This unit manages the IDE (or PCMCIA-ATA) interface, acting as the go-between the system and the flash drive's microprocessor and flash memory. This controller will typically be in the form of an ASIC.
- Miscellaneous - Other pieces that can be found within a flash drive include an error detection and correction unit (EDC), RAM used as a buffer and scratchpad, and a hardware data compressor/decompressor.

UPDATE OPTIONS

Flash memory's flexibility means that it can be erased and reprogrammed in many different ways, and at many different times during system lifetime. Three common techniques for updating flash memory are PROM programming, on-board update and in-system write.

Off-Board PROM Programming

For those of you with an existing hardware/software investment in PROM programming equipment for EPROMS or PROMs, you'll be happy to know that this very same equipment can also be used to program flash memories. What's new, of course, is that instead of putting EPROMs under UV light to erase them, you can both program and erase flash memories in the PROM programmer!

This flash memory update method is especially useful for easy-to-socket packages like DIP, PLCC and PSOP. If your PROM programmer only contains a DIP socket, you can purchase socket adapters for all flash memory packages.[11]

---

[11]Information on socket adapters, as well as PROM programmer vendors supporting flash memory, can be found in the Appendix.

PROM programming equipment for flash memory is most useful during system debug and prototyping, to aid in quick code revisions. It's also useful when programming the kernel boot code in block-eraseable flash memories such as Intel's Boot Block devices. Programming the boot block before installing the component on the board means that the requirement to ramp 12V on the $\overline{\text{PWD}}$[12] input for Boot Block flash memories does not need to be supported in-system.

On-Board Update

Contrary to the PROM programming method described earlier, on-board update programs or erases flash memories *after* they are soldered onto the system board. Designs that have large arrays of flash memory devices use this method to minimize component handling and maximize manufacturing efficiency. It's also often the method-of-choice for hard-to-socket component packages such as TSOP.

In on-board update, an external connection supplies all signals and voltages required for programming/erasing the flash memory, with an external processor (outside of the system) executing the update algorithm. If a board tester is used in production, its bed-of-nails component interface can be used to provide these inputs; otherwise a dedicated connector on the board is an option. In some cases, an adapter originating from a PROM programmer socket can even be used.

One important design consideration to keep in mind is that during on-board update, *all other logic* in the system that shares signals with the flash memory (common data bus, addresses, control inputs/outputs) should also be powered up (and held in reset). If not, this logic must be electrically isolated from the flash memory to prevent damage to the memory and/or the external device controlling the update. As Figure 4.16 shows, CMOS devices not powered up through their supply voltage inputs will instead attempt to power themselves via their inputs or outputs. This will most likely draw excessive current from the flash memory and external update control source.

---

[12]$\overline{\text{PWD}}$ is also known as $\overline{\text{RP}}$ in JEDEC notation.

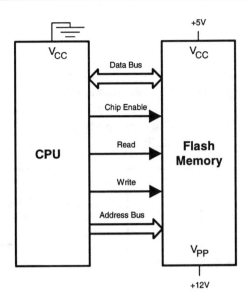

Figure 4.16: Design Considerations During On-Board Update

On-board programming adds flexibility to board manufacturing. For example, as a system moves down an assembly line, you can download diagnostic code to the flash memory to fully test system functionality under system CPU control. Also, the final software version can be downloaded to flash memory immediately before the hardware box leaves the warehouse. This enables just-in-time (JIT) manufacturing, and also allows one hardware design to service multiple markets and functions. For example, one personal computer hardware design can be customized for specific customers, specific market price points and/or specific areas of the world simply by varying the software programmed into its flash memory BIOS before shipping the PC.

Several companies making PROM programmers also offer board-programming fixtures and systems. These companies consult/advise customers interested in programming/erasing flash memory in this manner, and are a valuable resource.[13]

---

[13]See the Appendix for more information.

In-System Write

Like on-board update, flash memories being updated in-system are physically attached to the system motherboard. However, in this case, the entire system is powered up and operational, and the system CPU is executing the update routine. A simplified diagram of this process is shown in Figure 4.17. This key capability differentiates flash memory from earlier technologies like EPROM.

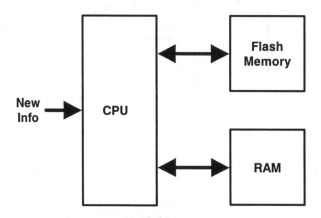

Figure 4.17: Key Elements of In-System Update

In Chapter 7 we'll review flash memory software update algorithms in great detail; let it suffice for now to say that registers internal to the flash memory devices decode the command sequences written to them and react accordingly to program or erase the memory. Therefore, although programming takes many microseconds or milliseconds to complete (erase being similarly slow), commands can be written to the flash memory at SRAM-like write speeds.

Figure 4.17 shows external RAM interfacing to the CPU in addition to the flash memory. Today, it is not possible to read data (or execute code) from a flash memory while it is being programmed or erased (some newer-generation devices allow you to *suspend* erase to read, however). Although the in-system update routines can be *stored* in the flash memory, they must be copied to, and executed from, some external device, such as RAM. After update is complete, the system can jump back to, and resume executing out of, the flash memory.

In-system write is most useful for updating code or data once a system is in the customer's hands, eliminating the need for a technician call and system disassembly to replace memory components. The new data or code to be stored in the flash memory can come from any of numerous possible sources; downloaded from a parallel or serial connector, supplied via a modem link or floppy or hard disk drive interface, etc. Using embedded code in cellular phones as an example, flash memory update could be as simple as the user calling the phone manufacturer on a special telephone number. After establishing the connection, new code could be downloaded to flash memory via the wireless link! The possibilities are limited only by your imagination and the unique characteristics of your system design and operating environment.

SUMMARY

This chapter has discussed the different flash memory packaging options available to you, and how these packages match up to the various methods that can be employed to update flash memory. In Chapter 2 we discussed different system applications that can take advantage of flash memory capabilities. These applications have unique needs, which often translate into optimum flash memory packaging selections, and allow/preclude various possible update methods.

Other areas of this book to reference for more information include the upcoming chapters on hardware interfacing (components and cards), power requirements, software algorithms and the PCMCIA memory card standard. Finally, the Appendix gives more detailed information on various socket, socket adapter and programmer vendors for your reference.

Chapter Five: Hardware Interfacing To Flash Memory Components

Chapters 1 and 2 explained what flash memory *is*, and discussed flash memory *applications*, ways that flash memory can make today's systems better and enable revolutionary new solutions that exploit its features. In Chapter 3, we reviewed several unique semiconductor technology approaches to solving the flash memory "puzzle". Now, beginning with Chapter 5, we'll show you how to integrate flash memory into your upcoming designs. In particular, this chapter outlines techniques for hardware interfacing to flash memory components. Interfacing to flash memory cards, as well as software interfacing to flash memory, will be saved for later.

HARDWARE INTERFACING FUNDAMENTALS

As you're already aware, flash memory is nonvolatile like ROM (Read-Only Memory) and equally important, in-system rewriteable like RAM (Random-Access Memory). With rare exceptions, most flash memories have minor variations on standard SRAM pinout interfaces. We'll review the SRAM interface in this section. Specifically, we'll cover the following input/output and control pins:

- Chip Enable (Chip Select)
- Addresses
- Data In/Out
- Output Enable (Read)
- Write Enable (Write)

Figures 5.1 and 5.2 give examples of standard processor/flash memory interfaces, while Table 5.1 shows a typical bus interface truth table for an "SRAM interface" flash memory.

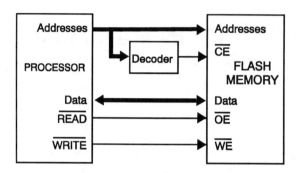

Figure 5.1: Processor/Flash Memory Interface (separate address and data buses, distinct read and write, one flash memory)

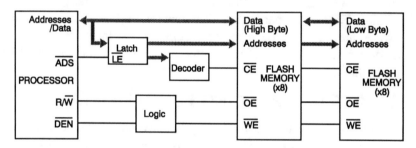

Figure 5.2: Processor / Flash Memory Interface (multiplexed address/data lines, multiplexed read/write, two x8 flash memories)

Mode	$\overline{CE}$	$\overline{OE}$	$\overline{WE}$	A_n	DQ_{0-7}
Read	V_{IL}	V_{IL}	V_{IH}	X	D_{OUT}
Output Disable	V_{IL}	V_{IH}	V_{IH}	X	High Z
Write	V_{IL}	V_{IH}	V_{IL}	X	D_{IN}
Standby	V_{IH}	X	X	X	High Z

Table 5.1: Flash Memory Bus Interface

Chip Enable

The system processor often connects to several other components through its external bus interface. These include memory (flash, RAM, etc.) and peripherals such as A/D and D/A converters, external interface chips and secondary processors (e.g., keyboard controllers, interrupt controllers, and graphics controllers). A specific external component is selected via its chip enable input, connected to an appropriate chip select signal generated by some type of decoding unit.

Some processors, such as the Intel 80C186 family, have dedicated chip select outputs activated when software accesses a defined address range. Chip enable inputs of corresponding external components connect directly to these processor chip select signals. Otherwise, external address decode logic generates chip enable signals from high order CPU addresses and port pins. This address decode logic can be as simple as a 3:8 demultiplexer, or, alternatively, more flexible programmable logic can be used. See Figure 5.1 for an example.

Addresses

Each flash memory stores many bits of data (8 million and growing at the time this book was published!). Typically, these bits are arranged in groups of 8 (byte-wide, or x8) or 16 (word-wide, or x16). To read or write a byte or word, the system logic must first select it, by specifying its location (or address) within the flash memory.

Just as the chip enable selects a device, the address inputs select data within that device. Think of a home address for an example of how the chip enable and address inputs coordinate with each other.

> Brian Dipert
> 123 Memory Lane
> Anytown, Anystate 45678

The city, state, and zip code select an area within the United States (the chip enable), and the street name and address select an individual house (the chip addresses).

Addresses originate at the system processor. As Figure 5.1 shows, the lowest-level processor address signals are common to all external components; the higher order addresses generate chip enables that select between them. Some processors minimize pin count by multiplexing addresses and data. In these cases, an external address latch (triggered by a processor address valid signal) stores these multiplexed addresses for use by external devices. See Figure 5.2 for an example of address latching in a processor design.

Data In/Out

The data bus transfers information between the processor and flash memory. Common processor data buses are byte-wide (x8), word-wide (x16) and double-word-wide (x32), transferring 8, 16 and 32 bits of data at a time, respectively. Depending on the specific processor and flash memory selected, multiple memories may be connected in parallel to satisfy the data bus bandwidth required by the interface (see Figure 5.2 for an example).

In some cases, an additional bus transceiver chip may be added between the memory and CPU. Later in this chapter, when discussing bus loading specifications, we'll show you if such a transceiver is required, either to mimimize processor loading or to eliminate the potential for data bus contention.

Output Enable

After selecting the flash memory and address within it, the processor must also communicate whether it wants to perform a read or write at that specific location. During a read operation, the processor activates its $\overline{\text{READ}}$ output, which connects to the flash memory output enable signal. This turns on the flash memory output buffers and drives data onto the processor data bus. When reading from a specific flash memory, outputs for all other devices on the data bus, including other flash memories, must be disabled. Dedicated chip enables ensure this, allowing the processor $\overline{\text{READ}}$ to connect to all interface devices. This concept is called two-line interface control. See Figure 5.1 for an example.

Some processors (notably those from Motorola and second sources) don't have a dedicated $\overline{\text{READ}}$ signal, and instead have R/$\overline{\text{W}}$ (Read/Write) and $\overline{\text{DEN}}$ (Data Enable) outputs. Figure 5.2 shows how these combine to form $\overline{\text{OE}}$ to the flash memory.

Write Enable

To write to flash memory, an approach similar to the "output enable" technique discussed earlier is taken. This is normally accomplished by connecting the flash memory write enable input to a $\overline{\text{WRITE}}$ output from the processor. Alternatively, R/$\overline{\text{W}}$ and $\overline{\text{DEN}}$ signals are decoded as shown in Figure 5.2. Again, two-line control allows common connection of one processor $\overline{\text{WRITE}}$ signal to all external devices, with per-device selection through individual chip selects.

Flash memory provides some unique challenges to the system designer with respect to its in-system write capabilities. Similar to EEPROM and battery-backed SRAM (for example), care must be taken to control the chip enable and/or write enable signals to flash memory during system power up and power down. Any glitches or active transitions on these signals may be misinterpreted by the flash memory as a valid write, with unwanted (and permanent) results!

Contrast this with ROM memories (which are nonvolatile but not in-system writeable and therefore unchanging) and RAM memories (which are writeable but volatile, guaranteed invalid after system power transitions and therefore requiring initialization by the startup software). The flash memory interface is complicated further by the fact that, in most cases, the chip enable and write enable inputs are "active low" signals, enabled at 0V. 0V is also the state of these signals when a system is first turned on, before the power supply reaches its operating voltage! Due to different capacitive loading, some control signals may ramp up faster than others, and similarly V_{PP} (the program/erase voltage) may reach high voltage before V_{CC} stabilizes.

Flash memory vendors provide several mechanisms that assist the system designer in eliminating the potential for unwanted data writes. Some include on-chip circuitry that monitors the supply voltage and blocks all write attempts below a specified value, called the lockout voltage (V_{LKO}). Others incorporate glitch detect circuitry that ignores excessively short active transitions on chip enable and write enable inputs. In some cases, lengthy multi-byte software command sequences must be used to enable flash memory write and erasure, lowering the probability that such sequences will be unintentionally written to the device. In other instances, a separate input to the flash memory acts as a write protect, such as the $\overline{PWD}$[14] input of some Intel flash memories. Finally, where a separate voltage is required to write or erase flash memory (i.e., V_{PP}), disabling this voltage when not needed will block unintended alteration of flash memory contents. We'll cover this additional V_{PP} voltage in the next section.

$\overline{WE}$-Less Flash Memories

In attempting to minimize pin count for their devices, some flash memory manufacturers have removed the $\overline{WE}$ input, resulting in the bus interface truth table shown in Table 5.2. This pinout eliminates separate two-line control for both reads and writes. A selected device distinguishes between a read or a write by the state of its $\overline{OE}$ input when it is selected (V_{IH} = write, V_{IL} = read). This functionality often complicates the system interface to $\overline{WE}$-less flash memories for the following reasons:

- $\overline{OE}$ must transition to its valid state (V_{IH} or V_{IL}) before $\overline{CE}$ selects the device. This is contrary to the design of most microprocessors, which provide addresses (for chip selects) before asserting $\overline{READ}$ or $\overline{WRITE}$. In many cases, this incompatibility impacts system performance by increasing the number of required wait states to read from or write to the flash memory.

- Spurious (involuntary) chip select generation is common in systems, as processor addresses transition through intermediate states at the beginning of, and between, external bus cycles. Interface logic between the processor and flash memory must

---

[14]$\overline{PWD}$ is also known as $\overline{RP}$ in JEDEC notation.

assure that these invalid chip select signals do not pass through to the $\overline{\text{WE}}$-less flash memory, where, without a clarifying write enable, they would cause spurious, unwanted writes.

Mode	$\overline{\text{CE}}$	$\overline{\text{OE}}$	DQ_{0-7}
Read	V_{IL}	V_{IL}	D_{OUT}
Write	V_{IL}	V_{IH}	D_{IN}
Standby	V_{IH}	X	High Z

Table 5.2: $\overline{\text{WE}}$-Less Flash Memory Bus Interface[15]

THE Vpp PROGRAM/ERASE VOLTAGE

Like all other logic devices in a system, flash memory requires an operating voltage (often referred to as V_{CC}) to power its circuitry and enable access to its contents. Common V_{CC} operating voltages are 5V ± 10% (4.5V-5.5V) and 3.3V ± 0.3V.

Program or erase of a flash memory cell[16] requires (in addition to V_{CC}) a high internal voltage to pull electrons onto or remove them from a cell's floating gate. This voltage is often referred to as V_{PP} in flash memory specifications.

Some flash memories generate this high internal voltage themselves from the existing V_{CC} input. However, the high V_{PP} current requirements and complex circuitry required can make the design of these internal voltage converters difficult. If they take up a relatively large percentage of the flash memory die, internal converters adversely affect the device's cost and manufacturing yield. Additionally, in a system design that uses a large number of flash memory components, it is often more economical to generate V_{PP} from an external source rather than to include this circuitry on every device in the flash memory array.

---

[15]Notice that, compared to Table 5.1, Table 5.2 has no entry for $\overline{\text{WE}}$.
[16]As we first discussed in Chapter 2.

For these reasons, other flash memory vendors require external V_{PP} voltage generation, and provide a dedicated input pin to supply this voltage to the internal flash memory cells. As an example, many NOR flash memories specify an external V_{PP} of $12V \pm 5\%$ ($11.4V$ - $12.6V$). If the existing system power supply already generates the appropriate voltage, the supply output can be connected directly to the flash memory. *Be sure that this supply falls within the 5% tolerance range.* Otherwise, use an external 12V regulator to up- or down-convert another available voltage to generate the required V_{PP} voltage. In Chapter 6, we'll cover flash memory power requirements in more detail, including specific examples on generating V_{PP}.

Switching V_{PP}

As mentioned earlier, a switcheable V_{PP} is one means of protecting flash memory data from unwanted alteration. Switching on V_{PP} only when required for program/erase also minimizes system power consumption. In many cases, the power supply or 12V converter circuit integrates a TTL-compatible V_{PP} $\overline{\text{ENABLE}}$ input; otherwise, an external switch can perform this function. Figure 5.3 shows an example circuit for switching V_{PP}. Note that a PFET is needed for compatibility with the TTL voltage driving the transistor gate.

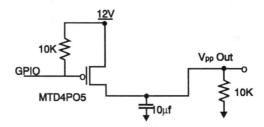

Figure 5.3: V_{PP} Switch Circuit

When using an external switch, factor in any voltage drops across the switch when matching the power supply to the V_{PP} requirements of the flash memory. The example Motorola MDT4P05 (or an equivalent) shown in Figure 5.3 makes an ideal V_{PP} switch. The calculations below show that given a power supply with an output voltage of $12V \pm 4\%$ and current draw of one flash memory being programmed or erased, the supply/MDT4P05 combination still satisfies the 12V ± 5% requirement of the flash memory. This calculation can be modified to fit the specifics of your design.

$$R_{DS} = 0.6 \ \Omega$$

I_{PP} = 30 mA (worst case, one component being programmed/erased)

$\Delta V_{SWITCH}DROP = $ (30 mA x 0.6 Ω) = 0.02 V

(12V - 4%) - 0.02V = 11.5V > 11.4V (OK!)

V$_{PP}$ Feedback

After switching V_{PP} on, the system must wait for the voltage to ramp up to the valid operating range before attempting the program/erase of flash memory. This delay is a function of the chosen power supply and of the amount of capacitance driven by the supply. In some cases, the hardware design engineer can characterize the performance of the power supply and determine the maximum delay. System software then simply inserts a software delay loop of sufficient duration to meet or exceed this maximum delay after enabling the power supply. In other cases, such as with removable memory cards, the varying number of flash memory devices from different densities results in a varying capacitive load. Under this circumstance, you should base the delay loop on a theoretical worst-case limit.

To obtain a more precise indication of V_{PP} status, or in applications where the system cannot tolerate the unusable delay of this software loop (i. e., real-time systems), hardware circuitry can be used to sense and report back "V_{PP} Valid" indication to the processor. Figure 5.4 shows the MAX705, which includes the system $\overline{\text{RESET}}$, V_{CC} monitoring (power-good sensing), *and* V_{PP} monitoring in one device. A multi-function device like the MAX705 is ideal in flash memory designs (see the next section on $\overline{\text{PWD}}$ usage). Simpler circuits (comparators, for example) are also available, if V_{PP} monitoring and feedback only are desired.

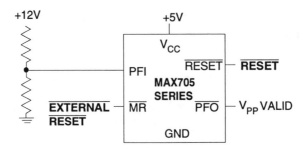

Figure 5.4: Maxim MAX705, Used for V_{CC} and V_{PP} Monitoring

ADVANCED HARDWARE INTERFACING

Second-generation flash memories have gone beyond the standard SRAM interface to provide additional functionality to system designers. This section of Chapter 5 discusses two additional pins offered in Intel Boot Block and FlashFile™ memories; the $\overline{\text{PWD}}$ input and the RY/$\overline{\text{BY}}$ output. RY/$\overline{\text{BY}}$ is also provided in Toshiba's NAND flash memories.

The $\overline{\text{PWD}}$ Input

This pin (explained most simply) provides a master ON/OFF switch for the flash memory. It has four distinct functions in system designs:

- Driving the input to a TTL low level (V_{IL}) puts the device in a very low power mode (referred to as Deep Powerdown), even with V_{CC} and V_{PP} still powering the device. Driving the pin fully to 0V (GND) allows the device to achieve the lowest power consumption.
- Acting as an ON/OFF switch, $\overline{\text{PWD}}$, when at V_{IL}, terminates any internal automation activity inside the flash memory. This is especially crucial when the entire system (including the processor) is reset, and the CPU attempts to fetch its reboot instructions from the flash memory. Toggling $\overline{\text{PWD}}$ low to reset the flash memory ensures that it will provide, when read, the stored instructions that the CPU anticipates, and not Status Register data or other unexpected information.

- Again acting as an ON/OFF switch, $\overline{PWD}$ at V_{IL} causes the flash memory to ignore all write attempts. This is ideal for protecting the flash memory from unwanted spurious writes during system power transitions.
- Finally, in Boot Block memories, $\overline{PWD}$ locks and unlocks the hardware-protected boot block (see the example memory map of Figure 5.5). The boot block is intended to store the kernel code to bring up (initialize) the system. Boot block memories are designed such that the boot block cannot be altered (programmed/erased) with normal TTL levels on $\overline{PWD}$. The boot block only unlocks by putting 12V on $\overline{PWD}$.

Normally, the boot block is programmed using a PROM programmer before installing the flash memory on the system board[17]. If the capability for generating 12V on $\overline{PWD}$ doesn't exist in the system, the boot code becomes completely nonvolatile and unalterable; the boot block essentially becomes a ROM block.

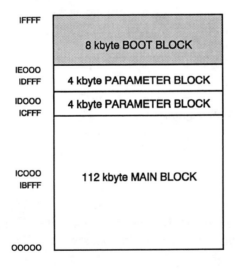

IFFFF	8 kbyte BOOT BLOCK
IE000 / IDFFF	4 kbyte PARAMETER BLOCK
ID000 / ICFFF	4 kbyte PARAMETER BLOCK
IC000 / IBFFF	112 kbyte MAIN BLOCK
00000	

Figure 5.5: Intel 28F001BX Boot Block Flash Memory Map

---

[17] As we first covered in Chapter 4.

Again looking at Figure 5.4, by connecting the MAX705 POWERGOOD output to the flash memory $\overline{PWD}$ input, the resultant design resets the flash memory in case of a system $\overline{RESET}$ and protects the flash memory from spurious writes on system powerup/down. Power management control can be added with a logic AND of the existing system $\overline{RESET}$ and an available I/O line, which is toggled low to put the flash memory in deep powerdown mode. The default state of this I/O line on reset and system powerup should be high.

RY/$\overline{BY}$ Output

The RY/$\overline{BY}$ output provides a hardware indication for monitoring the status of internal program or erase automation inside the flash memory. When the system initiates a program or erase, RY/$\overline{BY}$ goes low (to V_{OL}). Similarly, when program or erase completes, RY/$\overline{BY}$ returns to its default V_{OH} state. Its function is especially valuable during slow block erase. With RY/$\overline{BY}$ connected to a processor interrupt input or system interrupt controller, the system can initiate a block erase and then read from, program, or erase other flash memories (or execute any other desired system functions) as foreground tasks. The background block erase executes in parallel and alerts the system, when it completes, via the RY/$\overline{BY}$ output.

Keep in mind that flash memory programming may complete faster than execution of an interrupt service routine. Therefore, in this case, simple polling of the flash memory Status Register may make more sense[18]. System software can mask the RY/$\overline{BY}$-generated interupt for flash memory programming operations and re-enable it for block erase events.

RY/$\overline{BY}$ is a full CMOS (not a wired OR) output. To interface to an array of flash memory devices, you can run each RY/$\overline{BY}$ to a separate interrupt or can alternatively connect the multiple RY/$\overline{BY}$ outputs to one procesor input through circuitry like that shown in Figure 5.6.

---

[18]You'll also see the comparison of Status Register polling vs. RY/$\overline{BY}$ interrupt, from a software standpoint, in Chapter 7.

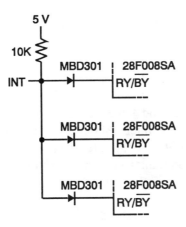

Figure 5.6: Wired-OR RY/$\overline{BY}$ Implementation

INTERPRETING DATASHEET AC PARAMETERS

What's the best way to insure that your flash memory-based system design will be "first-run functional"? Follow the datasheet specifications (*all of them*)! This section will help you interpret the abundance of information in typical flash memory technical documentation. Specifically, we'll cover the timing parameters, both for read and write operations. We'll save current and voltage information (the DC specifications) for Chapter 6.

Throughout the following discussion, please reference the following tables and figures:

- Figure 5.7, Flash Memory Read Access Time Partitioning
- Figure 5.8, AC Input/Output Reference Waveform
- Figure 5.9, AC Testing Load Circuit
- Figure 5.10, High Speed AC Input/Output Reference Waveform
- Figure 5.11, High Speed AC Testing Load Circuit
- Table 5.4, AC Characteristics, Read Operations
- Figure 5.12, AC Waveform for Read Operations

- Table 5.5, AC Characteristics, Write Operations
- Figure 5.13, AC Waveform for Write Operations
- Table 5.6, Input/Output Capacitance
- Figure 5.14, Ordering Information

These specific figures and tables are a subset of characteristics taken from Revision 3 of the Intel 28F008SA FlashFile memory datasheet, dated September 1992. They are representative of generic flash specifications from both Intel and other flash memory manufacturers.

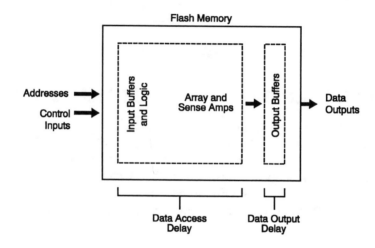

Figure 5.7: Flash Memory Read Access Time Partitioning

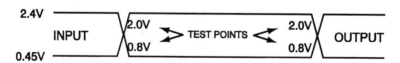

AC test inputs are driven at V_{OH} (2.4V TTL) for a logic 1 and V_{OL} (0.45V TTL) for a logic 0. Input timing begins at V_{IH} (2.0V TTL) and V_{IL} (0.8V TTL). Output timing ends at V_{IH} and V_{IL}. Input rise and fall times (10% to 90%) < 10 ns.

Figure 5.8: AC Input/Output Reference Waveform

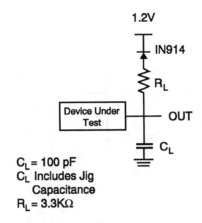

1.2V

IN914

R_L

Device Under Test

OUT

C_L

$C_L = 100$ pF
C_L Includes Jig
     Capacitance
$R_L = 3.3K\Omega$

Figure 5.9: AC Testing Load Circuit

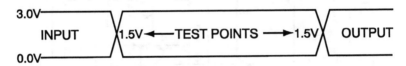

3.0V

INPUT

1.5V ◄——TEST POINTS——► 1.5V

OUTPUT

0.0V

AC test inputs are driven at 3.0V for a logic 1 and 0.0V for a logic 0. Input timing begins, and output timing ends, at 1.5V. Input rise and fall times (10% to 90%) < 10 ns.

Figure 5.10: High Speed Input / Output Reference Waveform

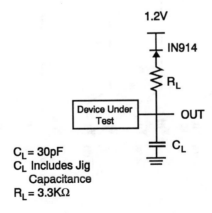

1.2V

IN914

R_L

Device Under Test

OUT

C_L

$C_L = 30$pF
C_L Includes Jig
     Capacitance
$R_L = 3.3K\Omega$

Figure 5.11: High Speed AC Testing Load Circuit

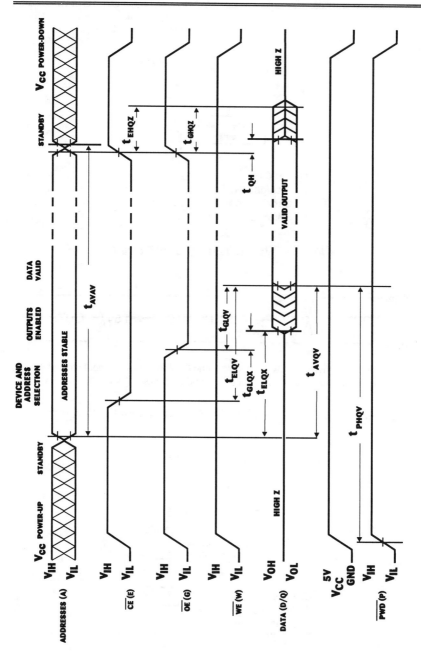

Figure 5.12: AC Waveforms for Read Operations

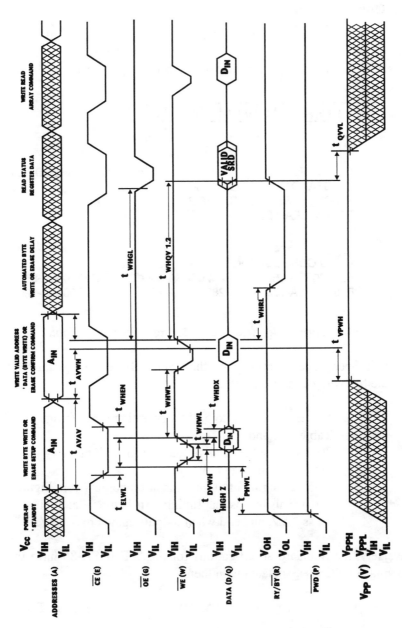

Figure 5.13: AC Waveforms for Write Operation

General Observations

Figure 5.14 and Table 5.4 indicate that the 28F008SA can be ordered in either of two flavors, the *28F008SA-85* and *28F008SA-120*. Notice that the "-85" version actually has two different sets of specifications.

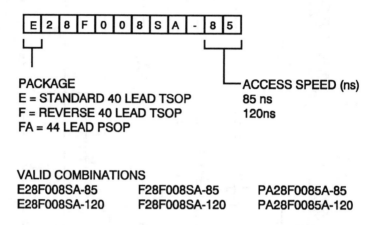

PACKAGE
E = STANDARD 40 LEAD TSOP
F = REVERSE 40 LEAD TSOP
FA = 44 LEAD PSOP

ACCESS SPEED (ns)
85 ns
120ns

VALID COMBINATIONS
E28F008SA-85   F28F008SA-85   PA28F0085A-85
E28F008SA-120   F28F008SA-120   PA28F0085A-120

Figure 5.14: Example Ordering Information Table

The High Speed specifications for the 28F008SA-85 are guaranteed under the following conditions:

- $V_{CC} \pm 5\%$ (4.75V to 5.25V) operating range (from Tables 5.4 and 5.5)
- 30pF (or less) capacitive loading on flash memory outputs (from Figure 5.11)
- 1.5V testing input/output transition points (from Figure 5.10). This means that timing tests begin when inputs cross 1.5V, and end when outputs again cross 1.5V.

Conversely, the Standard specifications for the 28F008SA-85 have the following conditions associated with them:

- $V_{CC} \pm 10\%$ (4.5V to 5.5V) operating range (from Tables 5.4 and 5.5)

- 100pF or less capacitive loading on flash memory outputs (from Figure 5.9)
- Full standard TTL testing input/output transition points (from Figure 5.8)

Since the 28F008SA operating under Standard specs has a wider allowable supply voltage range, more heavily loaded outputs, and more slew in its input and output testing points, its read specifications are slightly slower than those for the High Speed version. We'll discuss this in more detail below.

Naming Conventions

Most of the read and write specifications in Tables 5.4 and 5.5 have two different symbols associated with them. The first symbol for each specification reflects the JEDEC naming convention standards. The second of the two (i.e., t_{ACC}, t_{OE}, etc.) represents the common symbol which has been in use for many years with many different kinds of memories. Table 5.3 summarizes the JEDEC conventions for both flash memory signals and possible signal states.

Signals	
A	Address
E	Chip Enable
G	Output Enable
W	Write Enable
D	Data (Inputs)
Q	Data (Outputs)
P	Powerdown
R	RY/$\overline{BY}$
V	V_{PP}
Signal States	
H	High
L	Low
V	Valid
X	Low Z (Driven, Invalid)
Z	High Z (Not Driven)
P	High (12V)

Table 5.3: JEDEC Signal/State Naming Conventions

Capacitive Loading and Effects

One of the fundamental laws of electronics states the following:

$$I = C \times dV/dt$$

Any semiconductor device (like a flash memory) is capable of driving a constant finite amount of current from its outputs to the inputs of other devices. These inputs have a certain amount of capacitance associated with them, as do the board traces that route signals throughout the system.

Given a fixed current value (I), the above equation shows that an increase in the amount of capacitance (C) driven by a flash memory output results in a parallel increase in the output transition time (or stated in another way, its dV/dt decreases). The tradeoff here is clear; by minimizing the number of devices the flash memory's outputs drive, read performance will increase proportionally. Examining the 28F008SA-85 AC read specifications in Table 5.4 validates this. High speed access time is 85 ns; standard access time is 90 ns. Similarly, high speed output enable time is 40 ns, and standard output enable time is 45 ns. A difference of 5 ns may seem at first glance to be trivial, but in a tight design may result in one less wait state for processor accesses. Other flash memories may have similar or even more significant performance improvements at lower capacitive loading conditions.

The lesson: carefully analyze the amount of capacitance loading your flash memory outputs and minimize this loading wherever possible. After this analysis, choose the correct specifications for your design. Don't load outputs beyond their specified maximum capacitance and expect the flash memory to still perform as documented! In a heavily loaded design, buffers and/or transceivers can often be used to subdivide the number of inputs connected to each flash memory output resulting in a reasonable capacitive load that falls within specified limits.

Versions		$V_{CC} \pm 5\%$ $V_{CC} \pm 10\%$	28F008SA-85[1]		28F008SA-85[2]		28F008SA-120		
Symbol		Parameter	Min	Max	Min	Max	Min	Max	Unit
t_{AVAV}	t_{RC}	Read Cycle Time	85		90		120		ns
t_{AVQV}	t_{ACC}	Address to Output Delay		85		90		120	ns
t_{ELQV}	t_{CE}	$\overline{CE}$ to Output Delay		85		90		120	ns
t_{GLQV}	t_{OE}	$\overline{OE}$ to Output Delay		40		45		50	ns
t_{ELQX}	t_{LZ}	$\overline{CE}$ to Output Low Z	0		0		0		ns
t_{EHQZ}	t_{HZ}	$\overline{CE}$ High to Output High Z		55		55		55	ns
t_{GLQX}	t_{OLZ}	$\overline{OE}$ to Output Low Z	0		0		0		ns
t_{GHQZ}	t_{DF}	$\overline{OE}$ High to Output High Z		30		30		30	ns
	t_{OH}	Output Hold from Address, $\overline{CE}$ or $\overline{OE}$ Change, Whichever is First	0		0		0		ns

Table 5.4: AC Characteristics, Read Operations

Notes:
1. See High Speed Input/Output Reference Waveforms and High Speed AC Testing Load Circuits for testing characteristics.
2. See AC Input/Output Reference Waveforms and AC Testing Load Circuits for testing characteristics.

AC Read Characteristics

Next, let's define the various read timing specifications for our 28F008SA example flash memory.

t_{AVAV} (t_{RC})   Read Cycle Time-The shortest possible read cycle that a processor can execute when reading from the flash memory. It is measured from the active transition of the first signal (defining the beginning of the read) until data is valid.

t_{AVQV} (t_{ACC}) Address to Output Delay-The guaranteed longest time from when addresses stablize until data outputs become valid (assuming active $\overline{CE}$ and $\overline{OE}$ signals), during a read.

t_{ELQV} (t_{CE}) $\overline{CE}$ to Output Delay-The guaranteed longest time from when chip select is activated until data outputs are valid (assuming stable addresses and active $\overline{OE}$).

t_{GLQV} (t_{OE}) $\overline{OE}$ to Output Delay-The guaranteed longest time from an active output enable signal until data outputs are valid (assuming stable addresses and active $\overline{CE}$).

t_{ELQX} (t_{LZ}) $\overline{CE}$, $\overline{OE}$ to Output Low Z-The minimum delay from
t_{GLQX} (t_{OLZ})   activation of $\overline{CE}$ or $\overline{OE}$ (respectively) until the data outputs begin to drive (not necessarily with valid data).

t_{EHQZ} (t_{HZ}) $\overline{CE}$, $\overline{OE}$ to Output Low Z-The maximum delay from
t_{GHQZ} (t_{DF})   deactivating $\overline{CE}$ or $\overline{OE}$ (respectively) until the outputs are no longer driven.

t_{OH} Output Hold from Addresses, $\overline{CE}$, or $\overline{OE}$ Change, Whichever is First-The minimum valid data output hold time after deactivation of $\overline{CE}$ or $\overline{OE}$, or after address(es) change.

Read Specification Clarifications

The output delay from $\overline{OE}$ active (t_{GLQV}) is much shorter than the output delay from $\overline{CE}$ active (t_{ELQV}) or addresses valid (t_{AVQV}). As Figure 5.7 suggests, the time required to read from a flash memory (or any other memory, for that matter) consists of two general delays:

- Time to decode addresses and chip enable, select the correct bits in the array, and sense their stored data values, and

- Time to drive this information onto the data bus through the output buffers.

This latter delay is the t_{OE} or t_{GLQV}. t_{ACC} and t_{CE} incorporate both delays. Data may be read from a flash memory in as short a time as the t_{OE}, provided you ensure that valid data is internally sitting at the inputs of the output buffers (in other words, the first decode/sense delay has already been met). Interleaving is a hardware technique that takes advantage of this, and we'll cover it briefly at the conclusion of this chapter.

Specifications t_{ELQX} and t_{GLQX} show how quickly the flash memory could drive the output bus once enabled. The system designer must ensure not to drive other devices on the common bus at this time, to prevent bus contention. Similarly, specifications t_{EHQZ} and t_{GHQZ} show how long it could take for the flash memory to quit driving the output bus once deselected. Other devices should not drive the bus until this time has elapsed, again to prevent bus contention. If this is not possible, a high-speed external transceiver (which typically has very fast turn-off specifications) can be inserted between the flash memory outputs and the common bus.

AC Write Characteristics

We've looked at the specifications that describe a flash memory's read performance. Now, let's examine their counterparts: the flash memory write characteristics.

t_{AVAV} (t_{WC})   Write Cycle Time-Refers to the shortest possible write cycle that a processor can execute when writing to the flash memory. It is measured from the active transition of the first signal (defining the beginning of the write) to the inactive transition of the last signal (defining the end of the write).

t_{ELWL} (t_{CS}) $\overline{CE}$ Setup to $\overline{WE}$ Going Low-The minimum setup time from when $\overline{CE}$ is activated until $\overline{WE}$ is activated.

t_{WLWH} (t_{WP}) $\overline{WE}$ Pulse Width-The minimum $\overline{WE}$ active pulse width required to successfully write a command to the flash memory.

t_{VPWH} (t_{VPS}) V_{PP} Setup to $\overline{WE}$ Going High-The minimum time that V_{PP} must be at its high voltage before a program or erase operation initiates.

t_{AVWH} (t_{AS}) valid   Address, Data Setup to $\overline{WE}$ Going High-The minimum address and data t_{DVWH} (t_{DS}) setup time before $\overline{WE}$ is deactivated (a write pulse ends).

t_{WHDX} (t_{DH})
t_{WHAX} (t_{AH})
t_{WHEH} (t_{CH}) Data, Address and $\overline{CE}$ Hold from $\overline{WE}$ High-The minimum data, address and $\overline{CE}$ hold times from when $\overline{WE}$ is deactivated (a write pulse ends).

t_{WHWL} (t_{WPH}) $\overline{WE}$ Pulse Width High-The minimum $\overline{WE}$ inactive pulse width required before the processor writes another command to the flash memory.

t_{WHQV} Duration of Byte Programming, Block Erase Operations-Minimum duration of internally automated byte program and byte erase operations.

t_{QVVL} (t_{VPH}) V_{PP} Hold from Valid SRD-Minimum time that V_{PP} must be held at high voltage after the successful completion of an internally automated byte program or block erase.

Write Specification Clarifications

Examining Table 5.5 and Figure 5.13 closely gives us a great deal of useful information about the internal workings of the 28F008SA. First, specification t_{ELWL} shows that the flash memory must first be *selected*, before *writing* to it. Many flash memory vendors, including Intel, also provide alternate specifications in cases where $\overline{WE}$ is activated *before* $\overline{CE}$; this is called a "$\overline{CE}$-controlled write". Consult specific device documentation for more information.

Versions		$V_{CC} \pm 5\%$ $V_{CC} \pm 10\%$	28F008SA-85[1]		28F008SA-85[2]		28F008SA-120		
Symbol		Parameter	Min	Max	Min	Max	Min	Max	Unit
t_{AVAV}	t_{WC}	Write Cycle Time	85		90		120		ns
t_{ELWL}	t_{CS}	$\overline{CE}$ Setup to $\overline{WE}$ Going Low	10		10		10		ns
t_{WLWH}	t_{WP}	$\overline{WE}$ Pulse Width	40		40		40		ns
t_{VPWH}	t_{VPS}	V_{PP} Setup to $\overline{WE}$ Going High	100		100		100		ns
t_{AVWH}	t_{AS}	Address Setup to $\overline{WE}$ Going High	40		40		40		ns
t_{DVWH}	t_{DS}	Data Setup to $\overline{WE}$ Going High	40		40		40		ns
t_{WHDX}	t_{DH}	Data Hold from $\overline{WE}$ High	5		5		5		ns
t_{WHAX}	t_{AH}	Address Hold from $\overline{WE}$ High	5		5		5		ns
t_{WHEH}	t_{CH}	$\overline{CE}$ hold from $\overline{WE}$ High	10		10		10		ns
t_{WHWL}	t_{WPH}	$\overline{WE}$ Pulse Width High	30		30		30		ns
t_{WHQV}		Duration of Byte Programming Operation	6		6		6		µs
t_{WHQV}		Duration of Block Erase Operation	0.3		0.3		0.3		sec
t_{QVVL}	t_{VPH}	V_{PP} Hold from Valid Status Register Data	0		0		0		ns

Table 5.5: AC Characteristics, Write Operations

Notes:
1. See High Speed Input/Output Reference Waveforms and High Speed AC Testing Load
   Circuits for testing characteristics.
2. See AC Input/Output Reference Waveforms and AC Testing Load Circuits for testing
   characteristics.

CAPACITANCE $T_A = 25°C$, f = 1 MHz

Symbol	Parameter	Typ	Max	Unit	Condition
C_{IN}	Input Capacitance	6	8	pF	$V_{IN} = 0V$
C_{OUT}	Output Capacitance	8	12	pF	$V_{OUT} = 0V$

Table 5.6: Input/Output Capacitance

With the 28F008SA, the rising edge of $\overline{\text{WE}}$ (the conclusion of the active write pulse) latches both addresses and data. This simplifies the timing interface to the flash memory, as extra wait states can be added if needed to match flash memory requirements and processor timings. However, some flash memories latch addresses on the falling edge of $\overline{\text{WE}}$, and have a corresponding t_{AVWL} specification. Closely inspect specifications for various flash memories to identify if they latch addresses on the falling or rising edge of $\overline{\text{WE}}$.

PERFORMANCE ENHANCEMENTS

As raw processor performance continues to improve at a seemingly exponential rate, external memory's inability to follow a similar trend[19] has become acutely apparent. In fact, memory (especially nonvolatile memory) has become a limiting bottleneck to system performance. How have component designers (and how can you) overcome or "work around" these bottlenecks?

Caching

In one common technique, called *caching*, a portion of nonvolatile memory is replicated in faster SRAM. Accesses to this memory are from the SRAM (not nonvolatile memory) and thereby lessen the impact to system processor performance. Complex hardware and software algorithms have been developed that model memory subsystem characteristics and optimize interaction between cache memory and that memory which is being cached. Today's elaborate computer systems often contain multiple caches:

- External DRAM to cache disk drives
- External SRAM to cache DRAM and nonvolatile memory
- Even a primary internal SRAM cache (in the processor itself!) to cache the secondary external SRAM cache.

Shadowing

Another similar technique often used is called *shadowing*. Slower nonvolatile memory (such as ROM or flash memory) contents are copied

---

[19]At least, at a similar price/performance curve.

to an equivalent amount of faster DRAM for execution. Notable application examples of this technique include personal computers (where the BIOS is shadowed to DRAM) and laser printers (where code and fonts stored in nonvolatile memory are similarly shadowed to DRAM to speed system performance).

Fortunately, the latest generations of flash memory devices have read access speeds approaching or equaling those of DRAMs. Using a fast flash memory device in the design eliminates the memory duplication required for shadowing, lowering total system cost and improving reliability. Earlier in this chapter (capacitive loading and effects), we discussed the importance of minimizing capacitive loading on flash memory outputs. This loading minimization allows selection of the fastest possible flash memory devices, and therefore results in the highest system performance.

Hardware Interleaving

Hardware interleaving represents one final technique for improving read performance. Again referencing Figure 5.7, you'll remember that earlier in this chapter we talked about the different internal flash memory device delays that combined to form the read access time (t_{ACC}). These delays include:

- Time to decode addresses and chip enable, select the correct bits in the array, and sense their stored data values, ($t_{ACC} - t_{OE}$) and

- Time to drive this information onto the data bus through the output buffers (t_{OE}).

What would happen if we could access the data of multiple flash memory devices (the first delay) at the same time? In this scenario, after the initial decode/select/sense delay had passed, these devices would all have valid data sitting at the internal sense amplifier outputs, ready to be driven through the output buffers onto the system bus. Accesses to these components would take not the full t_{ACC} delay, but only the much shorter t_{OE} time. This, in a nutshell, is the concept behind hardware interleaving.

Hardware interleaving takes advantage of a common software concept called locality, which says that if a memory location is accessed, the next memory address accessed will likely be located very close by (often the very next address). Most of the time, a system processor executes code instructions which are sequential (with the exception of GOSUB and GOTO statements). With hardware interleaving, sequential memory reads access multiple flash memories (not the same device every time). Let's examine a specific example in more detail to make concrete sense of this abstract idea.

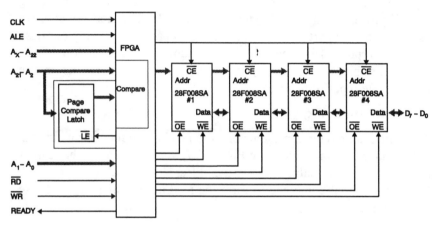

Figure 5.15: Hardware Interleaving - Utilizes Common $\overline{CE}$,
Unique $\overline{OE}$ and $\overline{WE}$

Figure 5.15 gives an example block diagram for a high-density interleaving design (possibly a laser printer or bridger/router) using Intel 28F008SA flash memories. 4-byte flash memory pages are selected by common addresses A_{21}-A_2; higher order addresses decode the 4 Mbyte flash memory array in the system memory map. Addresses A_1 and A_0, along with the $\overline{READ}$ input, generate $\overline{OE}$s for components 0-3. Therefore, system addresses are associated with flash memory components as follows:

System Address	Component and Component Address
0	Component 0 address 0
1	Component 1 address 0
2	Component 2 address 0
3	Component 3 address 0
4	Component 0 address 1
5	Component 1 address 1
etc......	

The step-by-step description below outlines a series of read accesses from this flash memory array:

1. The processor signals that it wants to read data from system address 0. This enables components 0-3 and provides them with address 0. Interface logic decodes system address bits A_1 and A_0 and, seeing that they are both zero, enables the $\overline{OE}$ input for component 0. Since this is the first access to the four byte page, it takes 85 ns.

2. The processor, executing sequential code, next reads from system address 1. Components 0-3 remain enabled, and address inputs to them remain as zeros. Interface logic decodes the "01" on system address bits A_1 and A_0, and enables the $\overline{OE}$ line for component 1. Component 1's data has already been selected and sensed, and access time for component 1, therefore, only has a 40 ns t_{OE} delay.

3. Similar 40 ns accesses follow for system addresses 2 and 3, reading from components 2 and 3, respectively.

4. Now the tricky part...the processor reads from system address 4 on its next cycle. This changes system address A_2 from a zero to a one, thereby incurring another full 85 ns t_{ACC} delay for this access from component 0 (we are now accessing a new 4-byte page, and therefore new data from each of the flash memories). However, once again, accesses to system addresses 5, 6 and 7 only have 40 ns durations.

One important (and possibly obvious) point; after the initial, relatively long t_{ACC} access to a flash memory in a page, *all* subsequent accesses within that page benefit from the shorter t_{OE} delay. These accesses need not be incrementally sequential; with a large enough page, a tight software JMP loop can also benefit.

The clearly apparent tradeoff in interleaving is between added hardware complexity and higher performance. First, let's quantify the performance gains. Over a four-byte series of sequential accesses, the average read delay from flash memory is no longer the 85 ns t_{ACC}, but is:

$$1/4 \ (85 \text{ ns} + 40 \text{ ns} + 40 \text{ ns} + 40 \text{ ns}) = 51.25 \text{ ns}$$

This performance improvement pertains to a four-byte interleaving page. A two-byte page will have average read delay of:

$$1/2 \ (85 \text{ ns} + 40 \text{ ns}) = 62.5 \text{ ns}$$

An eight-byte page, on the other hand, will have an average read delay of:

$$1/8 \ (85 \text{ ns} + 40 \text{ ns} + 40 \text{ ns} + 40 \text{ ns} + 40 \text{ ns} + 40 \text{ ns} + 40 \text{ ns} + 40 \text{ ns}) = 45.6 \text{ ns}$$

Now for the hardware complexity...the following functions (summarized in the state transition diagram of Figure 5.16), synchronized with the clock controlling the system processor, must be implemented in the interface logic between processor and memory array:

1. The logic must decode lower addresses and, correspondingly, generate $\overline{OE}$s to flash memory devices within an interleaving page. The earlier example was of a four-byte page, so addresses A_1 and A_0 must be decoded. For a two-byte page, only address A_0 must be examined, whereas an eight-byte page uses addresses A_2-A_0.

2. The logic must also examine all upper address bits, determine first if the flash memory subsystem is being accessed, and then if access to the same page is occurring, and adjust wait states back to the processor accordingly (via the READY output). The comparator logic block in Figure 5.15 serves this function.

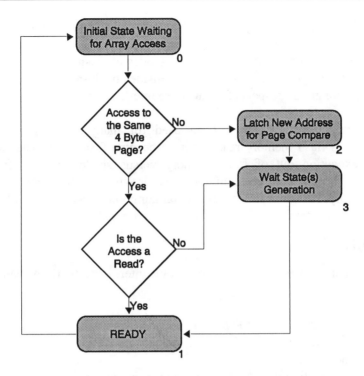

Figure 5.16: Hardware Interleaving - State Transition Diagram

3. Finally, the logic must be able to distinguish between a read or write
    to flash memory, and again adjust wait states accordingly. Note that
    flash memory writes cannot take advantage of interleaving as reads
    can; there are no t_{OE}/t_{ACC} equivalents for writes. Write timings are
    unique and must be treated as such when interfacing to flash
    memory. However, software interleaving (especially easy with
    automated flash memories) can be used to maximize program and
    erase performance.[20]

So is the performance improvement of an interleaved design worth the
added hardware complexity? Only you, the system designer, can make
this decision. Obviously, interleaving is only valid for designs that will

---

[20]See Chapter 7 for more information on software interleaving with both non-automated and
automated flash memories.

use multiple flash memory devices. The techniques described above can be used for all flash memories, but even when using 64 kbyte devices, a 4-byte page arrangement results in 256 kbytes of flash memory storage capability. Designs that require higher densities of flash memory storage are therefore good prospects for hardware interleaving.

Interleaving techniques have been used for many years in DRAM designs. As flash memory read accesses become faster and faster (and direct execution out of flash memory versus shadowing to DRAM therefore becomes more common), interleaving flash memory will increasingly be used to squeeze maximum performance out of the memory subsystem.

SUMMARY

In this chapter, we've discussed hardware interfacing to flash memory components:

*   The simple "SRAM" pinout,
*   Enhanced inputs and outputs in latest generation flash memories,
*   Interpreting datasheet read/write parameters, and
*   Optimizing designs for read performance.

Looking ahead, Chapter 6 explains how to pick the correct power supply for flash memory, and how to calculate the amount of bypass filtering for each flash memory device in the system. It also discusses the DC characteristic specification "companions" to the AC specifications explained in this chapter. Chapter 7 explains the software algorithms that control flash memory and its program and erase, as well as specialized software techniques to optimize program/erase performance and, consequently, flash memory write bandwidth. Beginning with Chapter 8, the book makes the transition from topics common to both flash memory components and subsystems to those primarily exclusive to flash memory cards and drives.

Chapter Six: Power Requirements and Design Techniques

Flash memory's very low power consumption (compared to alternative memory approaches) is one of the more compelling features driving its adoption into today's systems. Flash memory is not plagued by the refresh of a DRAM, the battery of a "nonvolatile" SRAM, or the motor of a magnetic disk drive. When not being accessed, flash memory can be placed in one of several very low power states, and conversely it can "wake up" quickly when the system accesses it.

Flash memory does consume *some* power, however, and as an emerging technology its fundamental voltage and current particulars are not widely known. More mature memories, like RAM or EPROM have simple and well-understood power profiles (in most cases), since they have been used in designs for many years. In contrast, flash memory's unique power requirements must be comprehended early in the design cycle (especially on your first flash-inclusive design!) to ensure proper and reliable operation throughout the system's lifetime.

This, then, is the purpose of Chapter 6; to assist you in creating a flash memory power profile for your system application, and thereby help you calculate (and minimize) the demands that flash memory will make of your system's power supply. The following topics, developed further in the pages that follow, outline the information in this chapter:

- The V_{CC} Operating Voltage
- The V_{PP} Program/Erase Voltage
- V_{PP} Generation Techniques
- Decoupling and Bypass Capacitive Filtering

- Mixed Voltage System Design
- Power Management Techniques

THE V_{CC} OPERATING VOLTAGE

V_{CC}, the main operating voltage for flash memory, originates in most cases from the same supply voltage that powers all other logic circuits in the system. Common voltages and tolerances for V_{CC} are 5V ± 10% (4.5V to 5.5V) and 3.3V ± 0.3V (3.0V to 3.6V). Many flash memories function essentially as read-only devices when powered by V_{CC} alone. This means that the data stored in the flash memory can be read but not altered (altering the memory requires an additional V_{PP} voltage, discussed later). However, some flash memories are "V_{CC}-only" devices that derive a higher internal program/erase voltage from the external V_{CC} input(s). We'll cover these as a special case at the conclusion of this section.

Flash memories operate in several different modes, dependent on the states of various input pins[21]. Predictably, flash memory V_{CC} current draw differs in each mode. As a representative example of flash memory specifications, we've provided DC characteristics for the Intel 28F008SA flash memory in Table 6.1, which we'll be referencing throughout the chapter. This table specifies maximum values at worst-case voltage and temperature conditions and manufacturing process "corners", and typical specifications at room temperature and nominal voltages. If the flash memory in question has multiple V_{CC} input pins (like the 28F008SA), assume that the various current specifications reflect total current drawn by the device. This current is divided (not necessarily evenly!) among the flash memory V_{CC} inputs.

Important note: The following information is representative of flash memories based on Intel ETOX™ and ETOX-like NOR technologies from other vendors. If the flash memory you are evaluating is based on an unrelated technology approach (EEPROM, NAND, etc.), contact your vendor for additional information[22].

---

[21]See Tables 5.1 and 5.2 in Chapter 5 for more information.
[22]Flash memory component and subsystem vendor contact information can be found in Appendices A and B.

Symbol	Parameter	Min	Typ	Max	Unit	Test Condition
I_{LI}	Input Load Current			± 1.0	µA	$V_{CC} = V_{CC}$ Max $V_{IN} = V_{CC}$ or GND
I_{LO}	Output Leakage Current			± 10	µA	$V_{CC} = V_{CC}$ Max $V_{OUT} = V_{CC}$ or GND
I_{CCS}	V_{CC} Standby Current		1.0	2.0	mA	$V_{CC} = V_{CC}$ Max $\overline{CE} = \overline{PWD} = V_{IH}$
I_{CCS}	V_{CC} Standby Current		30	100	µA	$V_{CC} = V_{CC}$ Max $\overline{CE} = \overline{PWD} = V_{CC} ± 0.2V$
I_{CCD}	V_{CC} Deep PowerDown Current		0.20	1.2	µA	$\overline{PWD} = GND ± 0.2V$ $I_{OUT} = 0$ mA
I_{CCR}	V_{CC} Read Current CMOS Inputs		20	35	mA	$V_{CC} = V_{CC}$ Max, $\overline{CE} = GND$ f = 8 MHz, $I_{OUT} = 0$ mA
I_{CCR}	V_{CC} Read Current TTL Inputs		25	50	mA	$V_{CC} = V_{CC}$ Max, $\overline{CE} = V_{IL}$ f = 8 MHz, $I_{OUT} = 0$ mA
I_{CCW}	V_{CC} Byte Program Current		10	30	mA	Byte Program in Progress
I_{CCE}	V_{CC} Block Erase Current		10	30	mA	Block Erase in Progress
I_{PPS}	V_{PP} Standby Current		± 1	± 10	µA	$V_{PP} \leq V_{CC}$
I_{PPS}	V_{PP} Standby Current		90	200	µA	$V_{PP} > V_{CC}$
I_{PPD}	V_{PP} Deep PowerDown Current		0.10	5	µA	$\overline{PWD} = GND ± 0.2V$
I_{PPW}	V_{PP} Byte Program Current		10	30	mA	$V_{PP} = V_{PPH}$ Byte Program in Progress
I_{PPE}	V_{PP} Block Erase Current		10	30	mA	$V_{PP} = V_{PPH}$ Block Erase in Progress
V_{IL}	Input Low Voltage	-0.5		0.8	V	
V_{IH}	Input High Voltage	2.0		$V_{CC} + 0.5$		
V_{OL}	Output Low Voltage			0.45	V	$V_{CC} = V_{CC}$ Min $I_{OL} = 5.8$ mA
V_{OH}	Output High Voltage	2.4				$V_{CC} = V_{CC}$ Min $I_{OH} = -2.5$ mA
V_{PPL}	V_{PP} During Normal Operations	0.0		6.5	V	
V_{PPH}	V_{PP} During Erase and Program Operations	11.4	12.0	12.6	V	
V_{LKO}	V_{CC} Erase/Program Lock Voltage	2.0			V	

Table 6.1: DC Characteristics

Note: All currents are in RMS unless otherwise noted. Typical values at $V_{CC} = 5.0V$, $V_{PP} = 12.0V$, $T = 25°$ C.

Read Mode (I$_{CCR}$)

In read mode, the flash memory is selected and its output buffers are enabled to drive data onto the output pins. Referencing Table 6.1, we see that Intel specifies the 28F008SA for two different maximum read currents, 35 mA and 50 mA. How do these two measurements differ? For the answer we need to look at the test conditions.

The 28F008SA is manufactured using CMOS logic. CMOS has an intrinsic characteristic of drawing very little power when fully on or off, but substantially more power when switching, or when not fully on or off (with transistors operating in saturation, to put it in more technical terms). We'll see this idiosyncrasy and its impact again at the conclusion of this chapter, when we talk about power management.

The lower of the two maximum I$_{CC}$ read currents (35 mA) is specified with the device controlled by full CMOS inputs (i.e., $\overline{CE}$ = GND, addresses = GND or V$_{CC}$). In this case, the transistors inside the 28F008SA are being driven to the power supply "rails", or fully on and off. The higher 50 mA value is specified at less stringent TTL levels (V$_{IL}$ = 0.8V and V$_{IH}$ = 2.0V), resulting in partially on/off transistors and, consequently, higher power consumption. For optimum power management, therefore, the flash memory should be driven with full CMOS inputs.

Notice, too, that I$_{CCR}$ is specified with I$_{OUT}$ = 0 mA. Current draw is tested with outputs "unloaded". This condition is essentially valid for system designs with optimized fanout (i.e., flash memory outputs driving only a few inputs) and where flash memory outputs are connected to high-impedance CMOS device inputs (therefore resulting in very low current draw). However, if your flash memory drives bipolar TTL logic, for example, or has excessive fanout, your measured I$_{CCR}$ may be higher than that specified.

Figure 6.1 shows an oscilloscope plot of the current profile for a flash memory device being read. Address A$_0$ toggles, alternating the eight data outputs between 55H and AAH. This plot (taken at room temperature with nominal supply voltage) shows I$_{CCR}$ at an almost-constant 12 mA, with slight current spikes when output buffers transition between 1 and 0.

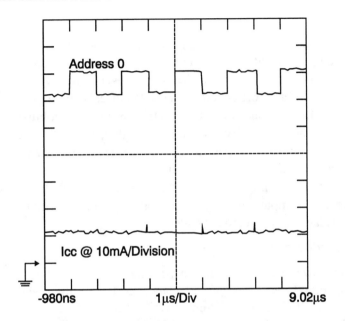

Figure 6.1: V_{CC} Current (Typical) - Read Mode

Variables that affect read current include the density of the device and its output architecture (x8, x16), since output buffer current constitutes a significant portion of I_{CCR}. Similarly, specialized high speed memories often use large output buffers with correspondingly higher current than their more mainstream counterparts. Newer flash memories include power saving circuitry that drops I_{CCR} to negligible levels after a short time period, as long as addresses do not toggle. Finally, it's intuitive that reading multiple components at the same time (such as when two x16 flash memories are selected in parallel for a x32 processor bus), causes a proportional increase in system current draw.

Standby Mode (I_{CCS})

In standby mode, the device is not selected ($\overline{CE}$ is inactive, regardless of the state of $\overline{OE}$). Examining Table 6.1, current consumption lowers dramatically in standby compared to read mode because much less of the flash memory circuitry consumes power. This has clear implications; the more time that the device is in standby mode, the lower the average energy drawn from the system power supply.

Similar to read mode above, Table 6.1 shows two different maximum standby current specifications; first with TTL and then CMOS inputs. Again, a full-CMOS design is the most power-thrifty. Notice that in standby mode, Table 6.1 specifies the states of only two inputs, $\overline{CE}$ and $\overline{PWD}$[23], in the test conditions. $\overline{CE}$ inactive disables input buffers for all other pins (save that of $\overline{PWD}$). This infers that, for this device[24], only $\overline{CE}$ and $\overline{PWD}$ must be driven to full-CMOS levels for lowest standby current consumption; other device inputs can be driven to TTL levels (although this will impact current draw in read mode). $\overline{PWD}$ inactive disables the $\overline{CE}$ input buffer, as well as almost all other circuitry on the chip. This latter device mode is called.....

Deep Powerdown Mode (I_{CCD})

This ultra-low power mode, currently available only on Intel Boot Block and FlashFile™ memories, provides an almost 100x improvement over the lowest CMOS standby current draw. The devices are put in the deep powerdown mode by driving the $\overline{PWD}$ input to GND. The deep powerdown mode disables almost all circuitry in the flash memory; an extended wakeup delay (several hundred nanoseconds) must be observed after exiting deep powerdown mode before the flash memory can again be successfully accessed.

Typically, systems will put flash memories in deep powerdown mode during "suspend" modes to conserve battery power. In this respect, an analogy can be made to a hard drive that is parked and spun down. In both cases, wakeup incurs a longer-than-normal initial access delay, but with flash memory this recovery time is many orders of magnitude less than for the HDD counterpart! Where the design includes a large number of flash memory components (in a flash memory card, for example), the

---

[23]$\overline{PWD}$ is also known as $\overline{RP}$ in JEDEC notation.
[24]Other flash memories may operate differently; look closely at device specifications.

specific devices being read, programmed, or erased can be kept awake while their non-accessed counterparts are asleep[25].

Program Mode (I_{CCW}/I_{CCP})

The flash memory draws current through V_{CC} (even while the device is deselected) during an internal byte program operation. This current includes the flow of electrons from source to drain through cell substrate areas (see Figure 2.5), as well as current draw of any automation logic. Table 6.1 lists the maximum I_{CCW} value as 30 mA; however as Figure 6.2 shows, substantial margin to this specification exists at typical conditions. Even the short-duration spikes fall short of exceeding maximum values.

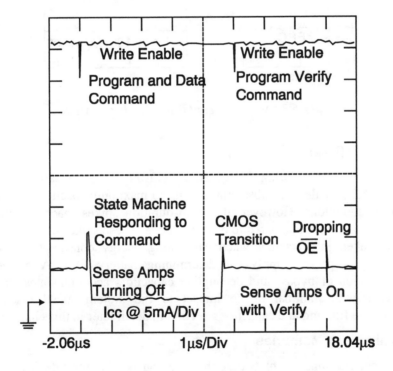

Figure 6.2: V_{CC} Current (Typical) - Program Mode

---

[25]See Chapter 8 for more information.

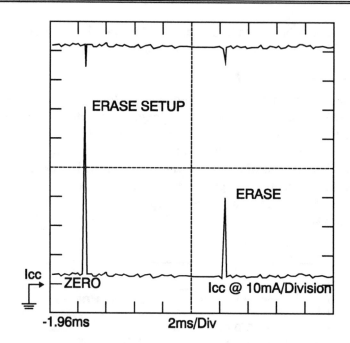

Figure 6.3: V_{CC} Current (Typical) - Erase Mode

Erase Mode (I_{CCE})

V_{CC} current draw during flash memory erasure is very small, and as Figure 6.3 reveals, has substantial margin to maximum specifications at typical conditions. However, the short-duration spikes reach a much greater magnitude compared to program mode. These spikes do not need to be taken into account when calculating energy consumption and choosing a power supply (or determining battery life). A correct combination of bypass and decoupling capacitors accommodates such glitches with minimal or no impact to the system. We'll discuss capacitive filtering and capacitor selection in detail later in this chapter.

V_{CC}-Only Flash Memories

The specifications and plots described previously were for a device with separate V_{CC} and V_{PP} inputs. As mentioned earlier, V_{CC}-only flash memories generate the V_{PP}-like voltage internally, from externally-supplied V_{CC}. Therefore, the I_{CC} profiles for V_{CC}-only devices will differ radically from those shown in Figures 6.1-6.3. As a rough approximation, they *may* appear to be a combination of I_{CC} and I_{PP} plots for each mode, with added input current for the internal voltage conversion (since power in = power out) and more even current to incorporate converter losses. The best recommendation is to closely analyze flash memory specifications in datasheets and other technical literature, and to contact the vendor for any additional information.

It's clear that the common conception that V_{CC}-only flash memories are lower power devices is not necessarily true. These are single-external-voltage devices, but they still must generate the higher program/erase electric fields inside. Their power profiles (current x voltage) must be derived from device specifications and should not automatically be assumed lower than their "V_{CC}/V_{PP}" flash memory equivalents.

THE Vpp PROGRAM/ERASE VOLTAGE

The externally-generated V_{PP} voltage, used when programming/erasing the flash memory, generates the electric fields that place charge onto, and remove charge from, the cell floating gate (see Chapter 3 for an explanation of cell program/erase). V_{PP} is also commonly tapped internally to produce verify voltages that ensure sufficient cell program/erase for extended data reliability.

The most common V_{PP} specification is 12V ± 5% (11.4V to 12.6V). This tolerance must be maintained at all times during program and erase. V_{PP} out of tolerance can impact device data integrity, and over-voltage can additionally damage the device.

Similar to V_{CC} discussed earlier, current consumption through V_{PP} changes dramatically depending on the operating mode of the flash memory. Where multiple flash memories exist in the system, their respective current draws must be combined to calculate total power consumption of the flash memory subsystem. This hints at a tradeoff between high data update performance (when multiple flash memories are programmed/erased at the same time) and low power consumption (when only one device is programmed/erased at a time). However, in either case total memory subsystem *energy* consumption (power **x** time) remains the same!

Read/Standby Mode (I$_{PPR}$ and I$_{PPS}$)

In both read and standby modes, the V$_{CC}$ supply exclusively powers the flash memory. The current drawn through V$_{PP}$, little more than leakage current, is very constant in magnitude and lacks the glitches seen on V$_{CC}$. As Table 6.1 indicates, the read and standby modes draw less current when V$_{PP}$ ≤ V$_{CC}$, compared to when V$_{PP}$ > V$_{CC}$, and no power is consumed when V$_{PP}$ = GND. Chapter 5 discusses example circuitry that switches V$_{PP}$ on/off for power management and write protection.

Deep Powerdown Mode (I$_{PPD}$)

Current draw in deep powerdown mode (again, currently available only on Intel Boot Block and FlashFile memories) is lower than in standby, but with a less dramatic difference than that seen with I$_{CC}$. Realistically, if the system designer is concerned with power consumption, you will most likely shut off the V$_{PP}$ supply completely to eliminate wasted current due to internal supply inefficiency losses. Deep powerdown mode power savings are most notable with respect to I$_{CC}$.

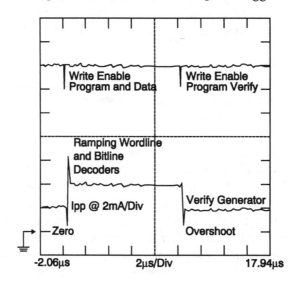

Figure 6.4: V$_{PP}$ Current (Typical) - Program Mode

Program Mode (I_{PPW}/I_{PPP})[26]

Figure 6.4 shows I_{pp} during a one-pulse byte program operation. The spike that occurs immediately after writing the program command is caused by the voltage ramp on the internal capacitance of the wordlines and bitlines ($I = C \times dV/dt$). Programming uses the external 12V directly, while program verify applies 6.5V (approximately) to the cell, tapped internally off the V_{PP} supply. Aside from the short-duration spike, typical programming current in this case is less than 4 mA, with program verify current of approximately 2 mA.

Erase Mode (I_{PPE})

In a bulk-erase flash memory, the transistor gates of all array cells are grounded, and 12V is applied to the transistor sources (see Figure 2.7). The flow of electrons from the floating gate to the source, as they are removed from the floating gate by the applied electric field, generates current through V_{PP}. Bulk-erase flash memories erase all cells in the array in parallel, whereas in block-erase devices erase occurs on a block-by-block basis.

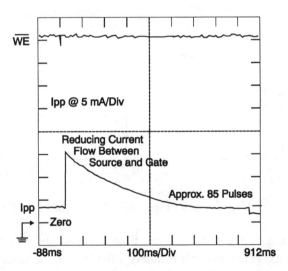

Figure 6.5: V_{PP} Current (Typical) - Erase Mode

---

[26]Both I_{PPW} (I_{pp} Write) and I_{PPP} (I_{pp} Program) are commonly found in flash memory documentation. They mean the same thing!

In either case, erase current decreases with increased time and, consequently, as more and more floating gate electrons are removed throughout the array or block of cells. Figure 6.5 displays this roughly logarithmic pattern. In this specific case, a full erase condition was achieved after 85 erase pulses. The number of erase pulses required is a function of technology, process, erase block size, applied voltage, and temperature. By altering these variables, the actual I_{PPE} curve will change correspondingly.

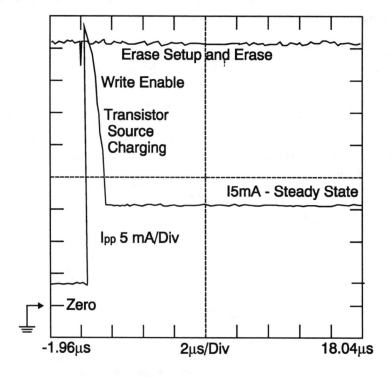

Figure 6.6: V_{PP} Current (Typical) - Beginning of an Erase Pulse

In Figure 6.6, we've tightened the time scale to show you the current spike that is generated immediately after initiating erase. Similar to programming described earlier, this spike is caused by the charging of capacitive transistor source lines for cells being erased. Bypass and decoupling capacitors easily handle this added short-duration current draw.

Vpp GENERATION TECHNIQUES

We've spent a lot of time so far in this book talking about the V_{PP} voltage; what it is, why it's needed, how much power it uses, and how to control it. What we haven't talked about yet (except in very general terms) is where it can come from. That's the purpose of this section. V_{PP} can be generated from any of several sources:

- Directly from a 12V regulated supply
- Converted from 12V unregulated
- Converted from a lower voltage
- Converted from a higher voltage

Today's state-of-the-art solutions are tomorrow's "yesterday's news", and as the flash memory market grows, the number of V_{PP} generation options (and the number of vendors providing these options) will increase and diversify to meet the needs of various application niches. We recommend that you consult the Appendices for the addresses and phone numbers of representative vendors and contact them directly for the most up-to-date information on their product lines.

Directly from a 12V Regulated Supply

If a 12V supply already exists in the system (to power RS-232 circuitry, a magnetic disk drive and/or a display, for example), this may be the ideal source for the flash memory V_{PP} voltage. However, the power supply must meet the V_{PP} tolerances specified by the flash memory vendor (usually 12V ± 5%). Since all internal voltages (program, erase and verify) stem from this single V_{PP} input, it directly impacts the accuracy of programming and erasing flash memory, and therefore the reliability of stored data. An out-of-spec V_{PP} may, for example, not place enough electron charge on the cell floating gate, thereby limiting data lifetime. An out-of-spec V_{PP} may also result in unwanted data alteration, caused by a disturbance from adjacent transistor cells. Finally, if V_{PP} is above specifications, permanent device damage may result.

When determining whether your existing 12V supply can be used to directly provide V_{PP}, make sure you include not only the tolerances of the power supply itself, but also any voltage drop of circuitry between the supply output and flash memory input. Examples of this circuitry include FET switches for on/off control[27], but excessively long or insufficiently thick board traces can also cause voltage droop.

Converting from 12V Unregulated

In general, this approach is not recommended, because currently-available solutions to regulate the 12V supply tend to be bulky, inefficient and expensive. A better solution will generate the 12V ± 5% from either a higher or lower voltage, such as the 5V or 3.3V that exists in most system designs (the V_{CC} voltage).

Converting from a Lower Voltage

Figures 6.7 and 6.8 show currently-available solutions from Linear Technology Corporation and Motorola Inc., respectively, that generate 12V from a 5V input. The LT1110 (or its lower-cost relative, the LT1109A), even with external components, occupies a small footprint (0.45 square inch total board area). The MC34063A, on the other hand, trades off higher component count for a lower total solution cost (approximately $2.25 in high volume quantities).

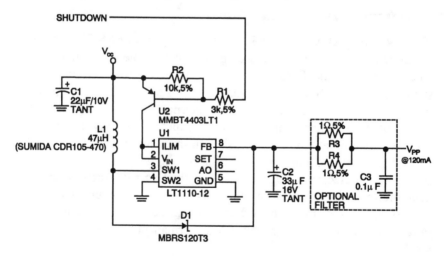

Figure 6.7: Linear Technology LT1110 5V to 12V Converter

---

[27]See Chapter 5 for an example calculation.

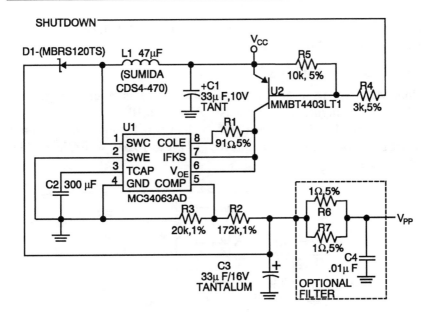

Figure 6.8: Motorola MC34063A 5V to 12V Converter

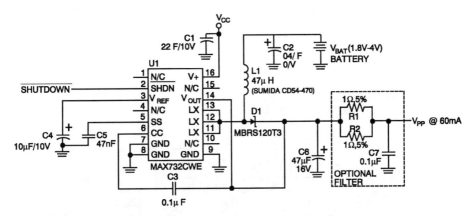

Figure 6.9: Maxim MAX732 3V to 12V Converter

Figure 6.9 shows the MAX732 from Maxim Integrated Products, a very flexible converter that can be configured to produce 12V at up to 60 mA output current, all from an input voltage as low as 1.8V. The MAX732 can also generate 12V at up to 120 mA from a 5V input, and has features similar to those of the LT1110.

Converting from a Higher Voltage

Both Maxim and Linear Technology also offer converters that generate 12V from a higher input voltage. Figures 6.10 and 6.11 show the MAX667 and LT1111, respectively, both of which output up to 120 mA. The MAX667 accepts input voltages of 12.1 to 16.5V, while the LT1111 input voltage range is 16-30V.

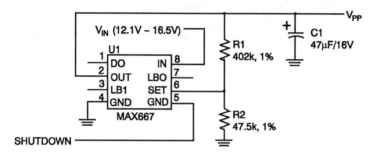

Figure 6.10: Maxim MAX667 12V Linear Voltage Regulator

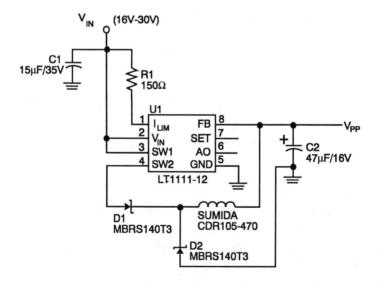

Figure 6.11: Linear Technology LT1111 Voltage Step Down Switcher

General Characteristics of Voltage Converters

When selecting a 12V converter, it's highly recommended that you do your homework in first identifying the important attributes of the system, and then matching converter features to these characteristics. As a general rule, 12V converters have been optimized by their manufacturers toward one (or several) of the following primary properties:

- **High Current Output**: They are capable of delivering high amount of current at the rated output voltage. This has importance for designs where several flash memories must be programmed and/or erased simultaneously. Some 12V converters can output currents in excess of 120 mA.

- **High Efficiency**: They transfer power (voltage x current) from input to output with very little loss as heat within the regulator. This has importance in power-critical designs, such as systems powered by batteries. Efficiencies of greater than 90% can be achieved with some 12V converters.

- **High Integration**: These converters combine all (or most) of the required circuitry within the device, including resistors, capacitors, inductors, and switching transistors. This simplifies system design, aids in manufacturing, and increases reliability. Note that the highest integration converter is not necessarily the *smallest* converter.

- **Low Cost**: These converters provide a low cost solution, albeit by potentially trading off one or several of the above properties. When calculating cost of a 12V converter, remember to add not only the regulator price but also that of all required external components and board assembly costs.

Secondary properties include input voltage range, output voltage tolerance, printed circuit board area, total solution height, rise time from enable, decay time from disable, and surface mountability. Some 12V converters have integrated shutdown or on/off capability via an input pin, another advantageous feature. Beyond disabling the 12V output, this shutdown feature puts the converter into a very low power consumption mode.

Totally Modular Solutions

A single-chip, totally integrated converter offers the ultimate in simplicity of design and testing. However, there are tradeoffs that must be considered. Typically, these products have lower efficiencies than their less-integrated counterparts. Also, the quality and reliability of discrete devices, being combined within the modular package, is no longer under the control of the system board designer. Finally, full integration usually comes at a price premium over alternatives. However, if the ease-of-design is attractive and your solution cost and efficiency needs are not stringent, a totally modular solution may be right for you.

DECOUPLING AND BYPASS CAPACITIVE FILTERING

Both small decoupling capacitors (one or more per device) and larger bypass capacitors (one per several devices) should be used in system designs for reliable flash memory operation. In general, capacitors smooth out the effects of AC transients on the DC supply voltages, by supplying excess charge (current) when voltage drops below the DC level and shunting off excess voltage spikes. Following the oft-mentioned equation that describes the current/voltage relationship for a capacitor,

$$I = C \times dV/dt,$$

we see that a smaller capacitor reacts more quickly to higher frequency AC transients. A larger capacitor, while reacting more slowly, responds for a longer duration and with much larger current capability. Therefore both types of capacitors have importance, and they work together to negate the potential impact of voltage spikes. Capacitors are relatively cheap (in the grand scheme of things) and take up little system board space compared to other devices. For all but the most space- or price-critical designs, therefore, it makes sense to design with plenty of margin.

For the example that follows, we've used the information in Figures 6.1-6.6. Different flash memories exhibit different behaviour with respect to transient magnitudes and durations. However, although your flash memory specifications may be different than those we've chosen, the methods used can (and should) be identical.

Decoupling capacitors in particular should be physically located as close to the input pin they filter (V_{CC} or V_{PP}) as possible, and connected between the particular supply voltage and GND. The bypass capacitor should also be located adjacent to the flash memory subsystem.

Decoupling Capacitors-V_{CC}

The largest-magnitude V_{CC} current transients occur when writing the erase command sequence to the flash memory (Figure 6.3). The decoupling capacitor assumptions and calculations are shown below:

Decoupling Capacitor Calculation

$$
I_{CC} \text{ (peak)} = 60 \text{ mA (I)}
$$
$$
\text{Max. Ripple Voltage} = 0.2\text{V peak-peak (0.1V dV)}
$$
$$
\text{Switching Time} = 20 \text{ ns (dt)}
$$

$$
\begin{aligned}
C = \ & = (I \times dt) / dV \\
& = (60 \text{ mA} \times 20 \text{ ns}) / 0.1\text{V} \\
& = 12 \text{ nF} \\
& = 0.047 \text{ μF (with approximately 4x margin)}
\end{aligned}
$$

Some flash memories have more than one V_{CC} input, each of which feeds a subset of the device logic. Unless you know the specific current draw of each V_{CC} input in all operating modes, it's best to calculate a worst-case bypass capacitor value and use it for each device's V_{CC} pin.

The above calculation assumes that the flash memory drives CMOS inputs (with corresponding high impedance and insignificant current requirements). If the flash memory outputs drive non-CMOS inputs and/or a large number of inputs (resulting in high load capacitance), output buffer current drive will be higher, and the transient current spikes during output switching will also increase in magnitude. In this case, the calculations for V_{CC} filter capacitance revise accordingly, to supply the extra current.

Bypass Capacitors-V_{CC}

A general rule of thumb is that one bypass capacitor should be used for each fifteen to twenty devices. Determine the value of the bypass capacitor by multiplying by ten the sum of the values of all decoupling capacitors, as shown below:

# of Flash Memories	= 4
Decoupling Capacitance	= 0.047 µF (per device)
Bypass Capacitor	= 10 x (0.047 + 0.047 + 0.047 + 0.047) µF
	= 1.9 µF (minimum)

A lower value for the filter capacitor will give a higher frequency noise response, while a higher value enables higher current drive capability.

Decoupling Capacitors-V_{PP}

The largest-magnitude V_{PP} current transients occur when writing the erase command sequence to the flash memory (Figure 6.6). The decoupling capacitor assumptions and calculations are shown below:

$$I_{CC} \text{ (peak)} = 45 \text{ mA (I)}$$
$$\text{Max. Ripple Voltage} = 0.2\text{V peak-peak (0.1V dV)}$$
$$\text{Switching Time} = 20 \text{ ns (dt)}$$

$$
\begin{aligned}
C = \ & = (I \times dt) / dV \\
& = (45 \text{ mA} \times 20 \text{ ns}) / 0.1\text{V} \\
& = 9 \text{ nF} \\
& = 0.033 \text{ µF (with approx 4x margin)}
\end{aligned}
$$

MIXED VOLTAGE SYSTEM DESIGN

The 1990s have seen the emergence of the new 3.3V standard for system supply voltage (V_{CC}). The lower voltage offers potential savings in power consumption and enables systems to operate cooler than their 5V counterparts. In designs and manufacturing processes optimized for 3.3V, the lower voltage can result in higher performance components, too. In today's reality, however[28], only a limited number of semiconductor devices exist that operate at 3.3V, and in many cases these are non-optimized "screened" parts with resultant lower performance than their 5V counterparts. In particular, a very small number of 3.3V flash memories are currently available, and read performance is generally inferior to 5V versions of the devices. This tradeoff for lower power consumption may or may not make sense for your specific design.

In most cases, therefore, system designs of the near future will be of the mixed voltage variety, with an intermingling of 5V and 3.3V devices, and corresponding multiple-voltage power supplies. Interfacing these mixed-voltage devices is often not as simple as it first appears, and following a few key guidelines will ensure proper operation and long system lifetime.

3.3 Volt to 5 Volt Interfaces

This scenario occurs, for example, when a 3.3V processor is driving a flash memory's addresses, $\overline{CE}$, $\overline{OE}$, and $\overline{WE}$ inputs. At a minimum, 3.3V devices must drive 2.4V for a logic 1 (TTL V_{OH}) and 0.4V for a logic 0 (TTL V_{OL}). As Figure 6.12 shows, these voltages exceed the thresholds for 5V devices with TTL-compatible inputs, making direct interfacing possible in this case. The only impact here is that the 5V device inputs are not driven to the supply voltage rails. As first mentioned earlier in this chapter, this may increase the 5V device's current consumption slightly.

---

[28]Hopefully, in the next revision of this book, 3.3V logic availability will improve and this section won't be necessary!

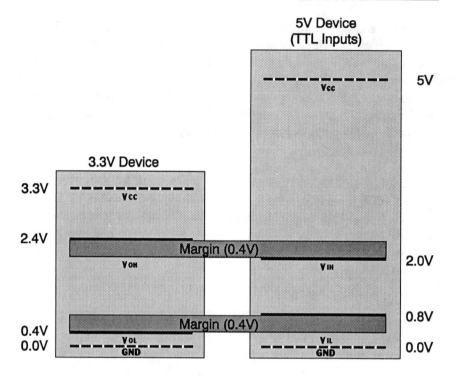

Figure 6.12: Interfacing a 3.3V Device to a 5V Device
(TTL Inputs)

Most logic devices, even if constructed of CMOS transistors, have TTL-compatible input structures (i.e., V_{IH} = 2.0V and V_{IL} = 0.8V). However, in rare cases, CMOS devices may follow the more stringent CMOS-compatible input voltage specifications (V_{IH} = 0.7 V_{CC}) and (V_{IL} = 0.3 V_{CC}). As shown in Figure 6.13, direct interface from a 3.3V device to a CMOS-compatible 5V device is not possible. In these cases, voltage translation logic at the output of-the 3.3V device must be used. Simple buffering with 5V-powered CMOS logic that accepts TTL inputs (i.e., HCT devices) provides one option, with the impacts being increased design complexity and lower performance due to the added logic.

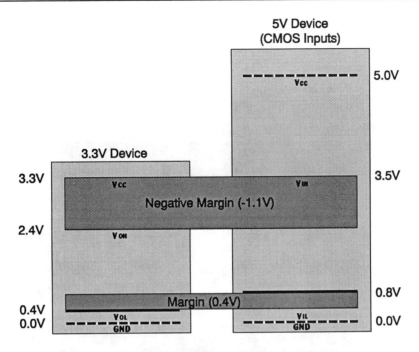

*Figure 6.13: Interfacing a 3.3V Device to a 5V Device
(CMOS Inputs)*

5V to 3.3V Interfaces

This interface is unfortunately more complicated than the one just described. A possible scenario here is a 5V flash memory $\overline{RY/BY}$ output driving a 3.3V processor interrupt input.[29]

Figure 6.14 shows the direct voltage translation from the 5V device to the 3.3V device. Although a 5V TTL-compatible device drives its logic one outputs to a minimum voltage of 2.4V, these outputs will eventually transition all the way to nearly the supply voltage rail (5V). As Figure 6.14 shows, this exceeds the absolute maximum input voltage specification for the 3.3V device (typically V_{CC} + 0.3V). The impact, shown in Figure 6.15, is forward biasing of the ESD protection diodes

---

[29]Note that we haven't talked about the data bus yet; we'll save bidirectional bus interface for the next section.

within the 3.3V device, and a resultant low impedance connection of the 5V and 3.3V supplies, with long term reliability impact.

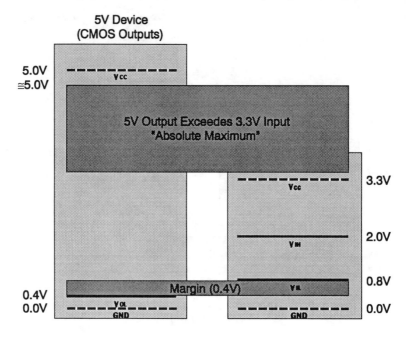

Figure 6.14: Interfacing a 5V Device to a 3.3V Device

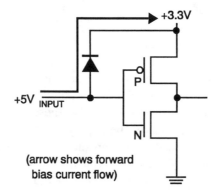

Figure 6.15: 5V to 3.3V Direct Interface.
Overbiasing the ESD Input Diode

Although a very small number of "5V-safe" 3.3V devices are entering the market, most still have the (V_{CC} + 0.3V) absolute maximum input voltage guideline. This means that the 5V output must be first translated to a 3.3V compatible level before driving the lower voltage device input. Figures 6.16 and 6.17 show two means of accomplishing this.

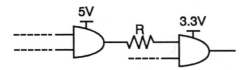

Figure 6.16: Interfacing a 5V Device to a 3.3V Device.
Series Resistor Voltage Drop

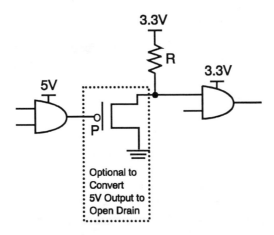

Figure 6.17: Interfacing a 5V Device to a 3.3V Device.
"Open Drain" Output Conversion

The first method (Figure 6.16) uses a series resistor at the output of the 5V device, to drop the voltage to an acceptable level for the 3.3V input. Resistor values must be carefully chosen to limit current into the 3.3V device input. Differences in ramp rates between the 5V and 3.3V supplies during system powerup must also be closely analyzed, to prevent even temporary forward-biasing of the 3.3V device ESD diode (make the worst-case assumption that the 5V supply is at 5.5V and the 3.3V supply is at GND, and calculate resistor values accordingly). The major impact in this case is speed; the 5V output now sees tremendously increased impedance on its outputs, and the output transition time suffers accordingly.

The other method, shown in Figure 6.17, assumes that the 5V device has open-drain outputs. The external resistor, connected to the 3.3V supply, automatically translates the output voltage to 3.3V-compatible levels. The lower the resistor value, the faster the 5V device outputs switch, and the higher the resistor value, the lower the current draw "penalty" through the resistor when the 5V device outputs a zero. If open-drain outputs are not available, an external MOSFET transistor and resistor will duplicate the functionality. An n-transistor will invert the output, while a p-transistor will pass the 5V device output with no inversion.

Bidirectional Bus Interface

The data lines, connecting a processor and external memory device, provide a common example of a bidirectional bus. Where a 3.3V processor and 5V flash memory exist, for example, two possible scenarios can occur:

- 5V outputs driving 3.3V inputs (during flash memory read), and
- 3.3V outputs driving 5V inputs (during flash memory writes).

A combination of the techniques described earlier for 5V-to-3.3V and 3.3V-to-5V interfacing is possible here, with the added complexity that logic outputs must be tri-stateable (since we're talking about the data bus in this case). A simpler solution uses one of several available bidirectional translation buffers with multiple V_{CC} inputs, one for each side of the mixed-voltage bus. The buffer handles all voltage translations internally. Integrated Device Technology Corporation (IDT) provides a full range of standard logic devices with this capability, and both Performance Semiconductor and Texas Instruments have also announced their intentions to provide similar products.

POWER MANAGEMENT TECHNIQUES

Throughout this chapter we've mentioned techniques for minimizing flash memory power consumption in system designs. In this final section, we'll summarize these recommendations. Not all of them may be applicable in every design; some applications are less power-sensitive than others, and in some cases the tradeoff in system complexity and cost does not make sense. However, each contributes incrementally, and we have listed them in increasing order of difficulty.

- The more a flash memory is in its standby mode, the lower its average power consumption over time. Make sure that when flash devices in the system are not being accessed, they are deselected.

- Interfacing to the flash memory with full-CMOS logic results in the lowest memory current draw. As described earlier in this chapter, CMOS-based semiconductor devices draw very little power when their transistors are driven fully on or off.

- Given the choice of storing data with flash memory or some other memory technology, flash memory usually draws the least power from the system (no motors, no batteries, no refresh requirements).

- Intel BootBlock and FlashFile memories provide the very low power consumption Deep Powerdown mode, which can be utilized keeping in mind the extended wakeup delay when exiting the mode. In a large flash memory array, for example, the majority of devices can be placed in Deep Powerdown mode, leaving only one or a few awake memories being accessed.

- The tradeoff between highest system write performance (where multiple flash memories may be programming/erasing at the same time) and lowest average power consumption (where flash memories are programmed/erased serially) is one you'll have to make yourself. Different applications have different needs, and you must choose accordingly. However, remember that given a fixed number of bytes (or kbytes or Mbytes) to be written, the amount of battery energy consumed (power x time) is equivalent whether flash memories are being erased and programmed serially (low average power draw) or in parallel (high average power draw).

- When simply reading from flash memories (not updating them), V_{PP} can be turned off for the lowest current draw. V_{PP} switching also inhibits unwanted alteration of flash memory contents. However, each time V_{PP} is switched on the system incurs a time delay as the voltage ramps to a valid level. An "intelligent" V_{PP} algorithm, based on modeling the anticipated frequency of program/erase and balancing power consumption with complexity and ramp delay tolerance, provides the solution. Depending on the power supply and/or voltage converter chosen, additional circuitry may be required for this V_{PP} switching.

SUMMARY

Chapter 6 has given you the tools needed to predict the anticipated power consumption model for your flash memory subsystem, and to appropriately design not only this subsystem but the power supply itself. Flash memory's full nonvolatility, in combination with its relatively fast update performance, offer tremendous benefit to designs that understand and fully harness its capabilities. As systems become more and more power-conscious in the future, flash memory will increasingly be used to meet the stringent requirements of these designs.

Chapter Seven: Software Interfacing to Flash Memory

An oft-repeated adage states that, "A computer's hardware gives it *potential*. Software makes that potential a *reality*". The latest and greatest microprocessor, a super-quick graphics subsystem and a fast, dense hard drive combine to make a computer nothing more than an expensive paperweight, without the software that harnesses this capability to do useful work.

A similar analogy can be inferred for flash memory. Flash memory designers can include all sorts of intricate and elaborate circuitry on their devices to enable powerful update flexibility. Yet, without system software to control it, flash memory is nothing but an expensive blank ROM! Flash memory internal hardware circuitry gives it update *potential*, but system software makes that potential a *reality*.

This chapter discusses how to integrate flash memory into your design and control it, from a software standpoint. To this end, we'll cover the following topics:

- Basic (First-Generation) Algorithms
- Fully Automated (Second-Generation) Algorithms
- Update Routines
- System Boot Code Contents
- Software Interface to Flash Memory Cards, SIMMs and Multi-Component Arrays

First, though, let's talk briefly about the basic command interface to flash memory, what these commands do, and why they simplify the update process.

WHY IS FLASH MEMORY CONTROLLED BY SYSTEM SOFTWARE?

To explain where we are today (and why we're there), it's often easiest to start with a description of where we *were*. Accordingly, Figure 7.1 shows the programming algorithm for the 27C010 EPROM. The EPROM is the technology foundation for NOR flash memory architectures[30], such as Intel's ETOX™ approach. Although EPROMs erase via ultraviolet light shining on the array cell floating gates (see Figure 3.6), EPROM and NOR flash memory cells both program electrically. However, you'll soon realize why EPROMs very rarely are programmed in-system.

EPROM Programming Algorithm

In explaining the EPROM algorithm below, we'll only highlight the steps of most interest in this discussion.

Step 2

Programming an EPROM location (byte or word, depending on the device) requires that it first be specified via its address, and this address must be held throughout the entire program algorithm. This requirement, along with having to multiplex pin functionality, is clearly incompatible with the normal bus interface of a system processor, and it means that the EPROM address must be a latched version of the processor address. Latching adds to system hardware complexity, and even slows EPROM read access time due to the extra logic propogation delay.

Step 3

In this step, V_{PP} (the program/erase voltage) is switched to 12.75V in preparation for a program attempt. Also, V_{CC} (the device operating voltage) is elevated from 5V to 6.25V. This means that V_{CC} to the EPROM must be switched, unique and electrically isolated from the

---

[30]As we discussed in Chapter 3.

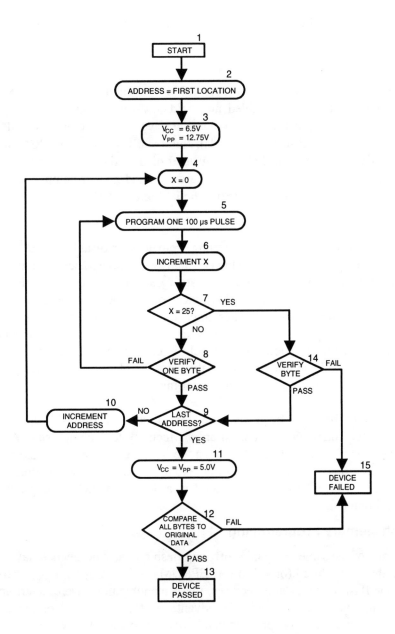

Figure 7.1:   EPROM   Programming   Algorithm   (Simplified Form)

V_{CC} connected to all other logic in the system (for which 6.25V clearly violates specifications).

Step 5

To initiate programming, the EPROM $\overline{CE}$ (chip enable) and $\overline{PGM}$ (program) inputs are enabled and held low for at least 100µs. Again incompatible with the normal bus interface (which toggles signals in periods measured in nanoseconds), this means that $\overline{CE}$ and $\overline{PGM}$ must be driven via separate I/O lines instead of directly from the processor. The impact reveals itself in extra hardware and greater complexity, and in slowed read accesses due to additional logic on $\overline{CE}$.

Step 8

The EPROM is verified by reading from it after disabling $\overline{PGM}$. This program verify, usually slower than a normal access, must be comprehended in the system wait state generation logic. The elevated V_{CC}, resulting in the EPROM logical one outputs ramping to nearly 6.25V, causes an even greater impact. Unless converted, this easily overdrives inputs of other logic in the system, violating absolute maximum specifications and severely impacting system lifetime. Again the undesirable solution to this reality is bus isolation logic between the EPROM outputs and system processor inputs.

It should be very clear by now that in-system EPROM update is extremely difficult and undesirably affects system complexity. Along with the fact that EPROMs must be removed from the system for erasure, this intricate interfacing explains why the vast majority of EPROMs in use today get updated in a dedicated PROM programmer environment.

Flash Memory Programming

Many of the same companies offering flash memory products today have in the past offered (or still offer) EPROMs. When they set out to define their flash memory architectures, these manufacturers were determined to improve ease-of-use to take advantage of the potential of these in-system updateability (programmable *and* eraseable) devices. To a large degree, they've succeeded admirably in their task. Figure 7.2 shows the

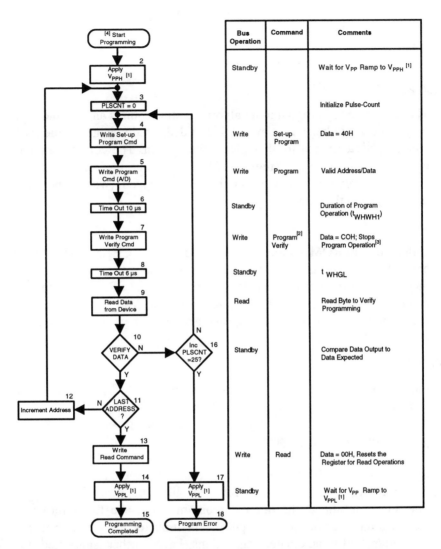

Bus Operation	Command	Comments
Standby		Wait for V_{PP} Ramp to V_{PPH} [1]
		Initialize Pulse-Count
Write	Set-up Program	Data = 40H
Write	Program	Valid Address/Data
Standby		Duration of Program Operation (t_{WHWH1})
Write	Program[2] Verify	Data = COH; Stops Program Operation[3]
Standby		t_{WHGL}
Read		Read Byte to Verify Programming
Standby		Compare Data Output to Data Expected
Write	Read	Data = 00H, Resets the Register for Read Operations
Standby		Wait for V_{PP} Ramp to V_{PPL} [1]

NOTES:
1. See DC Characteristics for the value of V_{PPH} and V_{PPL}.
2. Program Verify is only performed after byte programming. A final read/compare may be performed (optional) after the register is written with the Read command.
3. Refer to principles of operation.
4. CAUTION: The algorithm MUST BE FOLLOWED to ensure proper and reliable operation of the device.

Figure 7.2: Intel First Generation Flash Memory Non-Automated Programming Algorithm

flash memory programming algorithm used by Intel Corporation's first-generation bulk-erase devices[31]. We'll cover this algorithm in greater detail later, but for now let's look at the specific areas where the in-system interface has been improved.

Step 2

The flash memory programming algorithm still requires an external V_{PP} program/erase voltage. However, this is a dedicated voltage for the flash memory, not common to all logic in the system. The common system operating voltage, V_{CC}, remains 5V throughout the algorithm. All program/erase/verify voltages are internally tapped (within the flash memory) from the external V_{PP} input.

Steps 4 and 5

Unlike the EPROM example earlier, addresses, $\overline{CE}$ and $\overline{WE}$ (write enable) do not need to be held active throughout the 10 µs program interval. Specific data commands, written at normal SRAM-like speeds, control the flash memory. Logic internal to the flash memory decodes these commands and takes appropriate action, such as the enabling and disabling of internal program and erase pulses.

Step 9

Finally, referencing the flash memory data outputs to V_{CC} makes them compatible with other logic in the system. No voltage conversion is required between the flash memory outputs and processor inputs for program or erase verify operations.

Comparing Figures 7.1 and 7.2, we see that some elements of the old EPROM algorithm have been retained, like the need for software timeouts to terminate the internal program pulse, and the iterative if-then-else data verification and pulse repetition for each byte. Second-generation, fully automated algorithms have further simplified the update process; we'll cover these later in the chapter.

---

[31]Other manufacturers offer compatible devices; refer to the Appendix for vendor contact information.

One important point to note up front is that with all of today's devices (both automated and non-automated), the erase and reprogram code cannot be executed from the flash memory while it is being updated. Read-while-program/erase is not supported, although some devices allow the system to *suspend* erase to read, if needed. The update code can be *stored* in the flash memory, but it must be copied to external memory, such as a small RAM, for *execution*.

THE NOR BULK-ERASE FLASH MEMORY ALGORITHMS

As stated earlier, these algorithms were pioneered by Intel Corporation but compatible vendors such as Advanced Micro Devices, SGS-Thomson, Catalyst, Hitachi and Mitsubishi also support them. Flash memories using these algorithms include the 28F256A, 28F512, 28F010, 28F020 and Series 1 flash memory cards, and equivalents.

Command	Bus Cycles Req'd	First Bus Cycle			Second Bus Cycle		
		Operation	Address	Data	Operation	Address	Data
Read Memory	1	Write	X	00H			
Read Intelligent Identifier Codes	3	Write	X	90H	Read	IIA	IID
Erase Setup/Erase	2	Write	X	20H	Write	X	20H
Erase Verify	2	Write	EA	A0H	Read	X	EVD
Program Setup/Program	2	Write	X	40H	Write	PA	PD
Program Verify	2	Write	X	C0H	Read	X	PVD
Reset	2	Write	X	FFH	Write	X	FFH

Notes:

1.   IIA = Intelligent Identifier address; 0000H for mfg. code; 0001H for device code.
    EA = Address of memory location to be read during erase verify.
    PA = Address of memory location to be programmed.
    Addresses are latched on the falling edge of the write enable pulse.

2.   IID = Data read from location IIA during device identification.
    EVD = Data read from location EA during erase verify.
    PD = Data to be programmed at location PA. Data is latched on the rising edge of write enable.
    PVD = Data read from location PA during program verify. Address is latched during the Program command.

Table 7.1: Intel Bulk-Erase Flash Memory Command Definitions

Writing specific data command sequences (and corresponding addresses) into the flash memory command register enables device operations. Table 7.1 shows the full range of commands supported by the Intel-compatible, bulk-erase flash memories. A subset of these commands will be explained in greater detail in the following algorithm discussions.

The Program Algorithm

This algorithm is shown in Figure 7.2.

Step 1

This is the entry point for each program operation.

Step 2

Ramp V_{PP} to V_{PPH} (12V ± 0.6V). When programming a sequence of device locations at one time, V_{PP} does not need to be ramped down and then back up between each program operation. For that matter, it may be permanently enabled if desired[32].

Step 3

Initialize the pulse count (usually a system variable in RAM, or a CPU register) to value 0.

Step 4

Write the program setup command (40H) to the device. The address at this point is a "don't care", as long as the flash memory is selected via $\overline{CE}$.

Step 5

Write the data to be programmed, along with the address to be programmed. Note the absence of a 'program verify' command per se; the flash memory at this point assumes that the very next write after 'program setup' is data to be programmed.

To abort programming after writing the program setup command, write FFH as data to be programmed. Since programming only changes ones

---

[32]See Chapters 5 and 6 for discussions on V_{PP} generation and control.

zeros, writing data FFH (with no zeros in it) will leave the specified location unchanged. Writing another FFH resets the device to the read array mode.

Step 6

This step times the internal pulse, initiated in Step 5, that programs the specified location. The delay should be a minimum of 10 μs. Device datasheets specify the maximum delays that should be strictly followed to ensure reliable device operation. Either a hardware timer or a software loop can measure the 10 μs pulse.

If using a software delay, the designer must ensure the accuracy of the measured delay with respect to the system clock and CPUs instruction cycles. This is especially important when the same software could be run in different systems with different CPUs and clock frequencies (like a personal computer). In this case, the clock frequency can be initially determined by measuring the number of instructions that execute between real-time-clock interrupts, for example.

Disabling interrupts before step 6 helps to ensure that the maximum program pulsewidth is not exceeded. Also make sure that when debugging your software you do not single-step and pause within the timing loop, again to avoid exceeding the datasheet maximum delay timings.

Step 7

Writing the program verify command (C0H) terminates the internal program pulse. It also enables internal circuitry to apply the program verify voltages (derived from V_{PP}) to the array cells. The address supplied to the device with the program verify command corresponds to the location being programmed.

Some flash memories include stop timers that automatically terminate the internal program pulse after a specified delay, even if a program verify command has not been received. Even if these stop timers are available, the system designer should not rely on them, and should follow steps 6 and 7 for timing and terminating the program pulse[33].

Step 8

The 6 μs delay of this step allows time for the program verify voltages to stabilize at the array cells being programmed. This is a minimum delay; it has no maximum limit. However, to achieve the highest programming performance, this time should be adhered to as close as possible. The same guidelines explained in step 6 with respect to software delays should again be followed. Reading the device before 6 μs has elapsed may result in the output of inaccurate data.

Step 9

Read data from the device. The address being verified should match that of the location being programmed.

Step 10

Compare the data read from the device to the data being programmed. Remember that programming only changes ones to zeros, not zeros to ones. If bits within the location being programmed have already been set to zero by a prior program operation (and not yet set back to one by an erase), they will remain zero even if system software attempts to program them back to a one. In such an application, mask and examine only those bits you are attempting to program to a zero.

Steps 11-12

After a programming operation successfully verifies, subsequent locations can then be programmed by returning to the beginning of the algorithm as shown.

Steps 13-15

After completing device programming, write the "read array" command (FFH) to the device and disable high voltage on V_{PP} if desired. Bear in mind that for highest performance, you can leave V_{PP} on to avoid its

---

[33]Not all bulk-erase flash memories, even if they are otherwise compatible, offer stop timers. Stop timers are supported in all Intel products.

ramp delay (however, this may result in unnecessary power consumption).

Step 16

If the location being programmed does not verify successfully after one iteration, increment the pulse count and attempt another program sequence at the same location. Although most locations typically only require one program pulse, the actual number of pulses depends on the ambient temperature at which the device is being operated, the V_{CC} and V_{PP} values at the time of the programming attempt and the number of times the device has already been programmed/erased (cycled). A maximum of 25 program attempts are specified for each location.

Steps 17-18

If, after 25 attempts, the location being programmed still does not verify correctly, disable V_{PP} and return an error indication to the system. Inability to program most likely only occurs with an out-of-tolerance V_{PP} power supply, or if the device has been cycled far beyond its specifications. At this point, the system has several choices; it may mark the location as "bad" and continue, or it may attempt additional program pulses beyond the specified 25. This latter approach is a valid method of extending flash memory cycling[34].

The Chip Erase Algorithm

This algorithm is shown in Figure 7.3.

Step 1

This is the entry point for the chip erase operation.

Steps 2 and 3

The device must be pre-conditioned, or preprogrammed to all 0s, before erasing to prevent over-erasure of array transistors. To pre-condition, repeat the program algorithm of Figure 7.2 for *each* location in the array, programming to 00H in each case. Notice that we stressed the word *each* here. *Every* location in the *entire* device must be accessible for both

---

[34] See the "Extended Cycling; What Can You Do?" section of Chapter 3).

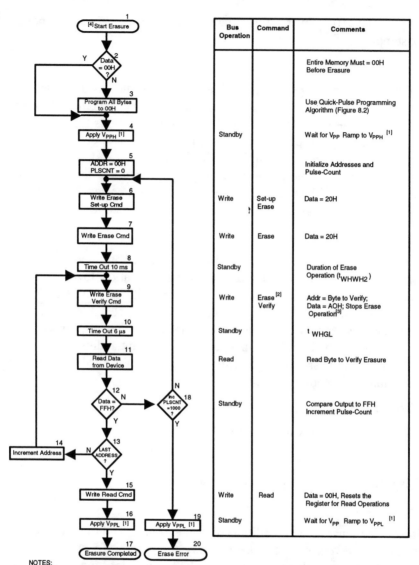

NOTES:
1. See DC Characteristics for the value of V_{PPH} and V_{PPL}.
2. Erase Verify is performed only after chip erasure. A final read/compare may be performed (optional) after the register is written with the Read command.
3. Refer to principles of operation.
4. CAUTION: The algorithm MUST BE FOLLOWED to ensure proper and reliable operation of the device.

Figure 7.3: Intel First Generation Flash Memory Non-Automated Erase Algorithm

reads and writes, so that it can be preprogrammed. Locations not programmed to 00H will eventually overerase (sooner versus later) rendering not only those locations but whole sections of the flash memory unusable.

Step 4

Ramp V_{PP} to V_{PPH} (12V ± 0.6V) before beginning the chip erase algorithm[35].

Step 5

Initialize the address and pulse count variables to zero. The address variable will be used to sequence through the array during erase verification, and the pulse count variable, as its name implies, will count the number of erase pulses applied to the chip. Both variables should be declared large enough to handle their maximum values; i.e., "address" will have values between 0 and 262,143 for a 2 Mbit x8 device, and depending on the flash memory and manufacturer, "pulse" can range from 0 to 3000.

Steps 6-7

Write the erase setup (20H) and erase confirm (again, 20H) commands to the device to begin the internal erase pulse. The specified address to the device is a "don't care" as long as the chip receives a valid $\overline{WE}$ and $\overline{CE}$, since the entire chip is being erased.

Step 8

Similar to the program algorithm described earlier, the system times the internal erase pulse. Erase should be enabled for a minimum of 9.5ms; specific device datasheets list the maximum times. Follow the same recommendations as first described earlier in step 6 of the Program Algorithm for accurately timing the erase pulse. Disabling interrupts before this step helps to ensure that the maximum erase pulsewidth is not exceeded.

---

[35]V_{PP} may already be at V_{PPH} from the previous pre-programming steps 2 and 3.

Step 9

Writing the erase verify command (A0H) terminates the internal erase pulse. It also enables circuitry that applies the erase verify voltages (derived from V_{PP}) to the array cells. The first device address to be verified is location 0000H, so the system presents this address to the device along with the erase verify command.

It is very important to accurately terminate the erase pulse after approximately 9.5 ms has elapsed, to prevent device overerasure. Although some flash memories include erase stop timers, these should be used as the exception, not the rule. For example, erase stop timers are useful during software debug when you single-step through your code. Without device hardware stop timers, the erase pulse length would be exceeded. In normal operation, though, follow steps 8 and 9 to time and terminate the erase pulse via writing the erase verify command[36].

Step 10

Similar to the program flowchart, the 6 μs delay of step 10 allows time for the erase verify voltages to stabilize at the array cells being verified. Reading the device before the 6 μs has elapsed may result in the output of inaccurate data.

Step 11

Read the data from the device. The address should match that of the location being verified, and therefore be the same address given in step 9 (at least for the first time through the loop).

Step 12

A fully erased location will read back as all ones. For example, a x8 component location will read back as FFH if erased, a x16 component or device pair will read as FFFFH, etc.

---

[36]Not all bulk-erase flash memories, even if they are otherwise compatible, offer stop timers, although stop timers are supported in all Intel products.

Steps 13 and 14

Continuing with device address 0001H and to the last location in memory (i.e. all ones for address inputs), repeat the sequence of steps 9-12.

Steps 15-17

After completion of device erasure, write the "read array" command (FFH) to the device and disable high voltage on V_{PP} if desired.

Step 18

It is very unlikely that the entire array will erase after one 10 ms pulse. In fact, as the "typical" erase times in flash memories indicate, erase time is often measured in tens of pulses, depending on temperature, cycling, device density and V_{CC}/V_{PP} values during an erase. It's also common for transistors within the array to erase at slightly different rates relative to each other. If the time differential between fastest-erasing bits and slowest-erasing bits is extreme, this can be an indication of a low-quality flash memory device that is headed for a quick cycling death. Assuming high quality flash memories, however, you will still commonly see a multiple-pulse difference between the first and last locations to erase.

If the location being verified does not read all ones after one iteration, increment the pulse count and begin another erase sequence. Verification then continues from *where it left off*, since previous locations were already confirmed as erased. Most devices permit a maximum of 1000 erase attempts, although higher density flash memories allow up to 3000 erase pulses.

Steps 17-18

If, after the maximum number of erase attempts, the device still does not verify correctly, disable V_{PP} and return an error indication to the system. Similar to program, the inability to erase will most likely only occur with an out-of-tolerance V_{PP} power supply, or if the device has been cycled very far beyond its specifications. At this point, the system has several choices; it may mark the non-erasing device locations as invalid and continue, or it may attempt additional erase pulses beyond the specified maximum. As discussed earlier in reference to programming, this latter method may be validly used to extend flash memory cycling.

Summary of First-Generation Programming/Erase Characteristics

We've shown in our bulk-erase flash memory algorithm discussions that first-generation flash memories dramatically improved upon the hardware/software interface required to update EPROMs. The following characteristics (and their impacts), however, are still evident in the steps required to successfully complete a flash memory "manual" program or erase attempt:

• The algorithms are extremely system-intensive, making it difficult if not impossible for the processor to service the needs of any other devices or functions in the system while performing a flash memory update. In fact, we recommended earlier that the system turn off interrupts during program and erase to ensure the generation of accurate timing delays. It is also very difficult to program or erase multiple flash memories at the same time, or to program one flash memory as a foreground task while erasing another in the background.

• The highly manual algorithms also require the system to maintain and increment pulse counts and address variables, use system software to generate timing delays and require the system to write multiple verify commands and execute location-by-location data authentication. The flash memory must also be manually preprogrammed before erasing. None of these issues are showstoppers, but they lead to software overhead beyond the raw flash memory program and erase times, increase the likelihood of software errors during prototyping and result in verbose code.

THE NOR FULLY-AUTOMATED FLASH MEMORY ALGORITHMS

Second-generation automated algorithms have been developed to further enhance the flash memory interface and overcome some of these first-generation manual shortcomings. Using the Intel automated algorithms as our first example, we note the following improvements and their positive impacts:

- The algorithms are fully automated, after system software issues program or erase command sequences. An internal oscillator measures all timing delays, on-chip counters increment through addresses and keep track of the erase/program pulses. Preprogramming of the selected block is automatically done before erasing the block. Flash memory automation allows the system to perform other functions during the program/erase operations. Automation also greatly simplifies read, program, and erase of multiple flash memories in parallel.

- Interfacing has been enhanced. A Status Register in the device informs the system as to the progress and success/failure of the internal automation. Integrated circuitry monitors the status of the V_{pp} voltage throughout program or erase, terminates the algorithm if V_{pp} falls out of tolerance and relays this information back to the system.

- Second-generation devices include the ability to suspend erase to read from the flash memory, and resume at a later time. This prioritizes high speed, high priority reads over slower, lower priority erase. In combination with automation and the $\overline{RY/BY}$ output (available on some devices), erase suspend/resume makes it possible to make slow erase a full background task.

We'll spend the majority of this section reviewing the Intel Corporation automated algorithms, shown in Figures 7.4-7.7. Intel's Boot Block and FlashFile memories and the Series 2 flash memory cards all support these algorithms. After this review, we'll follow with an analysis of

AMD's automated algorithms, and some general techniques and recommendations for automated program/erase.

Device operations are enabled by writing specific data command sequences (and corresponding addresses) into the flash memory command register. Table 7.2 shows the full range of commands supported by block-erase Intel flash memories. In most cases (erase confirm is an exception), these commands are backwards-compatible with those seen in Table 7.1 for bulk-erase flash memories. Additional commands have been added to comprehend device internal automation and Status Register operations.

Command	Bus Cycles Req'd	First Bus Cycle			Second Bus Cycle		
		Operation	Address	Data	Operation	Address	Data
Read Array/Reset	1	Write	X	FFH			
Intelligent Identifier	3	Write	X	90H	Read	IIA	IID
Read Status Register	2	Write	X	70H	Read	X	SRD
Clear Status Register	1	Write	X	A0H			
Erase Setup/Erase Confirm	2	Write	BA	40H	Write	BA	D0H
Erase Suspend/Resume	2	Write	X	C0H	Write	X	D0H
Program Setup/Program	2	Write	PA	FFH	Write	PA	PD
Alternate Program Setup/Program	2	Write	PA	FFH	Write	PA	PD

Notes:
1.   IIA = Intelligent Identifier address; 0000H for mfg. code; 0001H for device code.
       BA = Address within the block being erased.
       PA = Address of memory location to be programmed.
       Addresses are latched on the rising edge of the write enable pulse.
2.   SRD = Data read from Status Register
       PD = Data to be programmed at location PA. Data is latched on the rising edge of the write enable pulse.
       IID = Data read from location IIA during device identification.

Table 7.2: Intel Block-Erase Flash Memory Command Definitions

Intel Automated Program Algorithm

This algorithm is shown in Figure 7.4.

Step 1

Before beginning the automated program algorithm, ramp V_{PP} to 12V. When programming a sequence of data at one time, V_{PP} does not need to be ramped down and then back up between them.

Step 2

Write the program setup command (40H or 10H) to the device. The address corresponds to the address of the location to be programmed.

Step 3

Write the data to be programmed, along with the location to be programmed (i.e., the address), to the flash memory. Similar to the first-generation program algorithm described earlier, the flash memory assumes that the very next write after "program setup" is data to be programmed.

Note: To abort programming after writing the program setup command, write FFH as the data to be programmed. This *will* activate the automation, but since you are attempting to program ones, the internal programming will quickly complete. After ensuring that automation has finished (see Step 4), again write FFH (the read array command) to return the flash memory to its normal output mode.

Step 4

After receiving the written program command sequence, internal automation (the Write State Machine, or WSM) begins execution. As mentioned earlier, this automation controls many of the manual steps of the first-generation algorithms, including program pulse timing and termination, program verification and iteration of program/verify. System software (at its leisure) polls the flash memory Status Register (shown in Figure 7.5) to determine when automation has completed. Status Register bit 7, duplicating the function of the $RY/\overline{BY}$ output

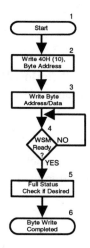

Bus Operation	Command	Comments
Write	Byte Write Setup	Data = 40H (10H) Address = Byte to be written
Write	Byte Write	Data to be written Address = Byte to be written
Standby/ Read		Check RY/$\overline{BY}$ V_{OH} = Ready, V_{OL} = Busy or Read Status Register Check SR.7 1 = Ready, 0 = Busy Toggle $\overline{OE}$ or $\overline{CE}$ to update Status Register
Repeat for subsequent bytes		
Full status check can be done after each byte or after a sequence of bytes		
Write FFH after the last byte write operation to reset the device to Ready Array Mode		

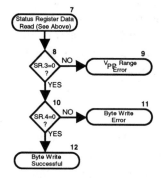

Bus Operation	Command	Comments
Optional Read		CPU may already have read Status Register data in WSM Ready polling above
Standby		Check SR.3 1 = V_{PP} Low Detect
Standby		Check SR.4 1 = Byte Write Error
SR.3 MUST be cleared, if set during a byte write attempt, before further attempts are allowed by the Write State Machine.		
SR.4 is only cleared by the Clear Status Register Command, in cases where multiple bytes are written before full status is checked.		
If error is detected, clear the Status Register before attempting retry or other error recovery.		

Figure 7.4: Intel Automated Flash Memory Program Algorithm

available on some flash memories, returns to logic one at the conclusion of the WSM-controlled programming.

Note that after writing the program command sequence to the flash memory, it automatically switches to a mode where it outputs Status Register data when read.

Step 5

After the system has determined that automation has completed, it may further analyze the Status Register to verify that programming was successful (steps 7-12). However, Status Register error bits will retain their values until explicitly cleared by the Clear Status Register command (50H). It may therefore be advantageous, when programming a large number of data locations at one time, to check these additional bits only occasionally or at the conclusion of all programming. For example, when programming a 16 byte string, poll only Status Register bit 7 (or the RY/$\overline{BY}$ output) between bytes, and save full analysis for the conclusion. Doing so minimizes system overhead and maximizes flash memory write performance.

Step 6

Programming of the desired flash memory location is complete. Another location can now be programmed, if desired, or the flash memory can be reset to its normal "array read" mode by writing the Read Array command (FFH).

Step 7

In step 4 above, we determined that the internal automation *completed*. In the following steps we'll determine whether the automation completed with a *successful outcome*.

Step 8

Examine Status Register bit 3 (see Figure 7.5). A one means that internal programming terminated unsuccessfully due to V_{PP} hard failure or momentary voltage transition below the valid low end of the V_{PP} range. Internal flash memory circuitry begins monitoring V_{PP} after the program command sequence is written to the device, and continues to periodically do so until automation completes.

Step 9

A reported V_{PP} error compels the system to determine whether this reflects a failure of the V_{PP} supply or a momentary glitch in the supply voltage due to excessive current draw by the system. In the former case, this reflects a hard system failure that must be repaired before flash memory can again be altered, and a message reflecting this supply failure should be relayed to the user. In the latter case, however, flash memory programming can again be attempted at the location. Occasional droop in the V_{PP} supply is sometimes caused by current draw by other logic/circuitry in the system that shares 12V with the flash memory, or it can be caused by attempting to program/erase excessive numbers of flash components at the same time, exceeding the current drive capability of the power supply. Appropriate action should be taken (turning off other circuitry, minimizing the number of flash memories being programmed/erased in parallel, etc.) before repeating the programming attempt.

Step 10

Now, check Status Register bit 4. A one means that the WSM has been unable to program the flash memory location after giving it the maximum possible number of program pulses. Inability to program (besides the "V_{PP} out of tolerance" case handled in steps 8 and 9) will most likely only occur if the device has been cycled far beyond its specifications.

Step 11

The system can mark the location as "bad" and continue (depending on the application), or it may issue another program command sequence to the flash memory to generate additional program pulses, as a means of extending device cycling.

The internal WSM-controlled verify only detects and reports errors for ones that do not successfully write to zeros, reflective of its function as a *program* verify. For example, what would happen if the system attempts to, at a location within the flash memory, write ones to bits that had previously been programmed to zero? These bits will of course remain at zero, but the program status bit of the Status Register will not reflect an

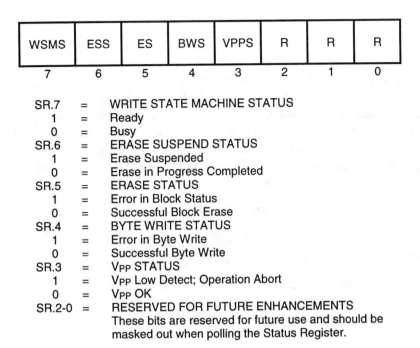

WSMS	ESS	ES	BWS	VPPS	R	R	R
7	6	5	4	3	2	1	0

SR.7 = WRITE STATE MACHINE STATUS
  1 = Ready
  0 = Busy
SR.6 = ERASE SUSPEND STATUS
  1 = Erase Suspended
  0 = Erase in Progress Completed
SR.5 = ERASE STATUS
  1 = Error in Block Status
  0 = Successful Block Erase
SR.4 = BYTE WRITE STATUS
  1 = Error in Byte Write
  0 = Successful Byte Write
SR.3 = V$_{PP}$ STATUS
  1 = V$_{PP}$ Low Detect; Operation Abort
  0 = V$_{PP}$ OK
SR.2-0 = RESERVED FOR FUTURE ENHANCEMENTS
       These bits are reserved for future use and should be
       masked out when polling the Status Register.

NOTES:

RY/$\overline{\text{BY}}$ or the Write State Machine Status bit must first be checked to determine byte write or block erase completion, before the Byte Write or Erase Status bit are checked for success.

If the Byte Write AND Erase Status bits are set to ones during a block erase attempt, an improper command sequence was entered. Attempt the operation again.

If VPP low status is detected, the Status Register must be cleared before another byte write or block erase operation is attempted.

The VPP Status bit, unlike an A/D converter, does not provide continuous indication of VPP level. The WSM interrogates the VPP level only after the byte write or block erase command sequences have been entered and informs the system if VPP has not be switched on. The VPP Status bit is not guaranteed to report accurate feedback between VPPL and VPPH.

Figure 7.5: Intel Automated Flash Memory Status Register

error. Remember, erasure (covered next) must be used to change zeros back to ones with flash memory.

Step 12

After first checking bit 7 of the Status Register to ensure that the internal flash memory automation has completed, and then verifying that the program attempt was successful via Status Register bits 3 and 4, the system can be assured that the specified location contains the desired programmed data. Unlike the first-generation program algorithm described earlier, actual read of the flash memory location to verify its value does not need to occur.

Intel Automated Block Erase Algorithm

This algorithm is shown in Figure 7.6.

Step 1

Before beginning the automated block erase algorithm, ramp V_{PP} to 12V. When erasing a sequence of blocks at one time, V_{PP} does not need to be ramped down and then back up between them.

Step 2

Write the erase setup command (20H) to the device. The address corresponds to any address within the block to be erased.

Step 3

Write the erase command (D0H), along with an address within the block to be erased, to the flash memory. Note that with this algorithm, only one block within a device can be erased at a time.

Step 4

After writing the erase command sequence, the WSM begins execution. Similar to automated programming, the erase automation controls many of the manual steps of the first-generation algorithm, including block preprogramming to 00H, erase pulse timing and termination, erase verification and iteration of erase/verify. System software (at its leisure) can poll the flash memory Status Register to determine when automation has completed. After it receives the erase command sequence, the flash

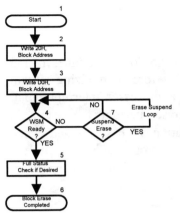

Bus Operation	Command	Comments
Write	Erase Setup	Data = 20H Address = Within block to be erased
Write	Erase	Data = D0H Address = Within block to be erased
Standby/ Read		Check R/BY 0V = Ready 0V = Busy or Read Status Register Check SR.7 1 = Ready, 0 = Busy Toggle OE or CE to update Status Register
Repeat for subsequent bytes		
Full status check can be done after each block or after a sequence of blocks		
Write FFH after the last block erase operation to reset the device to Ready Array Mode		

FULL STATUS CHECK PROCEDURE

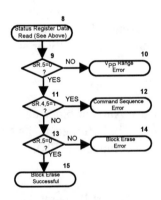

Bus Operation	Command	Comments
Optional Read		CPU may already have read Status Register data in WSM Ready polling above
Standby		Check SR.3 1 = Vpp Low Detect
Standby		Check SR.4,5 Both 1 = Command Sequence Error
Standby		Check SR.5 1 = Block Erase Error
SR.3 MUST be cleared, if set during a block erase attempt, before further attempts are allowed by the Write State Machine.		
SR.5 is only cleared by the Clear Status Register Command, in cases where multiple bytes are erased before full status is checked.		
If error is detected, clear the Status Register before attempting retry or other error recovery		

Figure 7.6: Intel Automated Flash Memory Block Erase Algorithm

memory automatically switches to a mode where it outputs Status Register data when read.

The RY/$\overline{\text{BY}}$ output can also be used to mask the slow erase time, freeing the system to execute other tasks and, therefore, minimizing system performance impact. When connected to a processor interrupt input, RY/$\overline{\text{BY}}$'s rising edge at the conclusion of erase interrupts the system. In most cases, RY/$\overline{\text{BY}}$'s interrupt configuration is best utilized when erasing the flash memory, versus during data programming. Due to the performance impact of interrupt latency and servicing, the speed of shorter programming events is often optimized by simple polling of the Status Register.

Step 5

After the system has determined that automation has completed, it may further analyze the Status Register to verify that block erase was successful (steps 8-15). However, Status Register error bits retain their values until explicitly cleared by the Clear Status Register command (50H). It may therefore be advantageous, when erasing a large number of blocks at a time, to check these additional bits only occasionally or at the conclusion of all block erasures.

Step 6

Erasure of the desired flash memory block completes. Another block can now be erased, if desired, or the flash memory can be returned to its normal "array read" mode by writing the Read Array command (FFH).

Step 7

If the system determines in step 4 above that the WSM is still operating, and it wants to suspend erase to read from the device, it can do so by issuing the Erase Suspend command (B0H). We'll cover the erase suspend/resume algorithm in detail after completing our review of automated block erasure.

Step 8

In step 4 above, we determined that the internal automation *completed*. In the following steps we'll determine whether the automation completed with a *successful outcome*.

Step 9

Examine Status Register bit 3. A logic one means that internal erasure terminated unsuccessfully due to V_{PP} failure or momentary transition below the valid low end of the V_{PP} range. Internal flash memory circuitry begins monitoring V_{PP} after the erase command sequence is written to the device, and then periodically until automation completes.

Step 10

The same guidelines for system response to V_{PP} error during erasure should be followed as those recommended earlier for automated byte programming. See step 9 under "The Automated Programming Algorithm" for more information.

Step 11

If Status Register bits 4 and 5 are both set to logic one, this reflects an invalid erase command sequence. The flash memory has correctly received the Erase Setup (20H) command, but the next command written to the device was something other than the Erase (D0H) command.

Step 12

The Erase Command Sequence error may have occurred due to bugs in the system software, or due to an unwanted glitch in a data line connecting the processor and flash memory. Whatever the reason, it is indicative of a critical system problem. This sort of error should be restricted to the lab during the debugging of a prototype design, and hopefully will not occur when the system gets in the customer's hands!

Step 13

Now check Status Register bit 5 alone. A one means that the WSM has been unable to erase the flash memory block after giving it the maximum possible number of program pulses. Inability to erase (besides the "V_{PP} out of tolerance" case handled in steps 9 and 10) most likely occurs only if the device has been cycled far beyond its specifications.

Step 14

The system will in most cases mark the block as "bad" and continue (depending on the application). Alternatively, an error message may be communicated to the system operator.

Step 15

After first checking bit 7 of the Status Register to ensure that the internal flash memory automation has completed, and then verifying that the block erase attempt was successful via Status Register bits 3, 4 and 5, the system can be assured that the specified block erased to FFH. Unlike the first-generation erase algorithm described earlier, actual read of the flash memory locations to verify their erasure does not need to occur.

Intel Automated Erase Suspend/Resume Algorithm

This algorithm is shown in Figure 7.7.

Step 1

Before this point, the system has already read from the flash memory Status Register and verified that the WSM is still running (see step 4 under "The Automated Block Erase Algorithm").

Step 2

System software writes the Erase Suspend command (B0H) to the flash memory. Since only one block within a device can be erasing at one time, any address within the device can be given.

Step 3

Write the Read Status Register command (70H) to the flash memory. You might ask why this is needed, since earlier we said that after writing the erase command sequence to it, the flash memory automatically outputs Status Register data.

It is possible that in the time between:

1.   When the system has read from the Status Register (to see that the WSM is still running), and

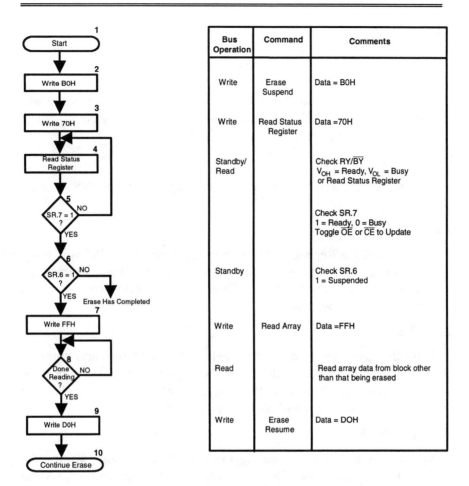

Figure 7.7: The Intel Automated Erase Suspend / Resume Algorithm

2.   When the system writes the Erase Suspend command (to suspend the WSM),

that the WSM may have already completed the erase algorithm and returned to "ready". In this case, the Erase Suspend command will be meaningless to the device, and will be decoded as invalid and cause the flash memory to return to its read array mode. In such a scenario, the system software would be polling what it thought was the Status Register, waiting for a suspend indication, when it was actually reading array data. An infinite loop would be the probable outcome.

Writing the Read Status Register command will ensure that, regardless of the status of the WSM, the flash memory will correctly output Status Register data when subsequently read, as expected.

Steps 4 and 5

Poll the Status Register repeatedly until receiving the WSM ready indication via bit 7.

Step 6

Next, read Status Register bit 6 to determine whether the WSM is ready because erase has been suspended (if bit 6 = one) or because erase has already completed (bit 6 = zero). If erase has completed, suspend is not possible, nor needed.

Steps 7 and 8

Write the Read Array command (FFH) to the flash memory, allowing code execution or data reads out of the device. Any block within the flash memory can be read at this point, but of course the block being erased when suspended will contain unknown data.

Steps 9 and 10

After the system finishes reading from the flash memory, writing the Erase Resume command (D0H) will continue the erase in progress and return the WSM to "busy".

Alternative Automated Algorithms

The first-generation bulk erase algorithms described early in this chapter are standardized and supported in flash memories from several manufacturers today. Automated algorithms, on the other hand, are to a greater or lesser degree unique to each manufacturer, and are essentially software-incompatible with each other. However, although specific implementations may differ, the general approaches used in many of these algorithms are similar and can be grouped together for review purposes.

As an example of an alternative automated approach, we'll cover AMD's embedded algorithms in the paragraphs that follow, and then discuss general techniques that can be applied to automated program/erase algorithms from multiple flash memory manufacturers.

Advanced Micro Devices Embedded Algorithms

Although AMD's flash memories are built on NOR technologies resembling Intel's ETOX approach, the software program and erase algorithms of their newest "5V-only" devices are most similar to those of flash EEPROM memories. Since these devices do not have the program/erase hardware protection of a separate Vpp voltage, they compensate by requiring multiple-byte command sequences to specific device addresses (software protection), shown in Table 7.3. Their methods of communicating internal automation status and success/failure, called data polling and toggle polling, are also similar to those of EEPROMs and flash EEPROM memories.

Command Sequence	Bus Write Cycles Req'd	First Bus Write Cycle		Second Bus Write Cycle		Third Bus Write Cycle		Fourth Bus Read/Write Cycle		Fifth Bus Write Cycle		Sixth Bus Write Cycle	
		Addr	Data	Addr	Data	Addr	Data	Addr	Data	Addr	Data	Addr	Data
Read/Reset	4	5555	AA	2AAA	55	5555	F0	RA	RD				
Autoselect	4	5555	AA	2AAA	55	5555	90	00/01	01/20				
Byte Program	4	5555	AA	2AAA	55	5555	A0	PA	PD				
Chip Erase	6	5555	AA	2AAA	55	5555	80	5555	AA	2AAA	55	5555	10
Sector Erase	6	5555	AA	2AAA	55	5555	80	5555	AA	2AAA	55	SA	30

Notes (addresses and data are shown in Hex):
1. Address bit A15 = X = Don't Care. Write Sequences may be initiated with A15 in either state.
2. Address bit A16 = X = Don't Care for all address commands except for Program Address (PA) and Sector Address (SA).
3. RA = Address of the memory location to be read.
   PA = Address of the memory location to be programmed. Addresses are latched on the falling edge of the $\overline{WE}$ pulse.
   SA = Address of the sector to be erased. The combination of A16, A15, A14 will uniquely select any sector.
4. RD = Data read from location RA during read operation.
   PD = Data to be programmed at location PA. Data is latched on the falling edge of $\overline{WE}$.

Table 7.3: AMD "5V-Only" Automated Algorithm Command Definitions

AMD's devices do not include a Status Register, but provide similar functionality via hardware sequence flags that can be read during automated program or erase. The description of the various flag bits below will aid in understanding the flowcharts of Figures 7.8-7.10.

DQ_7: $\overline{\text{Data Polling Bit}}$
During the execution of a programming operation, DQ_7 outputs, when read, the complement of the data last written to DQ_7. When the automated algorithm completes, DQ_7 outputs the true data last written to it. During automated erase, DQ_7 will be zero, and it will output a one when erase completes.

DQ_6:   Toggle Bit
During embedded program or erase, successive reads of the device result in DQ_6 toggling between one and zero. Upon algorithm completion, DQ_6 will not toggle, and valid data will be read.

DQ_5:   Exceeding Timing Limits
If DQ_5 outputs a one when read, the built-in timing limits for program or erase have been exceeded. This means that the program or erase cycle was not successful; it completed with error.

DQ_4:   Hardware Sequence Flag
If DQ_5 outputs a one, this bit informs the system whether programming (DQ_4 = zero) or erase (DQ_4 = one) was unsuccessful. During an automated erase attempt, this bit also reflects whether the timing limits were exceeded during block preprogramming or during block erasure.

DQ_3:   Sector Erase Timer
As Figure 7.9 shows, AMD provides the capability to erase multiple blocks within the flash memory with one sequence of commands. Writing successive 30H commands with corresponding block addresses tells the device to perform the multiple block erasure. The flash memory measures the time since the last 30H command was written to the flash memory, and if it exceeds a predefined delay, the internal automation sets DQ_3 to one and begins executing the internal algorithm.

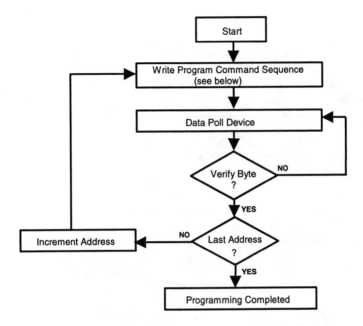

Program Command Sequence (Address/Command):

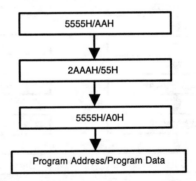

Figure 7.8: AMD "5V-Only" Automated Program Algorithm

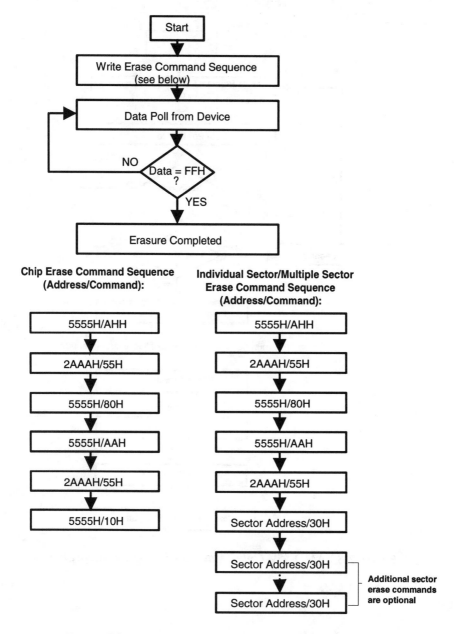

Figure 7.9: AMD "5V-Only" Automated Erase Algorithm

DATA POLLING ALGORITHM

TOGGLE BIT ALGORITHM

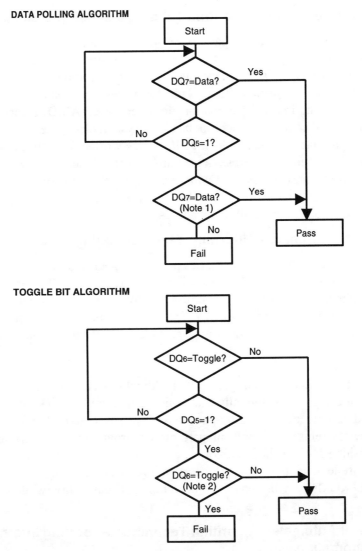

Note:
1. DQ7 is rechecked even if DQ5 = "1" because DQ7 may change simultaneously with DQ5.
2. DQ6 is rechecked even if DQ5 = "1" because DQ6 may stop toggling at the same time as DQ5 changing to "1."

Figure 7.10: AMD "5V-Only" Automated Data Polling and Toggle Bit Algorithms

General Automated Algorithm Techniques-Multiple Block Erase

The multi-block erase capability of AMD's flash memories also appears in flash memory devices offered by other manufacturers. In some cases (Toshiba's NAND, for example), after the multiple command/block addresses have been written to the flash memory, a specific command activates the internal automation. In other cases (AMD, Hitachi, NEC) an internal counter, asynchronous to the system clock, measures the time since the last command/block address was written, and after a specified timeout begins the erase algorithm. In the latter approach, system interrupts must be disabled while writing block addresses to the device. This prevents CPU distraction that may prematurely begin flash memory erase before entering all block addresses.

General Automated Algorithm Techniques-Page Programming

Toshiba's NAND flash memories program a page at a time (versus a byte or a word at a time), because of the requirements of the serial NAND architecture. After writing multiple data bytes to a page buffer within the device, a command sequence initiates the internal automated page programming. The devices also provide separate block and chip erase capability.

Flash EEPROMs (examples include Atmel devices), as you'll remember from Chapter 3, essentially function as defeatured EEPROMs that erase and rewrite on a page-by-page basis (versus byte-by-byte). On these devices, erase is a built-in part of the programming algorithm. Like Toshiba NAND flash memories, programming is initiated after writing multiple data bytes to a buffer on the flash EEPROM. Some flash EEPROMs provide separate block/chip erase capability, while others do not.

General Automated Algorithm Techniques-Aborting Internal Automation

Automated flash memories include internal oscillators to control the program/erase state machine logic. Since they don't run off the system clock (i.e., no CLK input), they operate asynchronous to the logic in the system. Once automation has been initiated, there is no software method to terminate the internal algorithms, until they complete by themselves.

As mentioned earlier, these devices automatically output status information once programming or erase have begun. They must be reset via software commands to output array data again, once automation completes. What happens, though, if the system is reset by hardware or software, including the CPU? If flash memory program/erase is occurring at this time, and if the flash memory contains the code that the processor boots from, the flash memory must also be reset to ensure that array data (not status information) is provided to the CPU.

Block-eraseable Intel flash memories are currently the only devices that provide hardware state machine reset capability, through their $\overline{\text{PWD}}$[37] inputs. Although the $\overline{\text{PWD}}$ toggle aborts the program or erase in progress, it also resets the flash memory to "read array" mode, enabling code execution from the boot block (see the section on "System Boot Code Requirements" later in this chapter). For all other automated flash memories, make sure that the system cannot be reset during the update of the flash memory, if using it to store the processor boot code.

General Automated Algorithm Techniques-The RY/$\overline{\text{BY}}$ Output

Intel's FlashFile™ memories and Toshiba's newest NAND devices include a RY/$\overline{\text{BY}}$ output that reflects the status of internal program/erase automation. RY/$\overline{\text{BY}}$ defaults to a high (or TTL-level one) state. During operation of the flash memory state machine[38], RY/$\overline{\text{BY}}$ is driven low, and its rising edge signals the conclusion of the internal algorithm. RY/$\overline{\text{BY}}$ reflects the state of the Status Register WSM Status bit (see Figure 7.5), and is implemented with the intent of connecting it to a system interrupt input or to a separate system register that can be software-polled. The primary difference between the Intel and Toshiba approaches is that Toshiba's RY/$\overline{\text{BY}}$ is an open-drain output (therefore multiple flash memory outputs can be wire-tied together) whereas Intel's RY/$\overline{\text{BY}}$ is a full-CMOS output.

---

[37] $\overline{\text{PWD}}$ is also known as $\overline{\text{RP}}$ in JEDEC notation.
[38] i.e. during flash memory program and erase.

Software polling or hardware interrupt: Which should you use?

The functions of RY/$\overline{BY}$ and its Status Register counterpart are interchangeable. Both methods of determining internal automation status (software polling and hardware interrupt) have their merits, depending on the type of operation(s) being performed. Recall that a NOR flash memory location programs in about 9 μsec, and a NOR flash memory block erases in about 1.6 seconds. Hardware interrupt configuration using RY/$\overline{BY}$ is very useful in hiding the slow erase time as a background function. It allows the system to prioritize and process flash memory reads/writes and other system functions as foreground tasks. For example, assume a real-time system with a flash card to continually accumulate data in a first-in-first-out manner. While writing the current blocks in the foreground, the system simultaneously starts erasing old blocks (background task) to get them ready for future block writes. When any of the background erase operations complete, RY/$\overline{BY}$ makes its low-to-high transition, generating the system interrupt that says, "Hey, I'm done!". The interrupt service routine now labels that block available for more data accumulation.

Now let's consider the foreground programming operation. What would happen if the system took an interrupt from this every 9 μsec? For performance reasons alone, system requirements usually will not be able to afford the time associated with interrupt latency and service routines for programming. In some cases, the interrupt latency may even be as long as the programming operation itself. Therefore, polling is generally suggested for programming, and may be performed by reading the RY/$\overline{BY}$ pin through an I/O port, or by reading the Status Register in the flash memory device. Make sure that if you choose software polling for an operation, you disable the interrupt that that operation's conclusion could generate.

UPDATE ROUTINES

Flash memory's easy in-system update capability makes it very useful for storing the embedded code that runs the system. What should such an update utility look like, and what will it contain? To some extent, the answer to this question will depend on the kind of system we're talking about, what kind of user interface it contains, and where the new code to be stored in the flash memory will come from. Following are some examples of systems that exist today that take advantage of flash memory update:

- If the flash memory stores the BIOS (Basic Input/Output System) in a personal computer, the update utility may be resident in the machine (accessed via a special keystroke sequence) or run from the HDD or a floppy disk. The new BIOS can be shipped on floppy disk from the manufacturer, or the customer can download the code from a BBS over a modem link.

- If the flash memory stores the operating software for a laser printer, the update utility can again be run from a connected computer, with handshaking and new software download over the parallel or serial link.

- If flash memory contains the embedded code of a cellular phone, the update utility can be resident in the handset or base unit, with communication between the user and phone over the keypad and screen. Conceivably, the user could call a computer at the phone manufacturer using a dedicated phone number, and after entering a unique keypad sequence, new code could be relayed over the wireless link to the phone, which would update itself automatically.

Only your imagination and the unique needs and capabilities of your application limit the specific update method chosen for your design. In general, however, if an end user is going to be doing the update, the interface should be as intuitive, simple and informative as possible. Think of a time when you've installed or updated an operating system or application on your computer. Like the authors, you've probably experienced setup routines that were very good, and those that were very bad! The end user's expectations, and the capabilities you provide, are no different when code resident in flash memory is being updated versus when updating software on a HDD.

The following pseudo-code routine applies to a BIOS update routine, but many of the concepts shown are equally useful for other applications. Spare no detail in designing the update utility; provide both keyboard and mouse interface if possible, make the display colorful and informative (while not distracting or overwhelming!), etc. Time spent up-front in making the update process intuitive and user-friendly will pay long-term dividends when customers take advantage of the capability you've designed into your system!

• Initialize the system; set up the screen, ensure that the system (if portable) has sufficient battery power for the update.

• Access BIOS update files (from floppy disc, modem link, etc.). If files are not present, send an error message ("Insert floppy disk, or press ESC to exit", or equivalent).

• Display BIOS update file information, prompt user for choice (have simple choices and perhaps even refer them to user's guide), load to memory and validate data via checksum or other means. If file is invalid, prompt for file or exit.

• Inform user that BIOS update is about to begin ("Press ESC to exit, or any other key to continue"). If user continues, display a message to the effect of "Do not power down or reboot the machine during BIOS update".

• Erase flash memory.

• Reprogram with new data (a "Percent Complete" indication is useful in both this and the previous step).

• Inform the user when the BIOS update completes.

• Reboot the machine.

Flexible Design Techniques

To ensure multiple flash memory sources, or to leverage one hardware design for several different end-system configurations, you may choose to create a flexible design that accepts several different flash memories. This flexibility may involve compatible flash memories from different manufacturers, different flash memory densities from the same manufacturer (i.e., a 1 Mbit or 2 Mbit flash memory in the same socket) or even incompatible flash memories (both a non-automated and an automated device, for example). In each of these cases, the software update algorithms probably differ for each flash memory that can be used in the design.

PCMCIA flash memory cards represent one likely example of this situation. Removability makes it very simple to install cards containing many types of flash memory devices in the same system.

Fortunately, most flash memories support software-accessible manufacturer and device IDs identifying the device and enabling the system to select the correct program/erase algorithms. For example, writing the Intelligent Identifier command (70H) to any Intel flash memory enables reading of the manufacturer ID (89H) at device address 0000H, and the specific device ID at device address 0001H. Other companies have different manufacturer and device IDs, of course, and both IDs can be found in device specifications.

Be careful if you use this procedure in a design that will accept either a flash memory or an EPROM. EPROMs do not support software access to device IDs. Writing the Intelligent Identifier command to an EPROM (thereby toggling its $\overline{\text{PGM}}$ input, usually located at the same pin as flash memory's $\overline{\text{WE}}$) with V$_{pp}$ at 12V may result in unwanted programming of EPROM locations!

SYSTEM BOOT CODE CONTENTS

When bulk-erase flash memories were introduced several years ago, there was some reluctance to using them for embedded code storage, precisely because erasure removed *all* data from the device. What might happen, for example, if in the middle of a code update (while the flash memory was erased and before new code was programmed) the system was reset, or it lost power? What would happen if the flash memory was unintentionally updated with corrupted code? When the processor attempted to reboot from the flash memory, it would not find the code it expected, leading to a brain-dead system. The realistic possibility of these scenarios was in most cases very unlikely, but it was a concern in some applications.

To better meet the needs of embedded code applications (and, quite frankly, to sell more flash memory!), several companies now offer blocked flash memories that allow selective erase of portions of the device without altering data stored in other device blocks. These products also offer hardware and/or software lockable boot blocks that, if desired, can make code or data stored inside unalterable once initially programmed by the system manufacturer. Examples include Intel's Boot Block flash memory line (see Figure 5.5), and AMD's 5V-only flash memories. The intent here is to provide a small kernel of stable, non-updateable code that will always be present, regardless of the state of other device blocks. This secure software will minimally bring up the system and download code to the other blocks of the device if required.

The contents of this kernel code vary from system to system and application to application, but the guidelines that follow apply in most cases. The core boot code should contain some, if not all, of the following functions:

- Minimally initialize the system (configure the processor, chipset, floppy drive to allow reading in of the update code, etc.)

- Perform a checksum of the remainder of the flash memory data

- If checksum verifies correctly, jump to the main portion of the system boot code, probably found in another block of the device.

- If checksum fails (meaning that one or several of the other flash memory blocks contain invalid code/data):
  -Alert the user through speaker beep, message on display, LED flash, etc.
  -Erase all other blocks of the flash memory[39]

---

[39] This means that the boot block must store the erase/program algorithms for the flash memory.

-Download new data from floppy disk, external connector, etc.
-Reboot the system

SOFTWARE INTERFACE TO FLASH CARDS, SIMMS AND MULTI-COMPONENT ARRAYS

This chapter, so far, has covered software interfacing to flash memory components in great detail. In its simplest definition, a flash memory card or SIMM is a *super-component,* a large array of flash memory devices in one package. Of course, some flash memory cards also include enhanced card identifiers and control registers[40]. Beyond this extra circuitry, system software interacts with the flash memory components in the card in the same way as it would interact with the flash memory *components* directly. A similar situation exists if the system design includes not just one resident flash memory, but a larger array of multiple flash memories on the motherboard, interfacing to the processor. To repeat, the same rules and guidelines we've already seen for individual flash memories also apply to groups of flash memories on the system motherboard, on a separate SIMM board, or in a removable card form factor. Each flash memory in the group is manipulated and controlled, programmed and erased using the same algorithms we've already covered in this chapter.

Parallel programming or *parallel erase* of multiple flash memories at the same time presents one area where things get a little tricky. Because they program or erase at slightly different rates relative to each other[41], multiple flash memories connected in parallel (to match the system buswidth) present a unique challenge. How do we ensure sufficient program/erase of the slower flash memories in a parallel configuration, while not overprogramming/overerasing faster devices? That's what this section will show you! Just as the system interface to individual automated flash memory components was much simpler than to their non-automated counterparts, automated flash memories make parallel program and erase much easier.

---

[40]Refer to Chapters 8 and 10 more for details.
[41]This results from process and cycling variations.

As a review, look at Figure 5.2, where we have shown two x8 flash memories connected in parallel (one to the lower half of the bus and one to the upper half) to match the processor x16 buswidth, and sharing a common $\overline{CE}$. This interface could have just as easily been four x8 or two x16 flash memories interfaced to a 32-bit processor. Similarly, Intel's Series 1 and Series 2 flash memory cards contain x8 flash memories connected in parallel, to match the 16-bit card interface. The components inside these memory cards can be accessed individually (via the $\overline{CE}_1$ and $\overline{CE}_2$ inputs). However, in this section we'll assume a simple 16-bit interface to the card, in which case both $\overline{CE}_1$ and $\overline{CE}_2$ will be active each time the card is accessed. Programming/erasing both components in parallel also maximizes performance by doing twice as much work in the same amount of time, albeit with twice the amount of current draw.

As we cover the parallel program and erase flowcharts in the next several sections, refer to the individual device program/erase algorithm discussions at the beginning of the chapter for step-by-step details, not repeated here for reasons of brevity.

Parallel Program of Non-Automated Flash Memories

Figure 7.11 shows a conceptual flow for parallel programming of non-automated flash memories. This procedure bases itself on the fact that writing data FFH to the flash memory is decoded as the reset command (see Table 7.1), which puts the device in its "read array" mode. Therefore, by writing FFH to flash memories that have already verified correctly, we avoid excessive programming. The parallel programming flow decreases total programming time, eliminates separate tracking of high-low byte addresses and per-device program pulses, and maintains a consistent interface (word, double-word, etc.) to the flash memories.

Step 1

Enable V_{PPH} for all devices to be programmed.

Step 2

When first entering this routine, the program setup command variable will be initialized so as to write 40H to each flash memory. Similarly, the program verify command variable will be initialized to write C0H to each flash memory. As an example, if two x8 flash memories are connected in parallel, the program setup and program verify command variables will initially be 4040H and C0C0H. For four flash memories, the commands will initially be 40404040H and C0C0C0C0H.

Similarly, the '"program" command variable will initially reflect the data to be programmed into each device. For example, for two x8 parallel flash memories, A and B, the program command variable will initially be AABBH, where AA and BB reflect the data for device A and B, respectively.

The program pulsecount is initially 0.

Step 3

Write the program setup and program command variables to the parallel flash memories.

Step 4

Time out at least 10 µs.

Step 5

Write the program verify command variable to the parallel flash memories.

Step 6

Time out at least 6 µs.

Step 7

Read from the flash memory interface, and compare each device's data to the program command variable written in step 3. Do all flash memories verify correctly after one program attempt at the location?

Step 8

If more data is to be programmed, the algorithm returns to step 2, to reset/clear all variables.

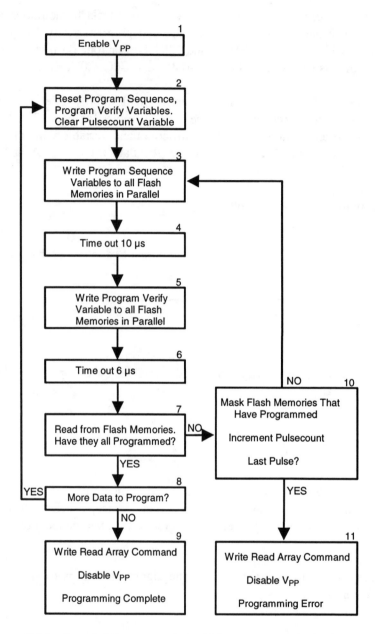

Figure 7.11: Parallel Programming of Non-Automated Flash Memories

Step 9

After programming all data, write the read array command (FFH) to all flash memories in parallel and disable V_{PP} if desired.

Step 10

What happens if some, but not all, of the parallel-configured flash memories verify correctly? Since some devices have not fully programmed yet, the algorithm will have to go through another program/verify iteration, but we don't need (or want) to do this for flash memories that have already passed. For these latter flash memories, then, we substitute data FFH for the program setup and program verify commands, and for the data to be programmed.

We also need to increment the pulsecount to make sure we haven't exceeded 25 pulses.

Example:
Two x8 devices are being programmed with variables initialized as follows:

Program Setup:	4040H
Program:	AABBH (A is the high-byte device, B
	is the low-byte)
Program Verify:	C0C0H
Pulsecount:	0

After one program/verify iteration, the high-byte device verifies correctly (to data 'AAH'), but the low-byte device does not. Therefore, we reset the variables as shown:

Program Setup:	FF40H
Program:	FFBBH
Program Verify:	FFC0H

Increment pulsecount now equals one. Since it is less than 25, we return to step 3 and repeat the program/verify sequence.

Step 11

If after 25 pulses one of the flash memories still does not verify correctly, write the read array command, disable V_{PP}, and return an error indication to the system. More comprehensive algorithms can return not only an error message but also reference to the specific flash memory that did not program to the calling routine, if this information is useful.

Parallel Erase of Non-Automated Flash Memories

Figure 7.12 shows parallel erase of non-automated flash memories. Like parallel programming, this algorithm depends on writing data FFH to avoid overerase of devices that correctly verify. As we first discussed in chapter 3, overerase is a much bigger concern (and much more damaging phenomenon) than is overprogram.

Step 1

Enable V_{PPH} for all devices to be erased.

Step 2

Preprogram all locations within the devices to 00H, by repeatedly following the parallel programming algorithm of Figure 7.11.

Step 3

After first entering this routine, the erase sequence command variable will be initialized so as to write 20H to each flash memory. Similarly, the erase verify command variable will be initialized to write A0H to each flash memory. As an example, if two x8 flash memories are connected in parallel, the erase sequence and erase verify command variables will initially be 2020H and A0A0H. For four flash memories, the commands will initially be 20202020H and A0A0A0A0H.

Initialize the erase pulsecount and address variables to zero.

Step 4

Write the erase sequence command variable twice in a row to the parallel flash memories, to reflect writing the "erase setup" and "erase" commands (same command data).

Step 5

Time out 10 ms.

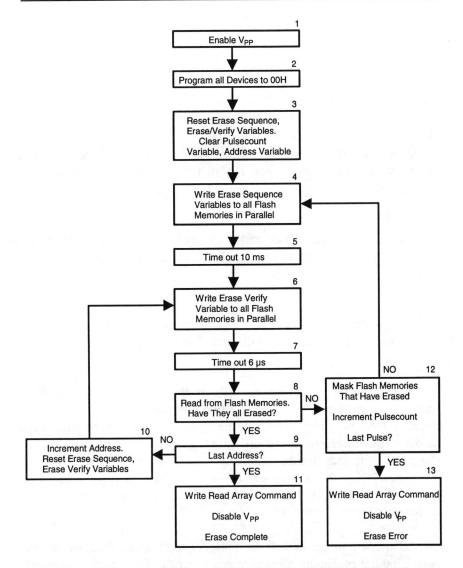

Figure 7.12: Parallel Erase of Non-Automated Flash Memories

Step 6

Write the erase verify command variable to the parallel flash memories.

Step 7

Time out at least 6 µs.

Step 8

Read from the flash memory interface, and compare each device's data to its valid erased value, FFH. Do all flash memories at the location verify correctly after one erase attempt (most likely not)?

Steps 9 and 10

Increment the address, and verify the new flash memory locations. Continue until all data in all parallel flash memories has verified as erased.

Step 11

When all flash memories have been erased, write the read array command (FFH) to them in parallel and disable V_{PP} if desired.

Step 12

What happens if some, but not all, of the parallel-configured flash memories verify correctly? Since some devices at the current address location have not fully erased yet, the algorithm will have to go through another full erase/verify iteration, but we don't need (or want) to do this for flash memories that have already passed. To do so would increase the potential for overerase! For these latter flash memories, then, we substitute data FFH for the erase setup, erase and erase verify commands.

We also need to increment the pulsecount to make sure we haven't exceeded the maximum allowable count for the flash memory (usually 1000; check specific device datasheets to be sure).

Example:
Two x8 devices are being erased with variables initialized as follows:

Erase Sequence:	2020H
Erase Verify:	A0A0H
Pulsecount:	0

After one erase/verify iteration, the high-byte device verifies correctly as erased, (to data FFH), but the low-byte device does not. Therefore, we reset the variables as shown:

Erase Sequence:	FF20H
Erase Verify:	FFA0H

Increment pulsecount now equals one. Since it is less than the maximum, we return to step 3 and repeat the erase/verify sequence.

Step 13

If, after 1000 pulses, one of the flash memories still does not verify correctly, write the read array command to all of them, disable Vpp, and return an error indication to the system. More comprehensive algorithms can return not only an error message but also reference to the specific flash memory that did not fully erase to the calling routine, if this information is useful.

Parallel Program/Erase of Automated Flash Memories

As explained earlier in the chapter, automated program/erase algorithms greatly simplify system interface software, by automatically and internally controlling verification, pulse repetition and iteration, and so forth. Parallel program/erase, shown in Figure 7.13, is similarly simplified.

Step 1

Enable Vpp before attempting the desired operation.

Step 2

Similar to the non-automated algorithms discussed previously, write the program or erase command sequence to each flash memory in the parallel configuration. Note that since the internal automation controls verify, repetition and algorithm termination, no provision needs to be made for device-by-device command masking with FFH.

Step 3

The system can poll the device Status Registers, or be alerted via RY/$\overline{BY}$ interrupt, to determine when program/erase completes. A full check of all Status Register bits will determine whether the desired operation was successful (see automated program/erase algorithm sections earlier in this chapter).

Steps 4 and 5

System software can loop back to step 2, if more data must be programmed or more blocks erased. Otherwise, it writes the Read Array command to reset all devices to their normal modes and disables V_{PP} if desired.

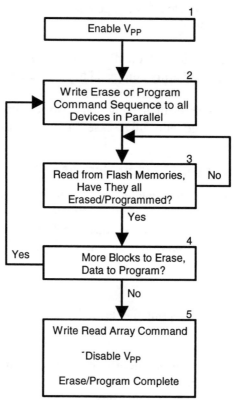

Figure 7.13: Parallel Program / Erase of Automated Flash Memories

SUMMARY

In this chapter we've shown you how to interface to flash memory components via *software*; to a single flash memory (or multiple devices) resident on the system board, to flash memories on an add-in board like a SIMM and to flash memories in a removable card form factor. The command interface and internal logic of flash memory makes in-system update a much simpler proposition than it was for earlier-generation memories like EPROM. Full automation on newest devices simplifies the process even further.

We've intentionally not covered some aspects of software interfacing in this chapter; specifically those that relate to PCMCIA flash memory cards and the extra logic and control registers that exist beyond the components themselves. The software architecture of flash-friendly file systems has similarly not been included in Chapter 7. Fear not, however; these topics have not been overlooked, just relegated elsewhere! See Chapters 8-10 for more information.

Chapter Eight: Hardware Interfacing Considerations for Flash Cards

In Chapter 5 we focused on the system hardware requirements for interfacing to flash memory components, from single to multiple device designs. This chapter runs in a parallel direction; in that it explains the hardware interfacing requirements for implementing a flash memory array inside a removable package, the memory card. Some of the things we'll cover include:

- The Personal Computer Memory Card International Association (PCMCIA) specification
- Fundamentals of memory card design from a system interface perspective
- Host system interface controllers
- PC Card insertion and removal
- Interrupt steering

A FLASH MEMORY ARRAY WITHIN A CARD

A flash memory card may consist of nothing more than a packaged array of flash memory devices, utilized primarily for easy removal and transfer. The simplest example of this is a card containing a single flash memory device that essentially plugs directly into the same socket that would be provided for a discrete component. Cards like this usually have a proprietary interface, typically designed for embedded equipment, or potentially even things like video games. The memory card packaging merely makes this component easier to handle when performing upgrades or removing it from the system for purposes of data security.

Taking this single-chip card a step further, some cards contain multiple components and incorporate a simple decoder to allow individual selection (chip enabling); not really much different than that required for an array of unpackaged discrete memories. These commercially available cards typically accommodate custom designs and have fine-tuning for a specific application. These "non-mainstream" cards tend to be more costly and generally do not allow interchangability from system to system.

PCMCIA FLASH MEMORY CARDS

PCMCIA/JEIDA (Personal Computer Memory Card International Association and Japan Electronics Industry Design Association) developed a detailed specification to standardize on a memory card format, including the electrical interface and card dimensions. Since PCMCIA/JEIDA represent the dominant memory card interface for flash memory, we will focus on it (and more specifically, only areas relevant to flash memory cards). This specification has the fundamental goal of allowing *any* PCMCIA-compatible card (ranging from flash memory cards to fax/modem cards) to be plugged into *any* PCMCIA-compliant system. To accommodate the wide variety of cards, the specification was defined to provide a generic card interface. For example, although flash memory cards do not require some signals (e.g., battery voltage detect, WAIT), they must still be supported to maintain a PCMCIA-compatible socket.[42]

PCMCIA 1.0

As described in Chapter 10, the PCMCIA specification actually represents two major versions, namely releases 1.0 and 2.0. Although the second release supersedes the first, there are still many low density, flash memory cards being sold, and systems designed, that only comply with release 1.0. The first PCMCIA-compatible flash memory card to enter the market, Intel's Series 1 Card, is basically an extension of the simple cards discussed above. The card contains between 8 and 16 flash memory components (Intel's 28F010 and 28F020), and an ASIC which supplies buffered signals for the PCMCIA interface and handles component-level decoding. Figure 8.1 shows a block diagram of this

---

[42]This may not be a concern for proprietary systems only using flash memory cards.

memory card. Other manufacturer's cards, such as Fujitsu's MB98A881223 (4 Mbyte flash memory card), also incorporate EEPROM devices that reside in the Attribute Memory address space.

PCMCIA 2.0

Along with the second release of the PCMCIA spec came a new generation of flash memory cards. In addition to maintaining backwards compatibility with the previous generation, Release 2.0 cards support new PCMCIA interface signals (occupying previously reserved pins). Intel's Series 2 Flash Memory Cards again provide a good example. Comparing their block diagram (Figure 8.2) with that shown in Figure 8.1, one can see a similarity in the basic structures. Closer examination reveals that the Series 2 Card not only contains different devices, but also supports a Card Information Structure[43] (CIS), reset capability, and ready/busy for automated write and erase operations (via the $\overline{\text{REG}}$, $\overline{\text{RST}}$, and RDY/$\overline{\text{BSY}}$ pins, respectively).

Although the PCMCIA evolution to release 2.0 focused primarily on the accommodation of I/O cards (modems, faxes, etc.), memory card vendors also took a step to add more complex circuitry, providing increased functionality and features. For example, the Card Information Structure, a feature originating with release 1.0, does not appear on most first-generation cards but is prevalent on cards designed to comply with the release 2.0 spec. The appendix lists different flash memory card manufacturers supporting the different levels of compatibility (release 1.0 or 2.0).

We'll begin our technical discussion of the PCMCIA flash memory card interface by defining the relevant signals (from a flash memory standpoint[44]). This will provide you with a knowledge base to understand and develop specific implementations. In the last part of the chapter we'll go over some general design guidelines such as buffering, card removal and insertion, power up and down protection, etc. To begin, Table 8.1 lists the 68 pins of the PCMCIA electrical interface and

---

[43]Chapter 11 discusses the Card Information Structure.
[44]For more information on the I/O interface, refer to the PCMCIA R2.01 specification.

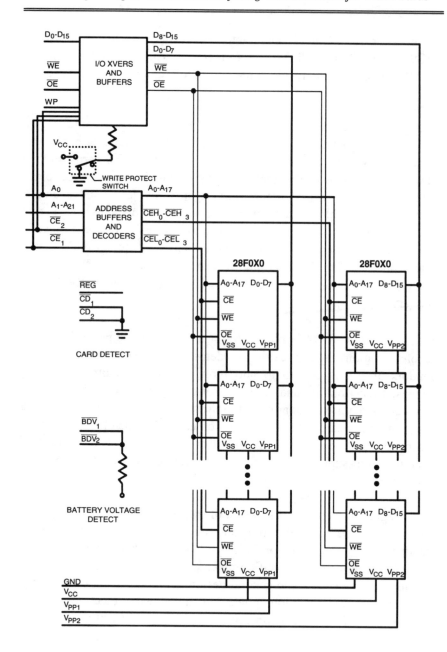

Figure 8.1: PCMCIA 1.0 Flash Memory Card

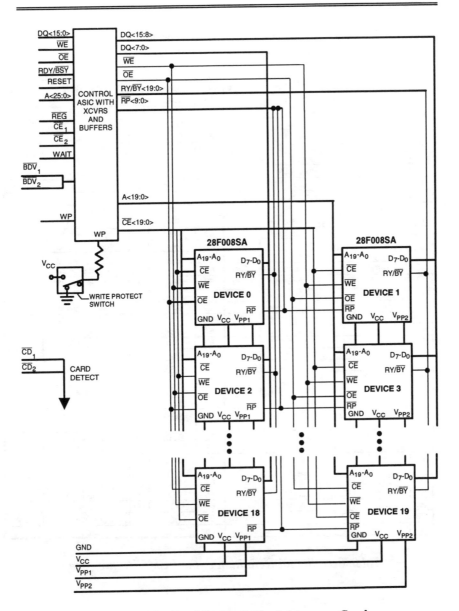

Figure 8.2: Intel Series 2 Flash Memory Card

Figure 8.3 displays the general categories. The text that follows defines these signals from a functional and electrical standpoint[45].

PIN	SIGNAL	I/O	FUNCTION	ACTIVE	PIN	SIGNAL	I/O	FUNCTION	ACTIVE
1	GND		Ground		35	GND		Ground	
2	DQ_3	I/O	Data Bit 3		36	$\overline{CD1}$	O	Card Detect 1	LOW
3	DQ_4	I/O	Data Bit 4		37	DQ_{11}	I/O	Data Bit 11	
4	DQ_5	I/O	Data Bit 5		38	DQ_{12}	I/O	Data Bit 12	
5	DQ_6	I/O	Data Bit 6		39	DQ_{13}	I/O	Data Bit 13	
6	DQ_7	I/O	Data Bit 7		40	DQ_{14}	I/O	Data Bit 14	
7	$\overline{CE1}$	I	Card Enable 1	LOW	41	DQ_{15}	I/O	Data Bit 15	
8	A_{10}	I	Address Bit 10		42	$\overline{CE2}$	I	Card Enable 2	LOW
9	$\overline{OE}$	I	Output Enable	LOW	43	VS1	O	Voltage Sense 1	
10	A_{11}	I	Address Bit 11		44	RFU		Reserved	
11	A_9	I	Address Bit 9		45	RFU		Reserved	
12	A_8	I	Address Bit 8		46	A_{17}	I	Address Bit 17	
13	A_{13}	I	Address Bit 13		47	A_{18}	I	Address Bit 18	
14	A_{14}	I	Address Bit 14		48	A_{19}	I	Address Bit 19	
15	$\overline{WE}$	I	Write Enable	LOW	49	A_{20}	I	Address Bit 20	
16	$RDY/\overline{BSY}$	O	Ready/Busy	LOW	50	A_{21}	I	Address Bit 21	
17	V_{CC}		Supply Voltage		51	V_{CC}		Supply Voltage	
18	VPP1		Supply Voltage		52	VPP2		Supply Voltage	
19	A_{16}	I	Address Bit 16		53	A_{22}	I	Address Bit 22	
20	A_{15}	I	Address Bit 15		54	A_{23}	I	Address Bit 23	
21	A_{12}	I	Address Bit 12		55	A_{24}	I	Address Bit 24	
22	A_7	I	Address Bit 7		56	A_{25}	I	Address Bit 25	
23	A_6	I	Address Bit 6		57	VS2	O	Voltage Sense 2	N.C.
24	A_5	I	Address Bit 5		58	RST	I	Reset	HIGH
25	A_4	I	Address Bit 4		59	$\overline{WAIT}$	O	Extend Bus Cycle	LOW
26	A_3	I	Address Bit 3		60	RFU		Reserved	
27	A_2	I	Address Bit 2		61	$\overline{REG}$	I	Attribute Memory Select	LOW
28	A_1	I	Address Bit 1		62	BVD2	O	Battery Voltage Detect 2	
29	A_0	I	Address Bit 0		63	BVD1	O	Battery Voltage Detect 1	
30	DQ_0	I/O	Data Bit 0		64	DQ_8	I/O	Data Bit 8	
31	DQ_1	I/O	Data Bit 1		65	DQ_9	I/O	Data Bit 9	
32	DQ_2	I/O	Data Bit 2		66	DQ_{10}	I/O	Data Bit 10	
33	WP	O	Write Protect	HIGH	67	$\overline{CD2}$	O	Card Detect 2	LOW
34	GND		Ground		68	GND		Ground	

Table 8.1: Signal Definition of the PCMCIA Interface

---

[45]Refer to Chapter 5 for more information on specific flash memory device signals.

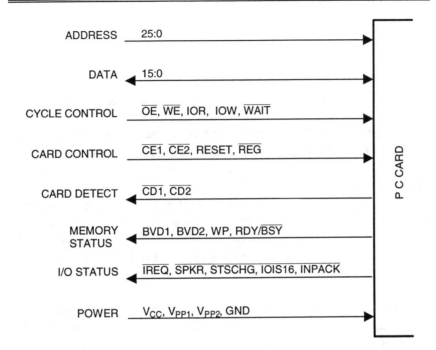

Figure 8.3: PCMCIA Electrical Interface Categories

PCMCIA Signal Definitions

Attribute Memory Select ($\overline{\text{REG}}$)

Memory cards supporting this signal contain two separate addressing spaces - a Common Memory Plane (CMP) and an Attribute Memory Plane (AMP). $\overline{\text{REG}}$ selects between the CMP ($\overline{\text{REG}}$ = V_{IH}) and the AMP ($\overline{\text{REG}}$ = V_{IL}). The following briefly describes their functions:

- The <u>Common Memory Plane</u> contains the flash memory devices, as shown in Figure 10.35.

- The <u>Attribute Memory Plane</u> contains:
  a.   The PCMCIA-defined Card Information Structure.

b.   Memory-mapped registers supporting PCMCIA-recommended functions and special functions designed by the card vendor.

c.   Reprogrammable memory for OEM or end-user customization, such as card format information.

Some host systems do not support the AMP because they lack support for the $\overline{\text{REG}}$ signal. Therefore, within the card this signal must be pulled up to V_{CC} to keep it inactive if it is not connected at the host. This will minimally ensure access to the CMP. For cards that do not support the AMP, the $\overline{\text{REG}}$ pin going into the card will be a no connect. This forces the determination of AMP presence onto the system software. For example, after the system asserts $\overline{\text{REG}}$, the system software attempts to read the CIS, and if invalid data appears, this indicates the AMP's absence.

When choosing the value of the pull-up resistor, the card vendor must maintain a balance between amount of current drawn and the switching speed of the signal. PCMCIA requires $R > 10$ kΩ with a load to the host of $C > 50$ pF at a DC current of 700 μA (low state) and 150 μA (high state). The DC current through a 10 kΩ resistor is 500 μA, leaving 200 μA available to drive the ASIC in the card. From the system perspective, the input capacitance value of this signal determines the amount of current that must be supplied to switch it in the desired amount of time. Notice from the read timing waveform in Figure 8.4 that the $\overline{\text{REG}}$ signal has the same timing requirements as the address signals.

Address Inputs (A$_0$ - A$_{25}$)

The 26 address bus lines enable direct addressing of 64 Megabytes of flash memory in the CMP ($\overline{\text{REG}}$ = V_{IL}) and 64 megabytes in the AMP ($\overline{\text{REG}}$ = V_{IH}). When designing a system, pay attention to the manner in which the different cards internally handle lower densities (i.e. less than 64 megabytes[46]).

---

[46]At the time this book was published, there was no such thing as a 64 megabyte flash memory card.

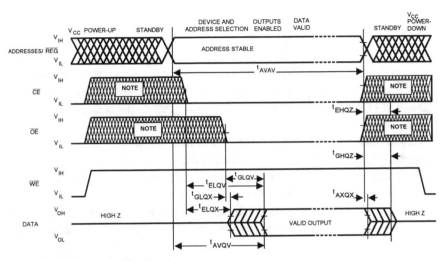

Note: The hatched area may be either high or low.

Figure 8.4: PCMCIA Read Timing Waveform

Some cards may only decode the address lines relevant to their densities. For example, if a 1 megabyte card only decodes from A0 to A19, any access above 1 megabyte will result in a wrap-around, or aliasing, because A20 - A25 are no-connects (Figure 8.5).

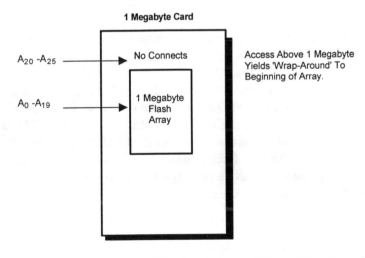

Figure 8.5: Aliasing Caused by Inadequate Address Line Decoding

Other cards decode all or most address signals, and will display invalid data when the system attempts to access an address above the card's known density (this is less dangerous than aliasing because it eliminates the possibility of overwriting data)[47]. In reality, neither situation should pose a problem, because properly designed system software checks with the card's CIS (or other means) to determine the card's density.

NOTE: System designs exist today where some of the address lines to the PCMCIA socket were left disconnected, or even where the upper unused address lines were tied low. These designs either took advantage of the wrap-around scenario or did this just to save on signal routing. The surprise comes during the discovery that not all cards are created equal (i.e., cards with all signals decoded). Perhaps an addressing scheme to standardize on card addressing could be proposed to PCMCIA! Until then, writing the software such that it doesn't access beyond the card's density provides the simplest and safest technique.

Data Bus (D_0 - D_{15})

These 16 lines represent the bi-directional data bus. The PCMCIA interface supports word-wide or byte-wide operations by decoding address line A_0 and the two card enables, $\overline{CE}_1$ and $\overline{CE}_2$ (Table 8.2). Decoding performed by the card's ASIC allows the system to access one word at a time or one byte at a time, referencing the high or low byte.

The flash memory architecture dictates how to arrange the components within the card (Figure 8.6). Flash memories with 8-bit interfaces must be paired to support PCMCIA-compatible word-wide accesses. 16-bit devices directly support the interface and provide the additional benefit of enabling a single-chip card (assuming the device supports selection at the byte-level). From a flash memory standpoint (i.e., erasable at the block level), the architecture also dictates the block size. In other words, a device pair doubles the effective block size because the odd and even bytes alternate between device pairs (provided the 8-bit and 16-bit wide devices have the same block size).

---

[47]For example, Intel's Series 2 Card returns FFH data when reading above the card's actual density.

MODE	$\overline{REG}$	$\overline{CE_2}$	$\overline{CE_1}$	A_0	$\overline{OE}$	$\overline{WE}$	Vpp2	Vpp1	D[15:8]	D[7:0]
STANDBY	X	V_{IH}	V_{IH}	X	X	X	VPPL	VPPL	HIGH-Z	HIGH-Z
BYTE - READ	V_{IH}	V_{IH}	V_{IL}	V_{IL}	V_{IL}	V_{IH}	VPPL	VPPL	HIGH-Z	EVEN BYTE
	V_{IH}	V_{IH}	V_{IL}	V_{IH}	V_{IL}	V_{IH}	VPPL	VPPL	HIGH-Z	ODD BYTE
WORD - READ	V_{IH}	V_{IL}	V_{IL}	X	V_{IL}	V_{IH}	VPPL	VPPL	ODD BYTE	EVEN BYTE
ODDBYTE - READ	V_{IH}	V_{IL}	V_{IH}	X	V_{IL}	V_{IH}	VPPL	VPPL	ODD BYTE	HIGH-Z
BYTE WRITE	V_{IH}	V_{IH}	V_{IL}	V_{IL}	V_{IH}	V_{IL}	XXX	VPPH	XXX	EVEN BYTE
	V_{IH}	V_{IH}	V_{IL}	V_{IH}	V_{IH}	V_{IL}	VPPH	XXX	XXX	ODD BYTE
WORD - WRITE	V_{IH}	V_{IL}	V_{IL}	X	V_{IH}	V_{IL}	VPPH	VPPH	ODD BYTE	EVEN BYTE
ODDBYTE - WRITE	V_{IH}	V_{IL}	V_{IH}	X	V_{IH}	V_{IL}	VPPH	VPPL	ODD BYTE	XXX

Table 8.2: Common Memory Accesses

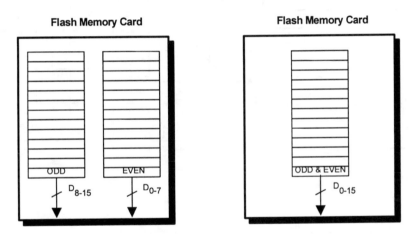

Figure 8.6: Internal Component Arrangement Dictated by Flash Memory Architecture

Special Considerations For 8-Bit Systems

The PCMCIA specification states that a card must also provide a byte-wide access mode for 8-bit systems. In other words, the high-byte (D8 - D15) access of a memory card plugged into an 8-bit system must be multiplexed to the low-byte (D0 - D7) on the system side. Figure 8.7 demonstrates the basic circuit design used for implementing this functionality. Address lines A_{18} and A_{19} decode the four pairs of devices[48], and $\overline{CE1}$, $\overline{CE2}$ and A_0 are decoded to select the low and high byte of each device pair. In the figure, the highlighted transceiver maps the high byte to the lower byte of the data bus.

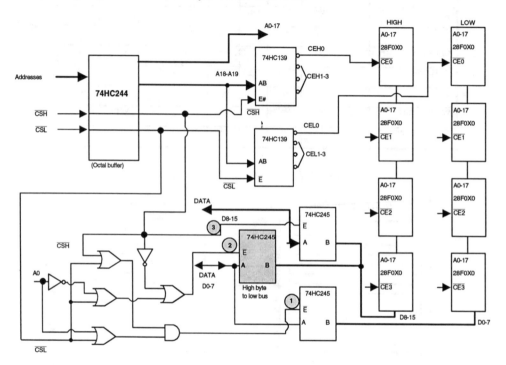

Figure 8.7: Byte-Wide Access Mode Circuitry for 8-Bit Systems

Card Enables ($\overline{CE}_1$ & $\overline{CE}_2$)

These active-low control signals, along with A_0, enable low and high byte accesses on the card. After inactivating $\overline{CE}_1$ and $\overline{CE}_2$, the card should enter a low power, standby mode, depending on the card's capability. As seen from Table 8.2, $\overline{CE}_1$ and $\overline{CE}_2$, in conjunction with A_0, support the 8-bit system's decoding scheme discussed in the previous section. The PCMCIA specification states that the AMP only supports

---

[48]More address lines would be decoded for higher density cards.

even-byte accesses. Therefore, activating $\overline{CE}_2$ when accessing the AMP ($\overline{REG}$ = V_{IL}) results in invalid data. As discussed in the CIS section of Chapter 10, some OEMs may use the first block of the CMP for additional CIS space. This situation allows the use of the even and odd bytes for storing the information.

Internal to the card, the $\overline{CE}_1$ and $\overline{CE}_2$ signals must be pulled up to V_{CC} (just like $\overline{REG}$, $\overline{OE}$ and $\overline{WE}$). The value of this becomes apparent during card insertion and removal, to ensure de-selection of the flash memory devices within the card.

Output Enable ($\overline{OE}$)

This active low signal gates AMP and CMP reads from the card. After the card's decoding circuitry selects the appropriate flash memory device, the PCMCIA interface $\overline{OE}$ signal activates the output buffers in the card's ASIC. The PCMCIA specification states that $\overline{OE}$ must be driven to V_{IH} by the host during write operations. This removes the possibility of bus contentions.

Write Enable ($\overline{WE}$)

This active low signal controls writes to the AMP and CMP. Similar to the situation for $\overline{OE}$, PCMCIA specifies that $\overline{WE}$ must be driven to V_{IH} by the host during reads, preventing unwanted write operations.

Write Protect (WP)

This signal reflects the status of the flash memory card's mechanical write protect switch. Prior to writing to the card, system software can check this signal and decide if it will permit the write. WP can also be used as a $\overline{WE}$ gate (at either the system or card level) to physically block write attempts to the flash memory devices or the memory card ASICs.

PCMCIA-interface controller chips, such as the 82365SL, support an interface status register that can be read by software. These controllers have WP as an input, and reflect its value within this register. This device also provides alternate write protect mechanisms such as that activated through Socket Service's *SetPage* function (Card Memory Offset Address High Byte Register). Some flash memory cards, such as

Intel's Series 2 Card, also have special control registers that will internally block writes to selected regions of the flash memory array.

Ready/Busy (RDY/$\overline{\text{BSY}}$)

When this signal was originally added to the PCMCIA specification, it was intended for devices like EEPROMs, to signal that an operation was being processed. Although the host's electrical interface supported this signal, first-generation flash memory cards (and the components within them) did not take advantage of this function, and replaced this signal with a no-connect. Some second-generation flash memories, such as Intel's 28F008SA, support automated write and erase operations, and therefore, provide a RY/$\overline{\text{BY}}$ signal to indicate operation status[49]. Using RDY/$\overline{\text{BSY}}$ essentially frees the host system to perform additional tasks after initiating an operation. In other words, the operation (erase or write) can become a background task, with completion signified by the host receiving a ready indication (Figure 8.8). In Chapter 9, where we discuss flash file systems, you will realize the significance of this capability for background cleanup.

The PCMCIA spec indicates that RDY/$\overline{\text{BSY}}$ (pin 16) supports alternative functions, depending on the type of PC card used:

- For I/O cards, this pin becomes the Interrupt Request ($\overline{\text{IREQ}}$) signal. $\overline{\text{IREQ}}$ asserted low indicates to the host that the I/O card requires service.
- For memory-only cards, this pin becomes an operation status signal that may be utilized by polling, or by generating a rising-edge interrupt to the host. Referring to Figure 8.2, witness how the Series 2 Card routes the RY/$\overline{\text{BY}}$ signal from each of its components into the ASIC, which in turn wire-ORs it onto the PCMCIA interface.

---

[49]Note that RY/BY refers to Ready/Busy at the device level; RDY/BSY refers to Ready/Busy at the card interface.

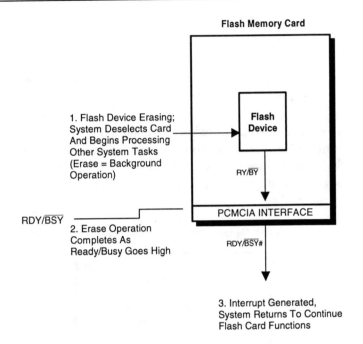

Figure 8.8: RDY/$\overline{BSY}$ Background Sequence

Optimizing RDY/$\overline{BSY}$ Functionality

In accordance with the PCMCIA specification, a flash memory card supporting this functionality drives the RDY/$\overline{BSY}$ line low when its circuits are busy processing an operation. When a single device within a multiple-device memory card processes an erase or write operation, the remainder of the card's devices may process subsequent operations if the system has the capability to support it. This means that ample current must be available to handle concurrent operations. It also adds to the complexity of system software.

For example, what if system software wanted to write data to (or read from) one device while another was erasing? Or, what if it was necessary to erase several devices simultaneously? How this is handled depends on the capabilities of the card:

•   Cards with manually programming devices require continuous attention. Chapter 7 discusses the techniques that must be applied here. Fundamentally, these devices do not support the RDY/$\overline{\text{BSY}}$ capability so when programming or erasing multiple devices, the software must perform all necessary steps.

•   The cards with automated devices and RDY/$\overline{\text{BSY}}$ capability can easily handle multiple commands to different devices (Figure 8.9). The software must have a method for determining which device/operation finished after detecting the busy-to-ready transition.

Flash Memory Card With Automated Devices

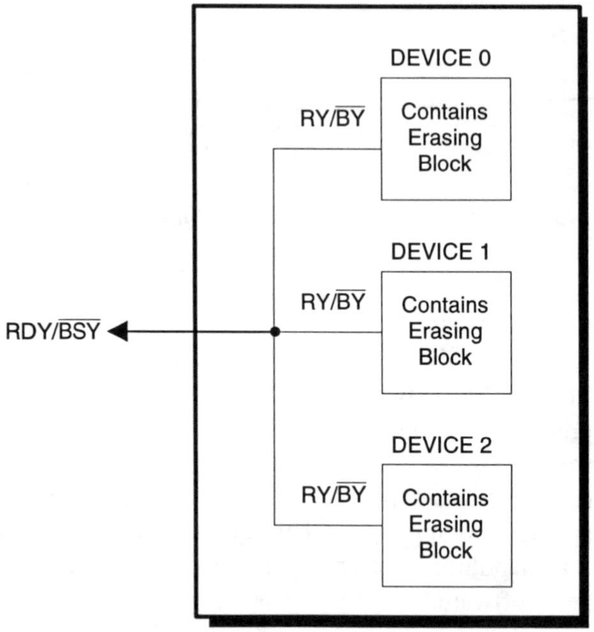

Any Busy Device Normally Results In The Entire Card Appearing Busy Because RY/$\overline{\text{BY}}$ Signals Are Tied Together.

Figure 8.9: Use of RDY/$\overline{\text{BSY}}$ in Multiple Device Operations

The RDY/$\overline{\text{BSY}}$ waveform for the standard PCMCIA implementation would appear as shown in Figure 8.10 for the situation where several devices were being erased simultaneously. Notice that RDY/$\overline{\text{BSY}}$ stays low until all devices in the card have completed their erase operations. Depending on the interrupt latency, this could impact the card's performance, because the system would not be notified that the first device had completed until the last one had completed. From a flash file system perspective, consider what happens during cleanup. For example, suppose an attempt to write a large file first requires the cleanup and erasing of several blocks. After copying the valid data, software begins the sequential erasure of the blocks in question. To avoid having to wait until the last one completed its erase, it would be most efficient to be notified instantly after the first block-erase completes. This would allow the flash file system software to immediately start writing the new file's data.

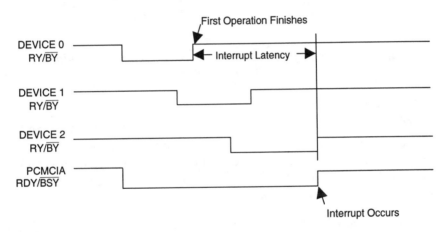

Figure 8.10: Standard PCMCIA RDY/$\overline{\text{BSY}}$ Waveform

How does the RDY/$\overline{\text{BSY}}$ signal indicate the completion of an operation with multiple busy devices, as in Figure 8.9? Remember, wire-ORing means that any busy device will make the entire card appear busy. Intel's Series 2 Card demonstrates one way to overcome this problem. The card's ASIC can be set up to detect and reflect the rising edge of RY/$\overline{\text{BY}}$

from any device within the card. This would generate a RDY/$\overline{\text{BSY}}$ waveform like that depicted in Figure 8.11[50]. To determine which device actually caused the RDY/$\overline{\text{BSY}}$ transition, software can interrogate each device's status register (see Chapter 7).

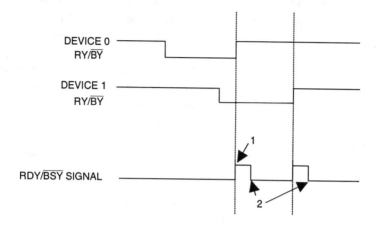

Figure 8.11: High-Performance RDY/$\overline{\text{BSY}}$ Waveform for Multiple Device Operations

An Alternate RDY/$\overline{\text{BSY}}$ Function

RDY/$\overline{\text{BSY}}$ may also be used to indicate to the host system when the card is ready for access after initial power up, if the card requires more than 20 milliseconds to initialize. If the card does not meet the 20 millisecond limit, the card must set RDY/$\overline{\text{BSY}}$ low within 10 microseconds of reset or V_{CC} being applied to the card.

Extend Bus Cycle ($\overline{\text{WAIT}}$)

Somewhat related to RDY/$\overline{\text{BSY}}$ is the $\overline{\text{WAIT}}$ signal. While RDY/$\overline{\text{BSY}}$ indicates the status of activity within the card, $\overline{\text{WAIT}}$ acts as a bus cycle indicator (and delay mechanism) between the card and the host system. It functions similar to the READY signal of a CPU interface used to add processor wait state cycles for slow peripherals. In flash memory cards this pin will most likely be pulled high to indicate the no-wait condition.

---

[50]For more details on how to implement this mode, refer to the data sheet.

$\overline{\text{WAIT}}$ is primarily utilized for I/O cards to delay completion of an I/O cycle in progress or when different access times are needed for the Attribute Memory Plane.

Card Detect ($\overline{\text{CD1}}$ and $\overline{\text{CD2}}$)

The card detect pins at opposite ends of the connector provide a means for the system to determine the presence (and proper insertion) of the card. From a top view of the card, notice that the card detect pins are the shortest (Figure 8.12). This ensures that they make host contact last during card insertion and break host contact first during card removal. We'll elaborate on the importance of this in the card buffering section.

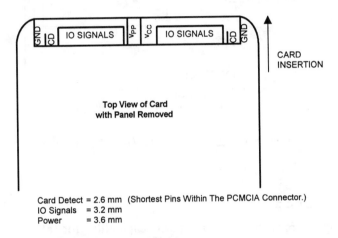

Card Detect = 2.6 mm   (Shortest Pins Within The PCMCIA Connector.)
IO Signals   = 3.2 mm
Power   = 3.6 mm

Figure 8.12: PCMCIA Pin Lengths Allow Proper Sequencing of Card Signals

Within the card, these pins connect to ground to allow a system to detect a low signal after inserting a card into the host's socket. The host must supply a pull-up resistor to V$_{CC}$ (with a value greater than 10 kΩ) to allow card detection to function after powering down the card slot. Most PCMCIA interface controller chips have inputs for these signals (refer to Socket Services in Chapter 10). Simple circuitry may also be used to tie these signals together and route them into the host's interrupt logic (Figure 8.13). Either method allows the system to detect a card's removal or insertion. Alternatively, the resultant wire-or'd signal may be periodically polled through an I/O port. One way of generating a polling time-period in a personal computer is to install an interrupt filter into the time-of-day interrupt. Every 55 milliseconds, when the system updates its clock, software also checks for card presence.

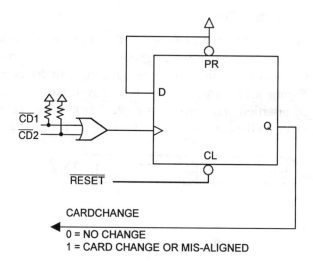

Figure 8.13: Example Card Detection Circuitry

Card Reset (RESET)

This signal provides a hard reset capability for all configurable PCMCIA-compatible cards. Intel's Series 2 Card (none others to date) provides an example of a configurable flash memory card, because its ASICs contain various registers (Component Management Registers) that must enter a default state on power-up, provided by reset. Within the Series 2 Card, the reset state also serves to hold the individual flash memory devices in a power down mode, to eliminate the possibility of accidental writes during noisy-system power transitions.

To be backwards-compatible with PCMCIA release 1.0 (where RESET had not yet been defined), a configurable card must internally generate its own power-on reset. This can be done with special V_{CC}-monitoring circuitry, which turns on after V_{CC} reaches a certain voltage during power up and forces a card reset. The PCMCIA specification requires that RESET be held in high impedance during card power up for at least 1 millisecond after V_{CC} becomes valid. Release 2.0 compatible cards must provide reset control by pulling up this signal (to V_{CC}) through a resistor greater than 100 kΩ. This will ensure that the card leaves RESET after the completion of the internal power up reset.

Configurable flash memory cards contain a PCMCIA-defined Configuration Option Register. Bit 7 of this register (Soft Reset bit, SRESET), provides the software equivalent of the hardware RESET signal. PCMCIA states that once software sets this bit, it must also clear it. A software-generated reset leaves the card in the same default state that resulted from a power up.

Program and Peripheral Voltages (V_{PP1} & V_{PP2})

These signals provide the programming voltages for writing and erasing the flash memory devices. Within the card, V_{PP1} and V_{PP2} can be tied together, or they can be arranged to separately accommodate even and odd byte components, respectively.

According to the PCMCIA specification:
- The host must supply the V_{CC} level (at a minimum) on the V_{PP} pins (3.3V or 5V).
- If a card requires a higher V_{PP} than the system can supply, that system may reject the card.

This specification results in a serious limitation. For example, a PCMCIA-compatible system designed for 5-volt-only cards (V_{CC} and V_{PP}), will not accommodate PCMCIA-compatible flash memory cards that require 12 volts for program and erase operations (constituting the majority of cards). To remove PCMCIA ambiguities such as the one described above, Intel developed the Exchangeable Card Architecture (ExCA) specification based on a specific implementation of the PCMCIA spec[53]. ExCA requires that host systems support a programming voltage of 12V ± 5%. Furthermore, the ExCA spec also provides a peak and average current supply and duration for V_{CC} and V_{PP}

---

[53]See the section in Chapter 10 on the PCMCIA-ExCA relationship.

(Table 8.3). This ensures successful operation of most flash memory cards, and most PC cards in general.

Signal	Voltage	Continuous Supply Current	Peak Supply Current	Peak Current Duration	Minimum Average Current	Average Current Duration
VPP (1 & 2 combined)	12.0V±5%	N/A	60mA	10ms	60mA	1 sec
VCC	5.0V ± 5%	200mA	300mA	10ms	200mA	1 sec

Table 8.3: System Power Requirements

The host design can provide a switchable or fixed V_{PP} supply (i.e., hardwired "on"). When using a switchable supply, account for voltage ramp time after enabling V_{PP} (via software delay or special V_{PP} monitoring circuitry) before attempting an erase or write operation. This provides time to charge up all the capacitance tied to V_{PP}. Be aware that ramp rate will depend on the capacitive loading on V_{PP}, which in turn depends on the number of flash memory devices in the card. The best thing to do is to use some type of hardware monitoring circuitry such as that built into one of the integrated voltage converter devices. Alternatively, design for the worst-case situation assuming 20 devices per card.

Chapter 6 discusses 12V generation for flash memories[52]. To re-emphasize, some of the key attributes to look for in a DC-DC converter include:

- Input Voltage Range - Depending on the host system, this will probably be 3.3V or 5V.
- Output Voltage Tolerance - As shown in Table 8.3, this value has a tolerance of ±5%.
- Output Current Capability - The value should be a tradeoff of performance desired and system power sourcing limits.
- Conversion Efficiency - This value ranges between 50-90%. Although this represents a very wide spread, most higher quality converters typically have an efficiency of 85%.

---

[52]The Appendix contains a list of DC-DC converter manufacturers.

Control over V_{PP} switching (and V_{CC}, for that matter) is most conveniently performed by a PCMCIA-interface controller chip, such as the 82365SL. PCMCIA controllers have several outputs that can be decoded to generate the appropriate switch[53]. Figure 8.14 depicts a controller chip interfaced to Maxim's MAX780A. Notice the data inputs on the Maxim device for controlling the voltage outputs. Some PCMCIA interface designs use discrete logic. In these cases, load switching control can be accomplished by using programmable I/O lines.

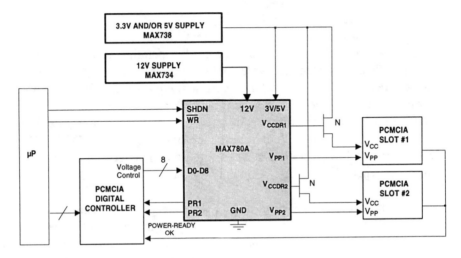

Figure 8.14: PCMCIA Controller Chip Controls Voltage Switching

Card Voltage (V_{CC})

Without this input to the card, all of the other signals would be meaningless. The majority of cards available today operate with V_{CC} = 5V, which for the most part, represents a pretty straightforward and standard requirement. Very soon, however, 3.3V cards and 3.3V systems will begin to appear.

What does this mean from a design standpoint? Two scenarios are possible:

---

[53]Refer to the *SetSocket* function in Chapter 10.

- A 5V card that doesn't function at 3.3V will not operate correctly in a 3.3V-only system. For this situation, consider using a DC-DC converter (as described in the V_{PP} section) that can also generate 5V. This may be important to allow the use of 5V cards. When the card requires 5V in a 3.3V, this converter can be switched on to pump the V_{CC} supply.
- A 3.3V only card will probably be permanently damaged if operated in a 5V-only system.

How do you resolve this problem?

The power description structure in the Card Information Structure's Configuration Table may indicate the card's operating voltage[54]. In the former situation, system software should provide a message to the user to the effect of: *"Improper voltage, card will not operate"*. In the future, cards may be capable of functioning at both voltages by incorporating voltage switching capabilities within the card or flash memory devices themselves. For example, a card may incorporate a 3.3V to 5V DC-DC converter to allow operation in a 3.3V system. This converter must be bypassed when placing the card in a 5V system.

On the other hand, how does a 3.3V card keep from frying in a 5V system? PCMCIA has been developing a keying mechanism for the card that will physically prevent a user from inserting the card. The keying will be flexible enough to allow the combination of dual voltage cards and systems.

Voltage Sense (VS$_1$ and VS$_2$)

Interface Pins 43 and 57 have been defined as the Voltage Sense output pins (43 was REFRESH in the PCMCIA R2.01 specification, 57 was reserved for future use). These signals notify the host of the card's V_{CC} requirements. The configuration of these pins describes the voltage requirements of the card which is also indicated in the card's CIS. Table 8.4 lists the various configurations. As an example, to comply with the PCMCIA pin configuration for a 3.3V/5V compatible card, pin 43 (VS$_1$) is grounded and pin 57 (VS$_2$) is open.

---

[54]Most cards on the market today have not integrated this yet.

CARD TYPE	VS$_1$	VS$_2$	DESCRIPTION
5V only CIS 5V key	OPEN	OPEN	Can be plugged into 3.3V socket without damage but it will not function properly.
3.3V only CIS Low voltage key	GND	OPEN	Will not fit in 5V socket. When plugged into 3.3V socket, signals and CIS indicate 3.3V only card.
3.3V/5V CIS 5V key	GND	OPEN	Fits into either socket and functions at 3.3V or 5V.

Table 8.4: Voltage Sense Pin Configurations

Battery Voltage Detects (BVD₁ & BVD₂)

At this point, we've covered all the PCMCIA card signals except for Battery Voltage Detect (BVD$_1$ and BVD$_2$). For flash memory cards, which do not require batteries to maintain information written to them and therefore don't use batteries, these signals have no meaning. To maintain compatibility, however, flash memory cards must pull the battery voltage detects high to trick the system into thinking the battery is good. A host may monitor the BVD1 and BVD2 signals to determine the completion of the power on reset cycle, because they remain low (inactive status) until that time.

HOST SYSTEM IMPLEMENTATIONS

The PCMCIA specification only defines the fundamental characteristics of the card interface. The previous discussion mentioned nothing about the interface beyond the socket (aside from a few pullup or pulldown resistors). How do we map the flash memory from the card into the host system's address space? In this section, we'll discuss three categories of memory mapping: register-based (or I/O), paged (by far, the most popular), and linear. Some of you may already be familiar with these techniques, as they have not been uniquely implemented for flash memory cards. As a matter of fact, they apply to any type of memory cards, or even to discrete memory devices.

Several IC vendors have developed single-chip PCMCIA 2.0-compatible card interfaces that support the I/O and paged memory mapping implementations. These devices enable simple, minimal glue-logic interfacing between the host CPU and a IC card socket, as the following discussion will point out.

Register-Based Memory Mapping

Register-based memory mapping has much similarity to that used for disk drives; the system uses a single I/O address (or minimal address range) to pass data to and from the drive's controller, which in turn takes care of writing to (or reading from) one of many locations on the drive. Likewise, for I/O-mapped memory, a single I/O port funnels data between the system and the flash memory card (Figure 8.15). The advantage of this approach is that it consumes the least amount of the host system's memory map resources; however, it incurs a performance disadvantage because the processor cannot access the memory directly.

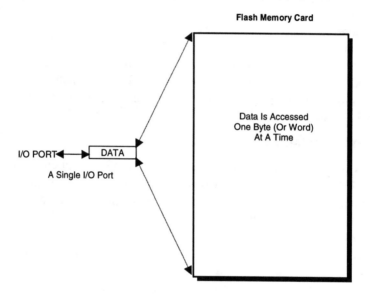

Figure 8.15: Mapping Memory Through an I/O Port

Standard I/O Access

The simplest I/O implementation can be designed with a latch(es) and a data transceiver(s). As shown in Figure 8.16, the system performs an I/O write (and latch) of the memory address on the data bus. With the memory address selected, use another I/O port to read or write through the transceiver. The latched data must be updated for each new flash memory address.

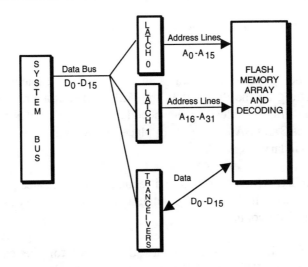

Figure 8.16: The Data Bus Generates the Flash Memory Addresses

High-Speed I/O Reads

By replacing the latches with counters, read performance can be considerably enhanced (Figure 8.17):

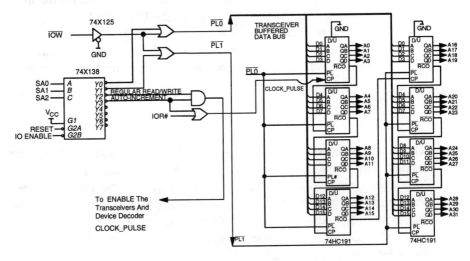

Figure 8.17: Counters Enhance I/O-Mapped Read Access

1.   A '138 decoder selects four sequential I/O addresses that service four different functions in this design.

2.   When the system generates an I/O address that matches with the setting on the dip switch, the '521 comparator provides one of the three enables for the decoder. Notice that the comparator uses SA_3 - SA_{10} as inputs to place the I/O port base on an 8-byte boundary.

3.   An I/O write to the first and second ports generates parallel load signals, with PL_0 and PL_1 latching the flash memory address into the 4-bit counters.

4.   The third I/O port provides the enable for the card enable circuitry (CE_1 and CE_2) to allow regular single byte or word reads and writes.

5.   Reading from the fourth I/O port address generates the clock signal for the counters. This causes them to automatically increment, providing the next flash memory address. By the time the address increment has occurred, the I/O cycle has completed and the data has been read from the I/O port. This fast read method works great for string reads (i.e., from sequential addresses). However, the counters must be reloaded for any out-of-sequence read.

Linear Mapped Memory

The linear-mapped, or direct-mapped, memory design delivers the highest performance memory-mapping technique - where the processor has direct access to the entire memory array. Unless you only use a very low density flash memory card, however, the processor had better have more than 20 address lines. In other words, if a processor has a 1 megabyte address space (as is the case with many embedded CPUs or even less with some microcontrollers), the memory map would be completely overtaken by a 1 megabyte flash memory card. From a hardware design perspective though, linearly mapped memory addressing is very simple (Figure 8.18). The number of address lines decoded depends on the maximum density of the flash card to be used.

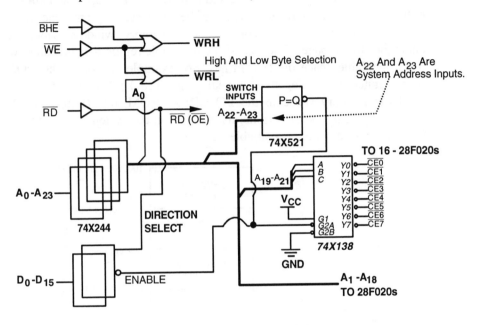

Figure 8.18: Linearly-Mapped Memory Addressing

From a software standpoint, linear-mapped memory designs have the most practicality in conjunction with system architectures with unrestricted operating system boundaries. These would include most 32-bit operating systems or proprietary embedded computers. But in a DOS-based machine (running in real mode), linear mapping requires continuous switching to protected mode to gain access to the large memory array, due to the 1 Mbyte memory restrictions.

Although, the majority of PCMCIA-interface controller chips for PCs utilize the page-mapped approach (described next), they can be configured with window sizes up to 16 megabytes (in a PC). This could essentially pass for a linear-mapped implementation.

Paged Memory Mapping

A page-mapped design accesses the flash memory in a LIM-EMS (Lotus-Intel-Microsoft) fashion where portions of the memory array get swapped in using special software and hardware[55]. This approach allows only limited regions of the array to be addressed at any one time (Chapter 10 discusses the concept of a memory window which is analogous to the page). The size of the mappable region depends on how much available space the system has. For example, a look at the DOS map, limited to 1 Megabyte, reveals only 128 kbytes of potentially available memory space in the I/O adapter ROM area (Figure 8.19). Depending on the other peripherals installed in the system, this memory space may or may not be available.

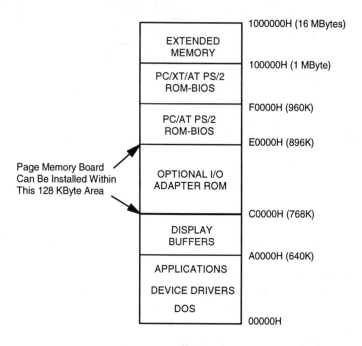

Figure 8.19: DOS Memory Map

---

[55]Most technical textbooks on developing with DOS cover this subject in detail.

Figure 8.20 demonstrates the basic circuitry involved in the memory paging scheme:

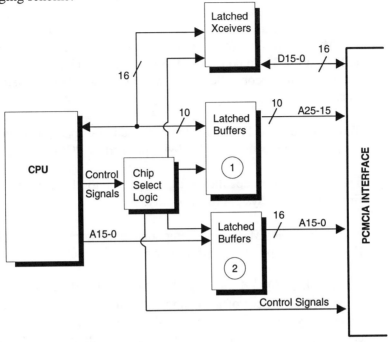

Figure 8.20: Memory Paging Circuitry

- The latched buffer provides the high order address signals (or page numbers) to the memory card. Notice that these address signals originated from the CPU's data bus.

- The system selects an address within the memory card by first writing and latching the page number, which then allows access to an address within that particular 64 kbyte region.

- This particular arrangement allows a fixed page size of 64 kbytes. The page size can be controlled by varying the number of address signals that come directly from the CPU versus those generated from latched data.

Variations on the theme described above can be implemented by replacing the discrete buffers, transceivers, and decoding circuitry with a single ASIC. An 8255 (parallel port device) can also be used to translate page numbers, as well as handle many of the control signals coming from the PCMCIA interface (e.g., card write protect, ready/busy, card detect, etc.). Figure 8.21 demonstrates the applicability of this concept, using a 80x186 microcontroller and a few other basic system components:

- The 80x186 only has a 1 Megabyte address space, but with paging can access the full 64 Mbytes defined by PCMCIA.

- The flash boot code allows easy updates to the controller's firmware to vary system functionality.

- The system's RAM services temporary data storage and holds flash memory update algorithms during their execution.

- Any number of I/O devices can be added to this flexible system to perform a variety of applications (by updating the firmware accordingly) which use the flash memory cards for data accumulation, such as remote weather stations or patient monitoring instruments.

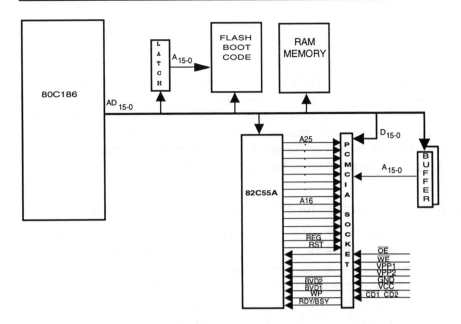

*Figure 8.21: Implementing a PCMCIA 1.0 Interface in an
Embedded Application*

IMPLEMENTING PCMCIA 2.0 HARDWARE

The implementations described above have one major limitation - they
only service PCMCIA 1.0 memory cards. A PCMCIA 2.0
implementation requires more complex circuitry, because several of the
interface pins must be multiplexed to handle different functions (e.g.,
RDY/$\overline{\text{BSY}}$ ←→$\overline{\text{IREQ}}$). Also, socket hardware must be capable of
mapping into the host I/O and memory space. The section on Socket
Services in Chapter 10 will provide the hardware designer with good
insight into the variety of functionality that can be implemented in the
design of a socket adapter.

Proprietary or Commercial Interface Controllers

In a PC platform, the large number of PCMCIA-interface controllers
available today greatly simplify the hardware design of a PCMCIA 2.0

implementation[56]. The most difficult step often lies in choosing which controller chip to use (refer to the appendix), but many of these chips are modeled after Intel's 82365SL (PC Card Interface Controller, PCIC) and have been designed to be ExCA-compliant (as described in Chapter 10). In non-PC platforms, these commercially-available controller chips can also be used, but more than likely, additional logic will be required to connect the controller ISA bus interface to whatever bus the specific platform supports. For the most part, non-ISA implementations may design proprietary ASICs that tightly couple PCMCIA to their desired interface.

Supporting Hardware for PCMCIA-Interface Controllers

Although the PCMCIA interface can be built out of custom ASICs, PLDs, or discrete logic, commercially available controllers offer the most convenient solution, even if you have no need for all the capability they deliver. Viewed from a price standpoint, commercial controllers eliminate non-recurring engineering design costs. From a software standpoint, these controllers have a variety of support available from most BIOS vendors in the form of Socket Services[57].

For the most part, the majority of PCMCIA controllers can be integrated into a system design with minimal effort. As Figure 8.22 demonstrates for a dual-socket design, the 82365SL requires a minimal amount of glue logic; voltage control and generation circuitry, data transceivers and address buffers placed between each socket and the system bus to allow card insertion and removal (more on this later). As another example, Databook's TCIC-2/N (DB86082) controller has built in transceivers which can drive up to 3.2 mA. In a very controlled system with a limited number of peripherals, 3.2 mA may be sufficient to drive the ISA bus without any buffers. Typically, systems will have multiple peripherals and may require additional buffering. On the card side, 3.2 mA may be a limiting factor if both sockets have cards in them. Depending on your design requirements, it may be desirable to use external transceivers and buffers anyway to boost up the current drive.

---

[56]Socket Services provides the software that controls the hardware.
[57]Refer to the Appendix for a list of BIOS vendors.

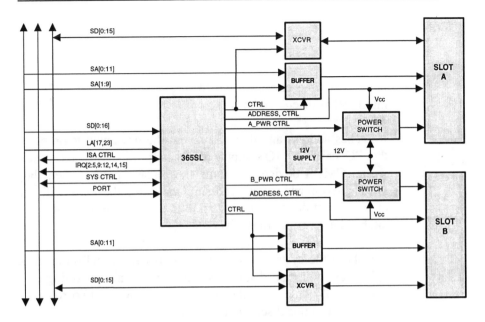

Figure 8.22: The Intel 82365SL PCMCIA Interface Controller
Requires a Minimal Amount of Support Circuitry

Accessing Flash Memory Cards with PCMCIA-Interface Controllers

The majority of controllers implement a memory paging mechanism using variable-sized windows to access a PC card's memory. This is similar to the page-mapped memory mechanism described earlier, except that the controller chips perform the address translations under software control. Furthermore, system software controls all hardware functionality of the socket and adapter (Chapter 10).

Software such as Socket Services configures the desired memory window and card offset via appropriate controller registers. Any access to the corresponding window in the system's memory map will generate the necessary address and control signals (including $\overline{\text{REG}}$ used to select between Common and Attribute Memory) to the card and its socket. In other words, the interface controller even handles all the decoding logic.

More On Buffering

In a PCMCIA socket design, buffering has several very important roles:

- It increases the current drive to the system bus and PCMCIA interface, as discussed above.

- It latches address and data to prevent the unwanted toggling of the PC card's CMOS inputs that leads to significant power waste. CMOS devices consume the highest power when they switch. Even when not accessing the card, the card will see every transition on the system bus unless the interface has latched buffers and transceivers.

- It isolates the system bus, so that the insertion and removal of PC cards will not disturb system operation. Satisfying this design goal inherently takes care of the previous two roles, so we will focus this discussion on this concept.

Isolating the System Bus

PC card insertion and removal can certainly wreak havoc on a system's integrity, if not handled properly. Consider the effects on a memory card's data integrity. For example, think about the potential noise generated on the PCMCIA interface during PC card removal. Table 8.5 defines the different card interface conditions that can exist.

Condition	Vcc	Card Enables & Address Bus Drivers	Data Bus Drivers
Cold	Off	High-Z	High-Z
Warm	On	Disabled	High-Z
Hot	On	Enabled	Enabled

Table 8.5: PC Card Interface Conditions During Insertion and Removal

The cold and warm conditions allow the safest removal and insertion of cards. The hot condition can also be handled by sequencing the PCMCIA interface signals to a warm or cold condition and ensuring that the card incorporates proper buffering and filtering capacitors to absorb voltage spikes on V_{PP} and V_{CC}[58]. The mechanical definition (i.e., length) of the PCMCIA pins, shown in Figure 8.12, allows the proper sequencing of card signals:

1. During the removal of a card, the card detect pins ($\overline{CD}_1$ and $\overline{CD}_2$), break connection with the socket first, since they're the shortest. Wiring these signals to hardware circuitry that controls power to the socket almost instantaneously turns off the socket's power. For example, the PCIC can be configured to perform automatic socket power switching based on the card detect signals[59]. The change in the card detect status also can be used for interrupt generation that notifies the application (analogous to the removal of a floppy disk).

DON'T TRY THIS AT HOME

Just for fun, assume 1 microsecond elapses from the beginning of card removal (when the card detect pins first break connect) until the PCIC automatically disconnects power to the socket. The difference in length between the card detect pins and the I/O signals is 0.6 mm. To travel the 0.6 mm distance in 1 microsecond means that the card would have to removed at a rate of 1,342 miles per hour! Now that's a "flash"!

---

2. By the time most pins start disconnecting from the socket, the power has already been switched off. However, due to capacitance, the voltages will probably not have ramped down yet. With power still present to the PC card, the various control signals will be pulled high, de-selecting the devices within the card. However, any data and address present on the bus at this time may be latched on the rising edge of write enable. However, the card enables will also be going high at this time and the devices will be deselected.

3. Finally, the power pins, the longest pins on the host connector, break contact. Their presence, until this point, have kept the

---

[58]The system's power supply must also be responsible for keeping voltages within the maximum operating conditions of the card.
[59]Using the 'Auto Power Switch Enable' bit of the 'Power and ResetDrv Control' Register.

other signals fairly stable. The system should now make sure that all power to the socket stays off until the next card insertion event.

Buffering

From a buffering point of view, the techniques for handling insertion and removal will vary, depending on the PCMCIA-interface controller used. For example, as shown in Figure 8.22, Intel's PCIC requires the use of external buffers to isolate the system's address and data bus from the socket. This particular design could be simplified by eliminating one set of buffers and transceivers and connecting the address and data lines from the two sockets together. However, this situation could create a problem with data integrity if one card was removed while a card in the other socket was being accessed.

Databook's TCIC-2/N uses internal buffers that force both sockets to share address and data inputs. This places the responsibility for card integrity on the user. To prevent card removal or insertion during a critical period, a BUSY LED (light emitting diode), in the system and visible to the operator, is recommended.

From a functional standpoint, Cirrus Logic probably provides the best solution with the CL-PD6720. This chip also has internal buffers for each socket, along with independent address and data pins[60].

The issue of card removal can also be resolved by using a socket-eject mechanism that physically prevents card removal during any card operations[61]. As the saying goes, "Prevention is the Best Medicine".

Interrupt Levels

A PC card and its socket have the capability of generating several types of interrupts. For example, a card status change interrupt can be generated from a change on the card detect pins, ready/busy, or battery warning (although not with a flash memory card). A system with multiple sockets, and therefore multiple cards, can experience conflicts

---

[60]A 208-pin package may be the drawback to this approach.
[61]The Appendix contains a list of socket vendors.

if they all try to utilize the same interrupt. In a closed system, the interrupt levels can be hardwired and never worried about again.

In an open system, a more flexible setup should be considered where interrupt steering can be configured depending on the resources needed at any given time. PCMCIA-interface controllers such as the 82365SL have the capability of directing a socket adapter's interrupt lines to any one of 10 interrupt levels (otherwise known as interrupt steering). Again, these chips are conveniently configured by software, as described by Socket Service's *SetAdapter* and *SetSocket* functions.

SUMMARY

In this chapter, we presented an overview of the PCMCIA interface. The most important lesson to learn is that for PCs, commercially available PCMCIA-interface controllers greatly simplify the socket adapter design. Before making a decision on what controller to use, study them carefully and don't be mislead by features that sound good on the surface (such as write FIFOs and on-chip timing generators). The Appendix lists the registers that control those features and the contacts for each of the vendors from whom to obtain more information.

For proprietary systems (i.e., non-ISA bus), you will more than likely have to design the logic from scratch. However, understanding the concepts developed within the ISA interface devices, will help to ensure that your design incorporates the necessary features.

Chapter Nine: Flash Memory File Systems

INTRODUCTION

Throughout this book, we have seen that flash memory can be designed into a large number of applications, with examples ranging from laser printers and cellular phones to medical instruments and portable PCs. The very nature of flash memory makes it a natural fit for code and data storage and data accumulation. A flash memory solid-state drive (which we've abbreviated FSSD), on the other hand, presents a new challenge to the designer. This chapter will not explicitly show you how to design a flash file system (this would take a whole book in itself), but points out key concepts and technical advantages and disadvantages of the various approaches. Although two basic categories of flash file systems exist, it seems like every month another company introduces a new flash file system, albeit incompatible with existing solutions. The issue of standardization amongst flash file systems must be resolved soon to eliminate confusion and incompatibilities in the industry.

Flash Memory Solid-State Drive Form Factors

- The direct flash memory interface (memory cards or resident flash array, for example), requires the host CPU to handle the flash file system software. This requires the file system to be compatible with both the host system's operating system and software applications run on it. For implementing this type of flash file system, you can select one of the ready-made solutions and take advantage of the many person-years of work that went into devising and developing it[62]. Alternatively, you may choose a proprietary approach (which may be very appropriate for a dedicated application), first taking into consideration the possibility that your choice could be incompatible with the existing solutions on the market.

• An integrated drive has the controlling software embedded within the drive itself (refer to Figure 4.15). The drive's internal processor takes care of making the flash memory interface transparent to the host system. This type of FSSD uses a standardized system interface (IDE or PCMCIA-ATA, for example) with a proprietary internal flash file system. Although distinct differences exist between this and the former approach, you will notice that while we focus on the direct interface approach, many of the file system concepts can be interchangeable.

Flash Memory Solid-State Drives Require Special Drivers

From the system perspective, the ideal FSSD should have comparable functionality to the mechanical disk drive. Naturally, there will be read performance, power, reliability, and space saving benefits associated with the FSSD, but to the end-user, all familiar functions should be available. In the future, as flash memory technology improves, the FSSD will also be used for execute-in-place (XIP) and other functions unforeseen today.

Besides flash memory, solid-state disk drives can be developed using several other types of memory technologies, such as RAM. Whatever the technology, special software drivers must be written to handle these non-magnetic disk mediums. For instance, the RAM-based solid-state drive can support the same functionality as the mechanical disk drive (using battery backup for data retention). Nevertheless, it still requires a special driver to translate the standard file operations from sector accesses into physical memory addresses. Many of you should be familiar with these drivers, as they include readily available programs such as VDISK and RAMDRIVE.

---

[62]Refer to the Appendix for a listing of available flash file systems.

The relatively new flash memory technology also requires special drivers to manage it. Flash file system developers are taking divergent approaches in dealing with the media. However, in working to drive a standard, companies, like Microsoft, will publicize their file structures. By following these formats, other developers (perhaps even running different operating systems) will be ensured of compatibility.

At the writing of this book, DOS was (and probably still is) the primary operating system using the FSSD to emulate disk drives[63]. Therefore, the remainder of this chapter, devoted to understanding the various flash file system designs, will evolve around this most widespread OS. However, bear in mind that a genuine flash file system can be divided into two portions (Figure 9.1). One portion concentrates only on managing the flash memory itself. The second portion provides the interface to the operating system of the host. By modifying or rewriting this second portion, the file system can theoretically be separated from DOS and ported to any other operating system, whether it be UNIX or proprietary dedicated control code.

DISK-DRIVE BASICS

To answer the question *"What is a Flash File System?"* and understand the need for such software, we will first review the basic functionality of the traditional mechanical disk drive. Although an FSSD services the same functions as the mechanical disk drive (storing application programs and data files), the two devices have entirely different structures. From a mechanical perspective, a disk drive looks like a compact disc (CD), containing a large number of concentric rings called tracks (See Figure 9.2). Instead of being divided up into songs, the disk drive is divided into sectors, typically representing 512 bytes of data storage capacity. A magnetic media coats the disk drive, microscopically subdivided into millions of individual magnetic fields (referred to as domains), one for each bit of data. An individual data bit is either a one or zero, based upon the polarity of its minute magnetic element.

---

[63] Personal Digital Assitants (PDA) and pen-based systems have created a growing market of non-DOS machines.

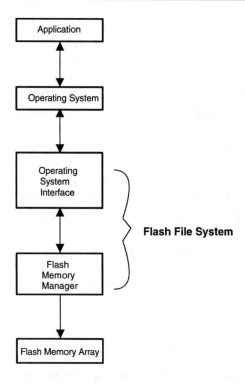

Figure 9.1: Flash Memory Manager and Operating System Interface

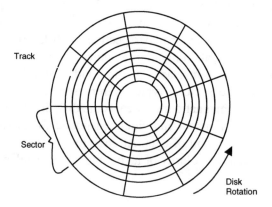

Figure 9.2: Disk Drive Tracks and Sectors

The data bits in a disk drive can be rewritten simply by changing the polarity of the magnetic elements. For practical reasons (such as the logistics of media management), the operating system controlling the disk drive manipulates the data in terms of one or more consecutive sectors. Many hard disks arrange these consecutive sectors into groups of four (referred to as a cluster) to make them even more manageable. Clustering also allows faster file access, because it ensures the grouping of at least four of a file's sectors. This implies that if the system user running a word processing application, for example, only modifies a single letter of a document, the entire portion of that document located within its particular cluster gets rewritten.

DOS Data Structures

DOS maintains two types of data structures on the disk drive; a File Allocation Table (henceforth referred to as the FAT) and a directory. Each of these data structures occupies its own cluster(s). The directory contains vital statistics of the files stored on the disk, including the file name, extension, time and date of creation, size, and the first cluster number of that file. The FAT serves two functions:

- Tracking available, allocated and bad clusters, and the last cluster in a chain (Table 9.1). It is interesting to point out that a free cluster is indicated as 0000H. For flash memory, this is a programmed state, and therefore not a free cluster.

- Maintains a chain for locating the clusters of a file (Figure 9.3). Each cluster has its own FAT entry.

12-bit entry	16-bit entry	Cluster description
000H	0000H	Free
001H-FEFH	0001H-FFEFH	In-use
FF0H-FF6H	FFF0H-FFF6H	Reserved
FF7H	FFF7H	Bad
FF8H-FFFH	FFF8H-FFFFH	End of cluster chain

Table 9.1: FAT Values for 12 and 16 Bit Entries

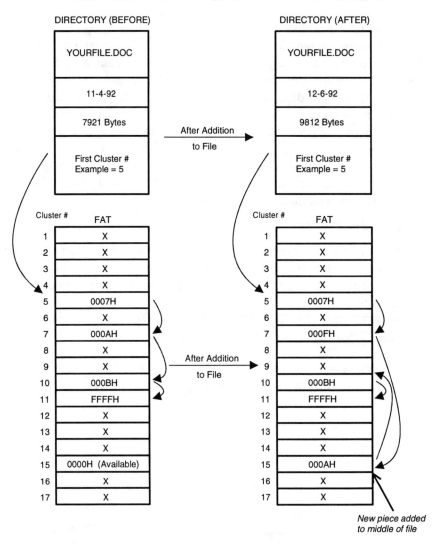

Unlike Disk Drives, a FFSD cannot rewrite the directory and FAT after file modification.

Figure 9.3: File Directory and FAT Modification

The clusters containing these data structures, as well as the remaining disk clusters, undergo constant modification as files are added, deleted and modified. Flash memory can only be rewritten to zeros after erasing the block or entire device to ones. This flash memory characteristic alone provides the key differentiator between the mechanical disk drive and flash memory. It also points out the need for implementing special file systems designed to handle the larger "cluster" size (typically 128Kbytes) and one-way writability of flash memory.

Device Drivers

Before leaving this discussion on disk drives, let's look at the methods in which application software accesses them. Whether interfacing to MS-DOS or any other operating system, the well-known device drivers represent special programs that provide the low-level interface between the operating system (called on by the application software) and the disk drive and all other peripheral devices within a system. Many books have been written on device drivers, so we will not reiterate the details that have long been standardized[64].

Device Driver Chaining

In the MS-DOS world, IO.SYS provides device drivers integral to the system's BIOS. The system uses these device drivers, sometimes referred to as default or built-in drivers, to communicate with the disk drive and other devices. During a computer's initialization, the system reads IO.SYS from the disk and MS-DOS loads each device driver into system memory using a standardized chaining method.

Installable and Built-In Device Drivers

New device drivers, commonly referred to as installable device drivers, may be added via CONFIG.SYS (with the *DEVICE=* command) to support additional peripheral devices. Each new driver gets installed at the front of the chain. Because the search always begins at the NULL driver (Figure 9.4), this guarantees that new drivers will be found before the built-in ones. Therefore, new drivers supersede the default drivers.

---

[64]For example, *Writing MS-DOS Device Drivers*, Second Edition, Robert S. Lai, The WAITE GROUP, Addison-Wesley Publishing Company, Copyright 1992.

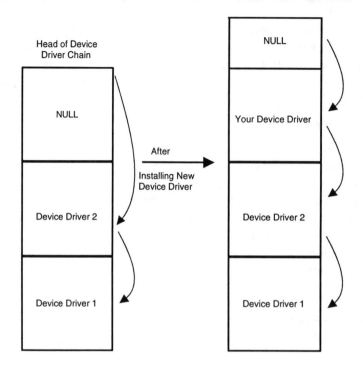

Linked-List Used to Locate Drivers.

Figure 9.4: New Device Drivers Supersede Default Drivers

Like the mechanical disk drive, an FSSD requires a device driver so that application programs can access files stored in the flash memory array. As a matter of fact, a flash file system is itself a special device driver. When designing a system with an FSSD, you must consider the manner in which the flash file system software hooks into the device driver chain. For after-market add-ins (i.e., MS-Flash) of an FSSD, the software loads during system initialization (through CONFIG.SYS) as an installable device driver. The cleaner route, not requiring end-user intervention with CONFIG.SYS (thereby eliminating the possibility of improper installation), calls for building the flash file system directly into the system BIOS. This allows the FSSD's device driver to be loaded along with the other built-in drivers.

The latter approach has the most usefulness when developing a bootable FSSD. This means that the FSSD has the bootstrap capability for loading MS-DOS and contains all the system files (i.e., IO.SYS, MS-DOS.SYS and COMMAND.COM). If the device driver must be installed to access the FSSD, but that device driver is located on the FSSD, how does it get installed? Chapter 10 discusses these concepts.

Character and Block Device Drivers

At the functional level, MS-DOS categorizes two types of device drivers, character and block. A character device performs input and output operations one byte at a time, such as a printer. A block device transfers data in blocks. Disk drives and FSSDs represent perfect examples of block devices. After a block device has successfully initialized, DOS checks the number of units (drives) installed by its device driver's initialization code. It uses this unit count to assign the next drive letter in sequence. For example, if you add an FSSD to your system that already supports a hard drive, the drive letter given to the FSSD will be D:. On the other hand, if the FSSD is the system's only drive, it will probably be assigned as drive C:.

Accessing the Disk Using Interrupt Services

We've said that the device driver provides the lowest-level interface to the device it controls. Disk device drivers can be accessed through several mechanisms. At one level above the device driver, the BIOS provides support using disk-drive service routines accessed through software Interrupt 13H (Figure 9.5). Its list of capabilities can be found in most MS-DOS programmer reference manuals.

As an example, let's examine the INT 13H setup required to read a sector:

Interrupt 13H
Function 02H
Read Sector

Register Setup

AH	= 02H
AL	= Number of sectors to read. This value depends on the available memory buffer space.
CH	= Cylinder
CL	= Beginning sector number
DH	= Head
DL	= Drive number (0-7FH for floppy disks, 80H-FFH for fixed disk)
ES:BX	= Segment:Offset of buffer to read into

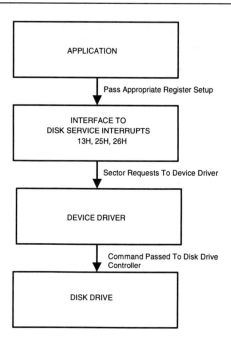

Figure 9.5: Using the Disk Service Interrupts to Access Disk Sectors

Generally, special utilities (such as CHKDSK) and games that go directly to the disk (i.e., bypassing DOS) use the INT 13H routines. The services of INT 25H and 26H (the Absolute Disk Read and Absolute Disk Write interrupts, respectively) provide a more popular solution because of ease of use. As a comparison, let's look at the setup required to read a sector using INT 25H:

Interrupt 25H
Absolute Disk Read

Register Setup
AL   = Drive number (0-7FH for floppy disks, 80H-FFH for fixed disk)
CX   = Number of sectors to read - This value depends on the
               available memory buffer space.
DX   = Beginning logical sector number.
DS:BX   = Segment:Offset of buffer to read into

Accessing the Disk at the File Level

Using INT 25H, the programmer does not get involved with head and cylinder determination, since requests are for logical sector numbers versus physical numbers. MS-DOS makes it even easier to deal with the details of the device driver interface by providing a group of file services through the functions of INT 21H[65]. These functions, used by the majority of application programs, allow disk accesses to be made at the file level.

Early versions of MS-DOS used file control blocks (FCBs) for file management, however more recent programs should be using file handle functions that take advantage of the increased capabilities and simplified programming interface[66]. With handle functions, an ASCIIZ string (an ASCII character string terminated by a null, or zero, byte) that can contain a drive letter, directory path, filename and extension designate the location of a file. For an application program to open or create a file,

---

[65]The disk related (FSSD included) functions of Interrupt 21H are listed in the Appendix.
[66]FCBs only support the current directory and do not offer support for the hierarchical file structure, for example.

it must pass the address of the ASCIIZ string specifying the file to MS-DOS. MS-DOS assigns a unique handle to that file and passes it back to the program. The program can then use the handle to access the file until the program closes the file. If the request is to a standard disk drive, the INT 21H takes this file handle and does all the work of translating the file request into the form supported by the BIOS (Figure 9.6). Otherwise INT 21H passes this request on to a flash file system, a network or tape drive, or any other type of non-standard drive.

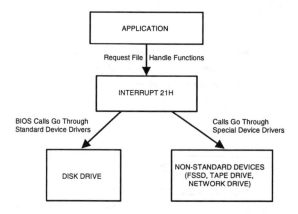

*Figure 9.6: Accessing Devices Using File Handles,
Not at the Sector Level*

FLASH FILE SYSTEM DESIGNS

Flash file system software for an FSSD may be designed in several ways. The chosen solution depends on the application's requirements and the desired complexity. As you will notice, each design has merits that relate to performance, functionality, design simplicity, degrees of disk-drive compatibility and even reliability. You will also notice that a programmer must undertake an exponential increase in flash file system development complexity to achieve a higher degree of functionality; the higher the degree of functionality, the closer the FSSD comes to appearing like a disk drive to the end-user. To achieve the ultimate goal, the FSSD must be completely self-contained and capable of managing all file and subdirectory manipulations without user intervention.

Measuring Drive Usage

When deciding the level of functionality to implement in an FSSD, consider the 80/20 model of operation: In typical disk-drive applications, reads constitute 80% of the accesses, and writes, the remaining 20%. This general rule serves only as a starting point, the exact usage model that fits your application may vary. So, at one extreme, your application may only use the FSSD for holding the applications and permanent data files which get downloaded into system memory for execution (i.e., a read-only FSSD). This minimal functionality FSSD is relatively simple to implement. On the other hand, your FSSD may need to handle frequently updated database records or interface to write-intensive operating systems, like UNIX. This latter scenario puts heavy demands on the FSSD write capability and requires much more sophisticated software algorithms to manage the flash memory media. The implications will become more apparent as you read through the remainder of this chapter.

In practice, flash file systems may be broken into two distinct categories:

The Disk-Drive Emulators

- Allow the FSSD to resemble the mechanical disk drive by possessing the standard disk file structures, such as a FAT, Directories, and sectors.

- Take advantage of all levels of disk-drive services (INTs 13H, 21H, 25H and 26H). This property allows the FSSD to run *all* software programs and potentially even serve as the boot drive.

- Function best using flash memory technologies, such as Toshiba's NAND, to take advantage of the smaller "sector" sizes (erase blocks).

- Function more as a device driver than a file system. As shown in Figure 9.7, the disk-emulator resides in the layer below the file system layer, serving as the device driver for the FAT file system.

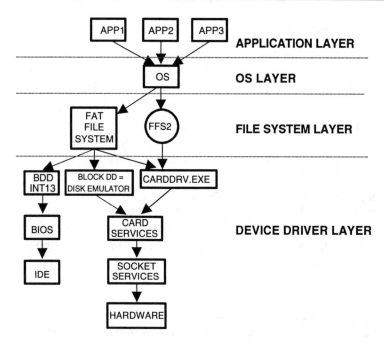

Figure 9.7: Flash Memory Solid-State Drive System Layers

- Have operating system independence from a functional standpoint. However, files stored on one media, such as a flash memory card, cannot be transferred (via the card) between systems with different operating systems. For example, the file structures wrapped around files stored on an Apple computer lack compatibility with the DOS data structures used in a PC.

- The positive traits of disk-drive compatibility tend to sub-optimize the flash memory benefits and add inefficiencies to the design. An example is the maintenance of sectors on a non-sectored media.

Flash Optimized File Systems

- Reside at the file system layer to allow direct management of the flash memory. Being true file systems, they may be ported to other platforms (i.e., they are operating system independent). OS independence has the most importance for FSSDs based on removable memory cards. The card may be transferred from system to system and still work even though the OS is different (by using OS data structure conversion).

- Have special properties (unlike mechanical disk drives) that *optimize* flash memory's functionality. This is exemplified in dealing with the block erases of flash memory, an operation completely foreign to the disk drive.

- Function best with the larger block sizes of ETOX flash because these file systems do not utilize small sector file structures.

- Only need to support the most common disk-drives features, thereby satisfying the typical end-user's expectations.

- Do not partition the flash memory media into sectors, and for this reason, only support the MS-DOS INT 21H functions (i.e., not INT 13H, 25H, and 26H).

THE DISK-DRIVE EMULATORS

Let's look more closely at the various types of flash file systems in existence today. Starting with the disk-drive emulators, we'll go from simple, limited-functionality implementations to complex and full featured designs.

When developing a device driver for a disk-drive emulator (DDE), first consider how it should interface to the operating system. In essence, the driver that controls a DDE consists of two portions. One portion represents the flash driver that manages the media and translates operating system calls into "flashable" operations. The other portion provides the standardized interface to the operating system. In DDEs, the flash driver will be minimal, compared to flash *optimized* file systems. This is because, as its name implies, to emulate a disk drive, it only performs the operations requested by the FAT file system (or equivalent). In this regard, it primarily manages the flash memory by hiding the large sector size of flash memory from the system.

The portion of the DDE that interfaces to the operating system will either hook into the existing disk-drive interrupt service routines or actually replace those routines. In other words, if you have the opportunity to write your system's BIOS from scratch, the interrupt service routines could contain direct support for interrupts 13H, 25H and 26H. But, for after-market add-ins (where you can't rewrite the BIOS), the developer must install filters in each of the disk interrupts to allow the requests to be intercepted (Figure 9.8). Using this filtering method, any requests to a non-FSSD drive in the system would simply be passed on to the original interrupt.

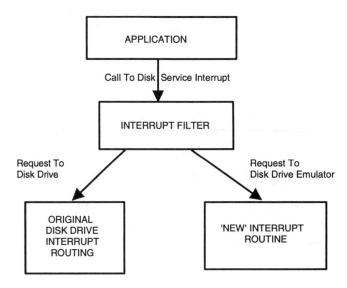

Figure 9.8: Using an Interrupt Filter

Primitive Flash File Systems

The first flash device drivers were designed to make the flash memory look exactly like the mechanical drive in terms of media organization, but definitely not in performance and functionality. These elementary device drivers employ most of the file structures (directory, FAT, and clusters, for example) known to the mechanical disk. Not much different than a ROM drive in some cases, they provide the simplest approach to FSSD development. Although it may seem that these drives have minimal functionality, they still offer solid-state reliability, high read performance, and low power consumption.

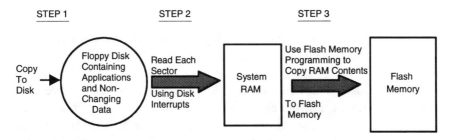

Figure 9.9: Creating a Disk Image in Flash Memory

Disk Imaging (the "Reusable ROM Drive")

Create this very primitive FSSD by superimposing a disk image (floppy or hard disk) directly onto the flash memory media. This type of FSSD can be likened to a glorified ROM drive, utilized in many embedded (or dedicated) applications even to this day. By using flash memory instead of ROM, the application benefits by having occasional rewrite capability. Implementing this FSSD requires a three-step sequence (See Figure 9.9):

1) Load a floppy or hard disk with the application software and data that will be accessed on the FSSD. This part of the sequence requires nothing more than using a few DOS commands, such as COPY or XCOPY.

2) Use a special disk transfer utility, written by the developer (or you), to transfer the disk image into a system buffer. The BIOS (INT 13H, Function 02H), providing the lowest-level services, can be called on by the utility to read the desired sectors from the mechanical disk into the host system buffer. Most developers will probably utilize the Absolute Disk Read Interrupt (INT 25H) available through MS-DOS. INT 25H allows the disk transfer utility to read and copy whole sectors on the disk to a program-specified buffer and only requires a limited number of parameters.

3)   After performing the disk read interrupt service, the utility copies the system's buffer contents into flash memory. The details of this operation can be found in Chapter 7, which discusses programming algorithms for flash memory. Loop back to step 2 and execute INT 25H until all disk sectors have been read and copied.

Getting the disk image into the FSSD's memory array only represents part of the design. For the end-user to access the files, a custom device driver (the actual flash device driver) must be used to translate the operating system's standard sector requests into flash memory addresses. This device driver resembles a RAM-disk device driver, with the exception that it is limited to performing read-only functions. With this type of design, the end-user changes the FSSD contents by erasing the entire flash memory array and running through the three steps listed above.

Disk-Drive Template

An approach that increases the functionality somewhat can be implemented by formatting the FSSD with a boot record[67], a blank root directory, and a FAT template, which gets filled in during the addition and deletion of files (Figure 9.10). Remember that with flash memory, these changes can only occur in a one-way direction (ones to zeros). Therefore, the flash device driver controlling these operations must prevent attempts to overwrite deleted sectors and find the first available, unused space. Once the flash memory array fills up (with a mixture of deleted and valid files), it must be erased and reformatted to allow the user to reclaim the deleted space and write additional files. Before doing this, copy the remaining valid contents to an alternate drive (using standard DOS copy commands) for temporary storage.

In maintaining the FAT, pay particular attention to the differences of standard FAT values used versus what flash memory accepts. For instance, a FAT entry on a disk drive ordinarily indicates a free sector (or cluster) with the value of 0000H (Table 9.1). This would force the

---

[67]The number of logical sectors specified in the boot record will be based on the size of the flash memory array.

FSSD's device driver to flip the bits to a non-zero value when using that entry. We all know by this time that flash memory doesn't allow this without first erasing the entire block. So the formatting on the FSSD must be reversed from the disk drive (a free sector would be represented as 0FFFFH in a flash memory FAT). The flash device driver must handle this reversal when processing standard requests from MS-DOS.

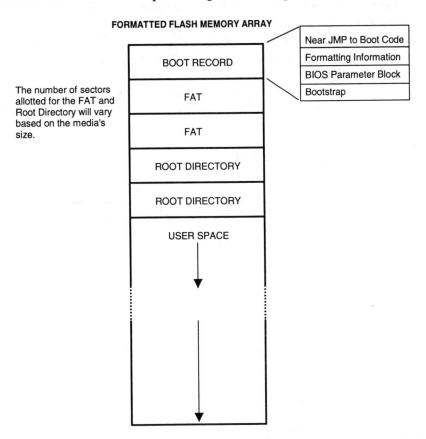

Figure 9.10: A Flash Memory Array Pre-Formatted with a Blank FAT and Root Directory

Sector-Level Modification Method

To achieve an even higher degree of functionality, a slightly more advanced flash device driver that performs sector-level modification may be employed. Every time the user modifies a file, the flash memory devices containing the FAT, directory, and associated file sectors get copied into system RAM. In RAM, the file system modifies the contents, updating the FAT and directory and inserting the user's changes into the file. (This method would not have to perform the FAT bit-flipping used in the previous example, because the FAT is completely rewritten with every change). Afterwards, the file system's software erases the corresponding flash memory devices and writes the modified file structures and file contents back into flash memory. Figure 9.11 shows this sequence for a simple single-device FSSD.

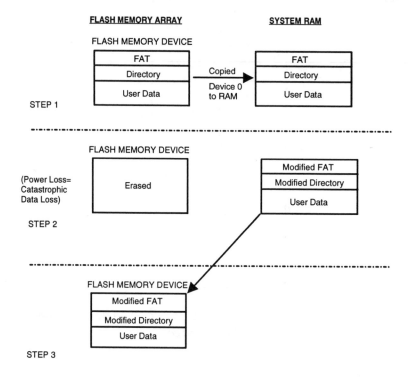

Figure 9.11: Sector-Level Modification Requires Considerable Overhead

If you're thinking, "Geez, this must be a long, slow process".....YOU'RE RIGHT! Remember that flash memory devices typically require one second to erase. A modification could constitute more than just a few erases for a file fragmented among many flash memory devices. Coming from a perspective that disk drives do not need to perform erases, these multiple one second erases become very visible in performance to the end user. Next you should ask, "What if power goes down during the erase process?". All the data temporarily stored in RAM goes away forever! However, analogous to the disk-image approach, if the user only requires occasional application changes, this flash file system may be adequate. Also realize that when performing excessive modifications, the flash memory devices in the FSSD experience an unequal amount of cycling, especially those containing the FAT and directory structures.

This type of flash device driver may function best using some of the smaller-sectored flash memory devices, such as Toshiba's NAND devices.

Full-Featured Disk-Drive Emulators

The example FSSDs we have seen up to this point have had very minimal functionality. Some of the noteworthy enhancements exhibited by real disk-drive emulators include:

- Virtually unlimited read and write capability
- Reclamation of memory space containing deleted files
- Compatible with all disk-related system commands

Today, several full-featured DDEs can be obtained from companies like M-Systems (True Flash File System, TFFS) and SCM. The file systems (e.g., FAT file system) supporting these drives access the DDE using all the standard mechanisms (disk interrupts and DOS function calls). When these file systems initialize, they install the disk interrupt filters we've discussed (just like the primitive flash file systems had to). Although these DDEs utilize a DOS FAT format and manage the media in terms of sectors, they differ considerably from the methods described earlier because they incorporate a logical (rather than physical) sector addressing scheme. This eliminates the dependency on any type of "fixed-in-flash" disk-drive data structures and allows the FAT and directories to move around. This means that the FAT, directory and user files can be modified simply by relocating them to free flash memory.

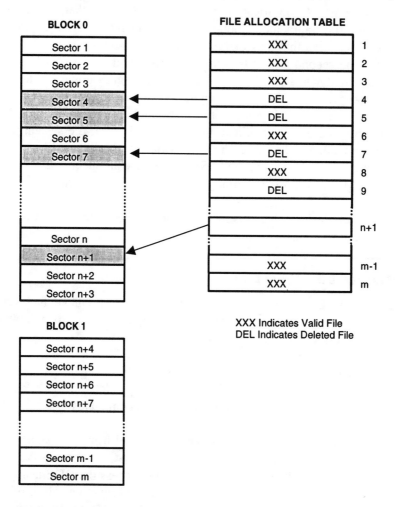

o Each block is an erasable flash unit.
o Fat entries point to physical location of a sector within a specific flash memory block.
o Full-featured DDEs can remove 'dirty' space occupied by deleted files.

Figure 9.12: One-to-One Correspondence Between FAT Entries and Sectors

Virtual Addressing

Let's look at what virtual addressing does for file management. First, think about the following important points with respect to the earlier disk-drive emulators (Figure 9.12):

a. Each formatted sector on the flash media maps with a physical address (or absolute index) to its associated FAT entry; and

b. The one-way write limitation of flash memory results in the development of "dirty" sectors (and ultimately dirty blocks) when deleting files.

The most notable enhancement of a full-featured DDE lies in its ability to remove the dirty sectors (containing deleted files) and therefore, reclaim the previously unusable memory space. To do this without user intervention or infringing on system memory, the file system manipulates the sectors completely within the drive. As an example of this capability, assume the flash memory media is originally depicted as shown in Figure 9.12. Basically, this represents the erasable blocks of flash memory in a DDE containing a mixture of valid and deleted sectors. Without knowing any better, one could say that this scenario doesn't look any different than the other designs we've discussed so far. But we said that these flash file systems perform dirty space reclamation, and that changes the story. Can you guess how it might work?

Spare Blocks

To proceed, we must introduce the concept of a *spare block*(s). As seen from Figure 9.13, we've added an extra block to the flash memory array of Figure 9.12. This block of free flash memory will be used for the transfer of the valid file data still remaining in the dirty blocks. This so-called spare block eliminates the need for using system RAM during the removal of dirty sectors (a process referred to as *clean-up*).

Clean-Up

Clean-up is fundamentally very simple. When the user writes a file to the DDE, DOS requests sectors to accommodate the file. Continuing on with the example above (Figure 9.13), also assume that the file to be

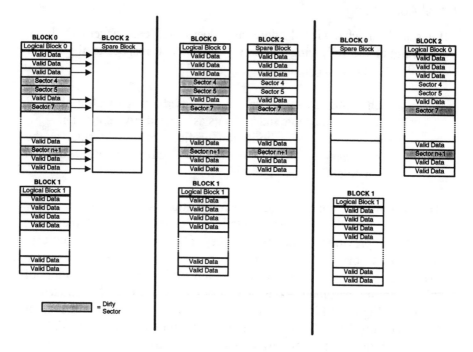

Figure 9.13: Three-Step Cleanup Operation: Copy, Erase,
and Block Renumbering

written ultimately occupies two sectors. However, assume that there are not enough clean sectors available. Also notice the assignment of a logical sequence number to each block. The flash file system executes the following steps to free up the necessary sectors:

1.   Copy the *valid* data contents (and sometimes the garbage sectors) of all the sectors to the corresponding sector spaces within the spare block. Any deleted sectors had been previously marked as dirty so they may not be copied (this depends on the capability of the DDE).

2.   Erase the dirty block. It becomes the new spare block.

3.   Renumber the previously spare block so that it reflects the number of the ex-dirty block.

Some disk emulators may do *exactly* what the operating system tells it to do. For example, if DOS only requested the use of five sectors, the remaining dirty sectors may have gone along for the ride. In other words, DOS does not know that the dirty sectors not needed for the file transfer even exist. These are dealt with at the device driver level. Remember, DOS normally deals with a disk drive; on disk drives, the concept of a dirty sector doesn't exist.

Clean-Up Efficiency

With respect to the clean-up operation, we should now discuss the subject of clean-up efficiency. From an efficiency standpoint, it is a waste of write operations to copy dirty sectors to a clean block. Ultimately, this also causes an increase in the number of erases that occur. On a drive that contains a high percentage of dirty sectors (i.e., not many valid files), this results in an inefficient use of battery energy and an unnecessary degradation in performance.

On the other hand, a drive with a high percentage of valid files may still have to move around lots of sectors, but these moves can be minimized by reducing the fragmentation of the valid files. This can be accomplished on a freshly formatted drive by storing all permanent files (rarely-updated application software, for example) first. Then most of the sector manipulation will occur within a few blocks, as opposed to scattered amongst many. To explain the latter condition, refer back to Figure 9.12. The sector holes, unless eventually filled up with permanent data, will always require the unnecessary movement of valid sectors. Besides using the method of "premeditated" permanent file storage, a type of defragmenting utility may be written (Figure 9.14). This utility can be periodically run to condense the valid sectors into fewer blocks. (Clean-up efficiency will be discussed in more detail later).

Modify the FAT and Root Directory

Before leaving this discussion on full-featured DDEs, it is also worth elaborating on the process of FAT and root directory modification. It's actually quite simple. Since the FAT and directory occupy their own sectors on the drive, they get moved around during clean-up, just like any other data sector. As a matter of fact, these their associated sectors get rewritten with every file addition, modification, or deletion. Because DOS requires that they be located within the first few sectors on a drive, they will always reside in logical block number 1. So after cleaning up block 1, the old spare block becomes logical block number 1.

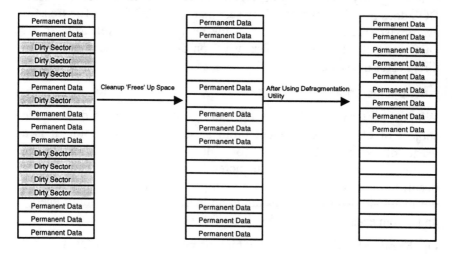

Figure 9.14: Defragmentation Utility Concatenates "Permanent Data"

FLASH *OPTIMIZE*D FSSD'S

Only Microsoft had a commercially available product for DOS (namely, MS-Flash) that can be placed in the "flash *optimized*" category of file systems at the time this chapter was written[70]. Working closely with Intel Corporation, Microsoft developed a unique approach to dealing with the large sector size of flash memory. Although MS Flash File System allows the FSSD to be compatible with the majority of MS-DOS and Windows software applications, its data structures differ considerably from those of the traditional mechanical disk drive. Furthermore, because it functions as an installable (or alternative) file system, MS-Flash has complete capability to actively manage the flash memory media.

---

[70]However, other companies are developing flash optimized file systems for alternative operating systems.

Accessing the Flash-*Optimized* FSSD

We discussed earlier how application programs access the FSSD drivers for the Disk-Drive Emulators. Contrary to this approach, the alternative file system does not utilize a BIOS Parameter Block (BPB), a FAT or other disk-drive compatible structures and the typical block device driver cannot be used. It could have been possible to develop a driver that hooked into INT 21H. Using this approach, every function call coming in would have to be watched (and potentially intercepted), requiring a considerable amount of overhead. To access MS-Flash, Microsoft chose instead to implement a redirector interface. In short, redirector interfaces allow alternative file systems to be transparently accessible by DOS and Windows programs. MS-Flash can receive calls from DOS by using INT 2FH (the Multiplex Interrupt) which provides the redirector interface (Figure 9.15).

During system initialization, the redirector interface "manufactures" a DOS drive(s) for the FSSD and provides fictional drive mappings (to generate drive letters in lieu of the standard block device method). The redirector interface unifies the two file access methods (FCB and file handles), so that the file system does not need to know by what method a file is being accessed. The work of resolving the drive and directory has already been done by the DOS kernel. The redirector operates at a level below INT 21H, and the code for INT 21H takes care of calling INT 2FH when appropriate. This access method independence saves a lot of code and further confirms the desirability of the redirector interface over the INT 21H hook as the means of implementing alternative file systems.

Microsoft's Flash File System Design Criteria

Microsoft initially entered the flash file system world with a design that more closely resembled a WORM (Write-Once-Read-Many) drive than a disk drive. Although this non-sectored file system (referred to as FFS1) found some usefulness in certain embedded applications, it mostly served as a flash memory test vehicle. Despite the fact that it had more functionality than any of the early disk-drive emulators (because it allowed files and directories to be added and deleted), it did not incorporate a method for reclaiming the dirty space created by the deleted files (as you have seen with the full-featured DDEs, this capability is needed to recreate the functionality of a disk drive). When the media became full using FFS1, the user had to *XCOPY* the non-deleted files to a backup drive, reformat the WORM, then *XCOPY* the files back (Figure 9.16).

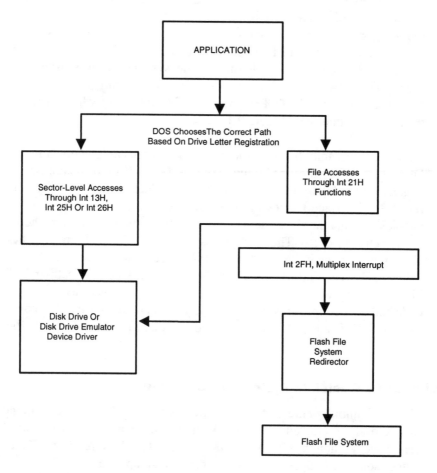

Figure 9.15: Flash Memory Solid-State Drive Accessing Methods

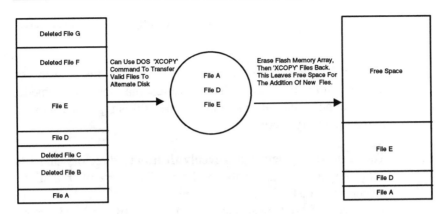

Figure 9.16: Microsoft's First FFS Functioned Like a WORM Drive

To explain the functionality of MS-Flash, we'll begin by elaborating on the design criteria of what a flash-*optimized* file system needs to be and do:

1. The flash file system must adapt to the erase block size of the flash memory devices that the FSSD uses. Erase block sizes range from 4 kbytes to 64 kbytes for symmetrically blocked devices (such as Intel's 28F008SA) and 32 kbytes to 512 kbytes (or the entire component size) for the bulk-erase devices (such as Intel's 28F020). Block size independence represents one key feature that makes this flash file system different from the mechanical disk, which usually deals with 512 byte sectors (disk-drive sector size can vary). Later, we'll look at the effects of block size on clean-up efficiency.

2. The flash file system must minimize the need to rewrite any fixed areas in the media. After programming a flash memory bit to a zero, that bit only becomes a one after erasing the entire block (or device). Basically, this functionality provides the biggest challenge to designing any type of flash file system.

3. The flash file system must first erase a block before it can reclaim deallocated space (created by deleting a file or subdirectory) within a block. Analogous to criteria number 2, a

programmed flash memory bit can only be rewritten after erasing the entire block.

4.   The flash file system must evenly distribute the erasure of blocks within the media. This ensures that the entire media cycles at an equal rate. The importance of this topic is discussed in the reliability section.

5.   The flash file system must evenly distribute directory and file control structures and data in the media. Remember that the mechanical disk drive has a centralized FAT and directory structure. Without even distribution, every file or subdirectory modification would require an erase and rewrite of the FAT and directory blocks[69]. Not only would this cause unnecessary cycling, but it also results in a performance degradation.

6.   The directory and file control structures must not rely on the absolute location of related control structures or data within the media. This capability allows relocation of the control structures (i.e., the boot record) during the cycle-leveling process[70].

Functional Description

To accommodate design criteria #2, MS-Flash stores all new files and directories in a stack-like manner, to sequentially free locations (Figure 9.17) in the flash memory array. The stack-like file storage serves two purposes:

1.   It overcomes flash memory's inability to turn zeros into ones without erasing the entire block. This satisfies a functional characteristic of flash memory and enables a performance increase by not requiring real time flash memory block erasure.

---

[69]Note that the DDEs had to rewrite the FAT and directory sectors with every file operation.
[70]Earlier we saw this could be done with the full-featured DDEs. When they moved the FAT and directory sectors, the new block that contained them was always assigned the number 1.

2.   It partially ensures that the entire media gets used equally, because writes are always made to unused sequential locations. We'll talk more about cycle-leveling concepts later.

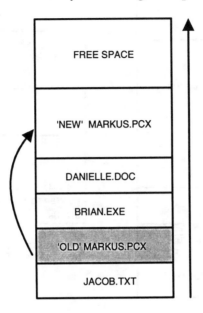

o   Modified File Saved To First Free Space.
'Old' File Marked As Deleted Until Cleanup.

o   Files Are Stored In A 'Stack-Like' Manner,
Always To Next Available Free Space. This
Avoids Rewriting Flash Memory Until Cleanup.

Figure 9.17: Files are Always Written to the Next Available Free Space

As demonstrated in Figure 9.17, a file modification (by a word processor, for example), results in the deletion of the old version after writing the new version to the first unused memory address (with the *save* command of the word processor, for example). The mechanical disk drive could simply overwrite the original file. In actuality, with an FSSD, the so-called deleted file remains intact until the cleaning of the block that contains it.

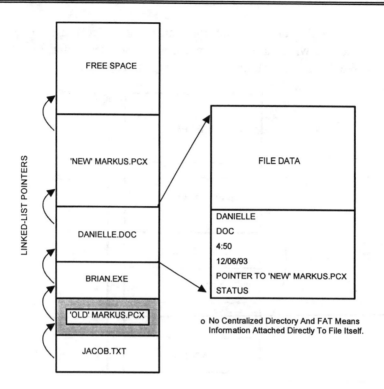

Figure 9.18: Linked List Pointers Locate Next File in the Chain

Linked Lists

Looking in a little more depth (Figure 9.18), notice that the file system stores files with their directory information functionally attached to the file itself. This eliminates the dependency on a fixed-location FAT and directory which would require modification with every file operation. In addition to the basic information that represents a file (Name, Extension, Time, Date, and Attributes), the file's attached directory contains, among other things, a set of pointers and a status word. The pointers, integral to a linked-list scheme, locate the files in lieu of a FAT and centralized directory structure. The status word indicates whether the file or subdirectory is valid or deleted. In many ways, the linked-list structure resembles the FAT of a mechanical drive. However, instead of linking the various clusters of a particular file together, the linked lists chain together all the files and subdirectories on the FSSD. The actual structure consists of many linked lists, essentially one for every subdirectory (Figure 9.19). The pointers within a file's directory point to the next file in the link.

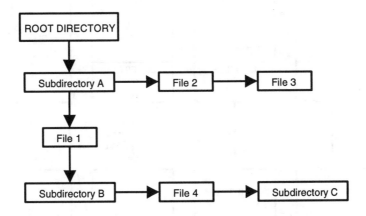

Figure 9.19: Each Subdirectory has Its Own Linked List

Besides eliminating a fixed FAT and directory, the pointers involved in the linked-list scheme also remove the dependency on fixed cluster sizes. The pointer values represent physical flash memory addresses, not fixed indices as with a FAT. This allows files to be stored more efficiently. For example, a ten byte file stored on a mechanical disk (or DDE) consumes a whole cluster, whereas that same file only consumes ten bytes on this type of FSSD (plus the overhead bytes).

Clean-Up

So far, we've described how the file system manages the storage of files and directories. However, dealing with deleted files represents the most important and complicated aspect of the file system - the part known as clean-up. We saw that some primitive file systems performed a type of clean-up operation, but at tremendous expense of the host CPU's bandwidth and user's time. The ideal file system should be able to remove deleted files without any noticeable impact on system performance (but, this isn't an ideal world, is it?). Before we get into the implications of that last statement, let's look at how to perform a clean-up operation.

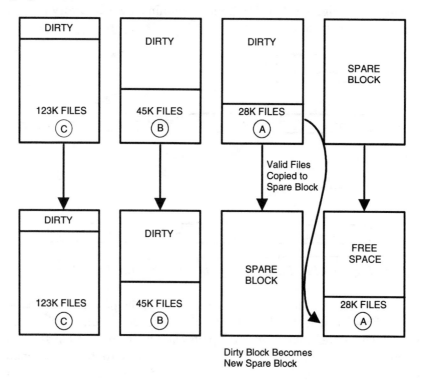

Figure 9.20: MS-Flash Performs a Three-Step Clean-up Operation

Figure 9.20 shows a simplified example of an FSSD with a minimal number of blocks. These blocks contain a mixture of valid and deleted files. Notice that one of the blocks, labeled the spare, is empty. MS-Flash performs a clean-up operation following these three steps:

1.   Identify the dirtiest block by referring to the records that the file system keeps on all allocated and deleted space on the FSSD. After removing the deleted files, this once-dirtiest block will contain the most free space for accommodating new files. This has significant impact on step two of the clean-up operation.

2.   Copy valid files to the spare block. This step consists of a varying number of byte transfers from one flash memory block to another. Obviously, the dirtier the block, the less valid files to copy and the more efficient and timely the operation will be. The spare block, a required overhead of the file system, eliminates the use of system RAM.

3.   Erase the dirty block. Immediately after copying all valid files to the spare block, two copies of the same files resides within the FSSD. Without going into details, this plays a significant role in data integrity if the power should go down in the middle of a clean-up operation. At this point, the file system orders the dirty block to be erased. After the erase completes, this block becomes the new spare block ready for its role in the next clean-up operation. After erasing the dirty block, the file system increments the erase count and stores it in that block for cycle-leveling information.

Background Clean-up

Although the clean-up operation seems like a busy activity, the trick is to get all this to happen in the background, transparent to the user[73]. In other words, the user would still perceive full use of the CPU's bandwidth; once the background operation was initiated, control would return to the application running. The file system has built-in checks to periodically search the blocks and look for a certain percentage of dirtiness that will trigger a clean-up operation. Obviously, this searching function cannot occur continuously because it would result in a degradation of system performance. Usually the search occurs after a certain number of FSSD accesses.

The background clean-up mechanism can be implemented in several ways. Let's look at the following steps to see the additional functionality required beyond the three simple clean-up steps outlined previously:

---

[73] Except for the integrated drive, only MS-Flash can implement background cleanup because it has 'complete knowledge' of the flash memory array that it manages; it doesn't require the operating system to tell it what to do.

1.   Identify the dirtiest block.

2.   Copy valid files to the spare block. The actual programming
      method employed for this step depends on the specific type of
      flash memory used (the various programming methods were
      discussed in Chapter 7). Regardless of the device used, or
      whether the operation is automated or not, the bytes (or words)
      of data can only be written one at a time. Without going into the
      specifics of the write algorithms, individual write operations
      occur in a relatively short time (approximately 10-20
      microseconds). Assuming that even if a write operation were
      automated, it occurs in too short a time period to practically
      return control to the system after the initiation of each operation.
      Therefore, the host CPU must monitor the completion of the
      operation. This means that this step cannot really be a
      background task and again stresses the importance of identifying
      the dirtiest block to obtain the highest clean-up efficiency.

3.   Erase the dirty block. The flash memory devices employing
      automated erase (for example, Intel's 28F008SA) have been
      optimized for this step of the background clean-up. The erase
      operation, once initiated, occurs in approximately one to two
      seconds. During this time, the host CPU does not need to
      monitor the erase progress for automated flash memories; it can
      temporarily return control to the user's application (and wait for
      a transition on the Ready/Busy signal).

Foreground Clean-Up

Another circumstance can occur, which we call "on-demand" clean-up,
where a file write request forces minimally dirty blocks to be cleaned to
accommodate this file. Typically this would only happen on a relatively
full FSSD, where all reclaimable space is crucial. Figure 9.21 shows a
worst-case situation where the FSSD has a few reclaimable bytes
scattered throughout the array. For this example, every block requires
cleaning to accommodate the file write request. Obviously, this could
severely impact system performance. In practice, the situation does not

seem to get this bad. Nevertheless, it can be minimized by techniques described below in the section on hot and cold file management.

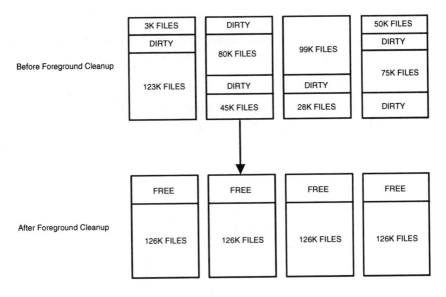

-Flash Memory Block Size is 128 KBytes
-Attempt to Write 9 KByte File Results in 4 Block Cleanup.
-Cleanup Concatenates Valid Files Within Each Block.

Figure 9.21: Worst-Case Foreground "On Demand" Cleanup

Implementing Cycle Leveling

Back in Chapter 3, we discussed the cycling characteristics of flash memory devices. However, intelligent media management with MS-Flash allows it to deliver very low failure rates. To achieve the highest possible performance and longest flash media life, the file system must cycle all erase blocks at an equal rate (also known as "wear-leveling").

From the example that follows, it should be very easy to see that without an intelligent cycle-leveling mechanism, serious hot spots would develop in the media:

A.   Assume files stored as depicted in Figure 9.22.

B.   The first two blocks contain non-changing files (perhaps applications). The *dirty detect* algorithm will always find these two blocks very clean and stable.

C.   Block 3 contains a splattering of stable files and a few deleted files. Sequence 2 in Figure 9.22 shows what happens after clean-up.

D.   In sequence 3, the user had previously stored and then deleted a file within the available free space. What happens on the next clean-up?

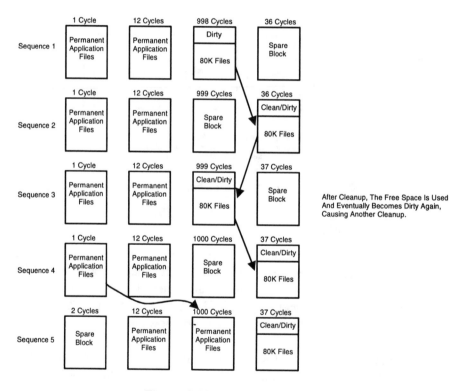

Figure 9.22: File Clean-Up

It looks like blocks 3 and 4 are playing a game of ping-pong. But, the cycle leveling algorithm, who has been watching this game, finally says, "All right, this has been going on long enough!". "Long enough" in this case refers to a large enough cycling delta between the four blocks in the picture; pick 1,000 as a nice round number. Sequence 5 shows what happens next. Block 1 becomes the new spare block. It undergoes cycling until the next time the appropriate cycling delta between the blocks is reached.

FLASH FILE SYSTEM EVALUATION

Developing a sufficient evaluation of a flash file system requires careful scrutiny. Although you must work out your own personalized test details and file system requirements, we have provided a basic list of things to consider. The tests are divided into categories consisting of performance, power consumption, reliability, and system-level issues.

Performance - File Transfer Rate

The end-user inevitably asks the fundamental question: "How fast is it?" Publicly-available benchmark programs, designed to test mechanical disk-drive performance, can be used for various types of read and write tests. Because these benchmark programs specifically target disk drives, most have been designed to function at the sector level and only operate on the DDEs. These benchmark programs will not be compatible with the file level functionality of Interrupt 21H used by MS-Flash. Furthermore, they're unaware of (and therefore, do not stress) the unique characteristics of any flash file system, such as the need to perform clean-up operations.

Benchmarking at the File Level

Benchmark programs can be written which use the INT 21H functions, thereby working with all types of FSSDs, including those with a redirector interface. The Appendix lists code providing a rudimentary example in which a specified file(s) is copied from a source (be it a hard disk, RAM drive, or even another FSSD) to the FSSD being benchmarked. A simple timer routine calculates the time for the operation. Beware that this does not eliminate any system overhead or timer inaccuracies.

From a read standpoint, most FSSDs perform at RAM-disk speeds. Therefore, most benchmarking efforts should be focused on write performance (except for the minimally functional FSSDs we discussed earlier). Referring back to the 80/20 model of disk-drive accessing, you may want to consider averaging out the read and write times to provide an overall performance indicator.

The file write transfer rate for a given FSSD will be condition dependent:

- A clean FSSD (no files) yields the fastest file write transfer rate. Under these conditions, the FSSD theoretically delivers file write rates equivalent to a disk drive. Most people find this surprising because flash memory actually has a much slower write transfer rate than the disk drive. However, rotational latency, seek time and system overhead limit the disk drive except when these factors average out with files exceeding approximately 100 kbytes.

- A dirty FSSD results in a noticeable decrease in performance due to the necessity to do clean-up in order to accommodate additional files. We referred to this earlier as "on-demand" clean-up.

Before running a benchmark program, precondition the FSSD so that these various situations can be properly studied. Obviously, it's up to you to determine the exact level of dirtiness an FSSD should be to provide a generalized evaluation. A good technique is to fill the entire FSSD with randomly sized files (ranging from 5 kbytes to 200 kbytes). Now delete files here and there so your FSSD's file arrangement looks like that depicted in Figure 9.21 and you've regained approximately 15% of the capacity. Remember, deleting files does not cause a clean-up, so the FSSD will contain a bunch of dirty blocks. The next file copy requires a clean-up before it can be written. You can repeat this procedure using various file sizes, causing more or less blocks to be cleaned. Again, consider an overall performance indicator because in reality, file copies will not always require a clean-up operation to accommodate a file.

Performance - Clean-Up Efficiency

Clean-up efficiency affects performance, power consumption, and cycling of the FSSD. Let's reiterate what clean-up efficiency means. To explain this, first recall the clean-up steps:

1.   Copy valid file data (and potentially some dirty data, in the case of the DDEs) from the dirty block to the spare block.

2.   Erase the dirty block.

Step number 1 implies that the fewer valid bytes (i.e., the dirtier the block) to copy, the faster this operation occurs. This also translates to a secondary (but important) benefit - power savings. An FSSD performing on-demand clean-up has no control over clean-up efficiency because the algorithm simply looks for the dirtiest block to clean-up. On an FSSD that is relatively full of valid data, the dirty space may be just a few bytes . Clean-up efficiency becomes important during background clean-up operations, where the algorithm decides how dirty a block should be before it kicks off a clean-up. If the dirtiness is too low, decreased performance, increased power consumption and increased cycling will result. In this situation, the background clean-up operation can noticeably steal CPU bandwidth away from the user's application. However, a very high dirtiness requires more on-demand clean-ups. In writing or evaluating a flash file system that can perform background clean-up, you must really have an appreciation and understanding of this fine balance.

You can work through the math to determine the "visible" time spent during the background clean-up steps. Depending on many factors, including the number of bytes to copy, the type of flash memory devices and the CPU speed, this time can range from a few microseconds to several seconds. Flash memory erase block size plays an important role in determining overall cycling efficiency. The smaller the block size, the more blocks that must be erased to reclaim an adequate amount of free space. The larger the block size, the more valid file data that potentially has to be copied to the spare block during the clean-up.

Performance - Hot and Cold File Management

The user will probably store both permanent (cold) application programs and temporary (hot) data files on the FSSD. Executable files or application programs fall into the category of permanent files, as they rarely change. User files created with the application programs may be frequently updated, classifying them as temporary. These files will probably be randomly arranged throughout the FSSD. Now, assume that some of the data files are deleted creating dirty holes amidst the application programs. A clean-up operation transfers the application programs to the spare block, but eventually that block contains dirty holes too. The non-changing application programs are getting bounced around needlessly. This wastes block-erase cycles and decreases efficiency. In an ideal situation, the algorithm will eventually sort out the hot and cold files. You could also consider writing a utility to allow the end-user to perform this sorting task periodically. The hottest files would then be located within the dirtiest blocks. Since the hot file activity would then be happening within the most efficient blocks (i.e., the dirtiest), the overall cycling efficiency will be highest. The algorithm that separates the hot and cold files could be designed to look at file creation dates to determine its relative warmth. Therefore the files could be stored in approximate order of age.

Reliability - Cycle Leveling

You may recall the ping-pong game that occurred during the clean-up operations. If it weren't for cycle-leveling stepping in, those blocks would have aged much quicker than the remaining blocks in the FSSD. Without further discussion, we must conclude that for the typical FSSD application replacing the mechanical disk drive, cycle leveling should be considered a very important feature. The lack of cycle leveling will dramatically affect the mean-time-to-failure (MTTF) of the FSSD.

It can be shown that based on cycling performance alone, the MTTF of an FSSD running an intelligent algorithm (includes cycle-leveling) such as Microsoft's Flash File System, will exceed one million hours. To demonstrate this assume the following simplified situation[74]:

- A clean 20 Megabyte FSSD uses ten pairs of Intel's 28F008SA devices.
- Each erase block equals 128 kbytes and can be cycled 100,000 times.
- A 20 kbyte file is copied to FSSD every five minutes, 24 hours a day. This equates to writing about 5.7 megabytes every day.
- Each block gets cycled once for every 1000 file copies (20 Meg/20K = 1000).

(1000 files/cycle) (5 minutes/file) (1 hour/60 minutes) (100,000 cycles) = 8 million hours[75].

Believable? Plug in your own numbers!

In reality, other factors will reduce the MTTF. For starters, this example showed a perfect situation for cycling efficiency; in reality, the efficiency will range from about 50-95%. This means that more cycles will occur to accommodate the same amount of files from the example above. Other non-cycling related components will also reduce the MTTF. These include things like failures of other devices within the FSSD.

Reliability - Failure Recovery Modes

1. How does the file system respond to unsuccessful byte writes, or worse yet, to an entire block of flash memory going bad? Keep in mind that as reliable as the flash memory media may be, the possibility exists that a write or erase operation will fail for one reason or another. The file system should be capable of handling these types of failures without a catastrophe. For example, it

---

[74]Chapter 3 contains a similar evaluation.
[75]Notice that this greatly exceeds the average user's life expectancy.

may use the spare block to replace the bad block. Although this may render the FSSD incapable of performing subsequent clean-ups, at least the data can still be read and recovered. Most of the full-featured DDEs and MS-Flash possess varying degrees of failure recovery capabilities.

2.   Since flash memory does not make audible noise like the mechanical disk, it could be difficult for the user to detect an operation in progress. The user may turn off power or remove the memory card during a critical event, such as clean-up or storing a file. You should understand the flash file system and confirm that the algorithms handle all possible events.

System Level Issues - File System Overhead

Whatever the type of flash file system, there will be varying amounts of data structures stored on the flash memory in addition to the user's data. This should not be a big concern, but the amount should not be excessive; typical numbers range between 2 kbytes and 200 kbytes, depending on the density of the FSSD (these numbers exclude spare blocks).

A file system, being a device driver, also uses some of the system's RAM. The amount of RAM required may not be important (again, as long as it's not excessive) if the device driver can be loaded high or if it runs in a protected mode environment.

System Level Issues - Ease of Use

How easily does it install? We've already discussed this subject in regards to built-in or installable device drivers. Almost all prominent BIOS vendors have been working on the solutions that will allow simple installation of the flash file systems[74]. Specifications like ExCA strive to turn all file systems into "plug-n-play" device drivers. In the next chapter, we'll take a look at how flash file systems fit into the overall PCMCIA and ExCA software solution. The key result to look for is simplicity - for a system integrator and for the end-user.

---

[74]Refer to the Appendix for a list of BIOS vendors developing PCMCIA software.

SUMMARY

A Flash Memory Solid State Drive provides the highest level of integration for flash memory devices. Although the hardware itself can be quite simple, the software required to deliver the functionality of the mechanical disk drive provides a challenge even to the most experienced software designer. This chapter was written to allow you to become familiar with the possible implementations of flash file systems and perhaps even tempt you to write your own.

Ultimately, whatever approach you select, you must ask some final questions:

✓ Does this product provide complete Windows and DOS compatibility (or compatibility with whatever operating system you are using)? Is this needed?

✓ Does the flash file system meet or exceed the requirements of your application?

✓ What are the end-user's perceptions?

Chapter Ten: PCMCIA Software

INTRODUCTION

In this chapter we'll be discussing the various pieces of software associated with integrating a flash file system into a host computer system. Chances are, when you hear the term "glue-logic" you think of hardware. The hardware glue-logic connects the major pieces of a system together (Figure 10.1). In Chapter 8 we saw that a few buffers and transceivers provided the glue-logic between the PCMCIA-compatible flash memory card and the card's interface controller (Intel's 82365SL, for example). Similarly, in the software environment of a flash file system, glue-logic connects the file system to the operating system on one end, and the flash memory card and socket adapter hardware on the other. Glue-logic software isolates a generic file system from a computer system's specific implementation.

Implementing the software glue-logic is not as simple as it may seem from this high-level view. In an ideal situation, a single file system can be used interchangeably in a variety of different machines. To do this, the file system must use standardized interfaces (i.e., glue-logic). When you buy a DOS-compatible (or Windows) application, you probably don't question whether it works on a i386 or i486 system or, for that matter, a Dell™, Compaq™ or NCR™ machine. Thanks to MS-DOS and the PC-AT specification that exists to ensure this level of standardization, common software runs on widely divergent hardware without (or with little) problems.

HARDWARE

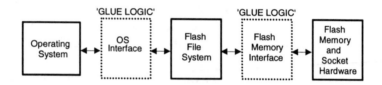

SOFTWARE

Figure 10.1: Glue Logic Holds Together the Major System Pieces

A similar situation exists within the realm of flash file systems. Specifically, the glue-logic that links the flash file system to the other system elements must adhere to some type of specification in order to achieve independence and compatibility.

THE AREAS OF SOFTWARE COMPATIBILITY

Three major software components must be comprehended for implementing a flash file system design. Later, it will become obvious how the glue-logic ties them together:

1.   *Flash File System* - As discussed in Chapter 9, flash file systems come as two basic implementations: as a disk drive emulator or as a redirected file system. A flash memory card formatted for a particular file system will not be recognized in a system running an alternative file system, even if they belong to the disk-emulator variety, for example. This fundamental issue can only be resolved by defining a media format specification that the

entire industry willingly (or unwillingly) adopts. Such specifications are currently being discussed in PCMCIA, and sooner or later standardization will be a reality. Microsoft has been contributing to this standardization by publicizing their flash file system's data structures for adoption by other flash file systems, or even by other O/S implementations of the Microsoft Flash File System. A common file structure format will eventually allow multi-platform and multi-OS inter-operability.

2.   *Host System Hardware* - Chapter 8 described multiple ways of designing the system hardware to accommodate IC cards for PCMCIA compatibility. At the system level, these cards may be accessed through memory windows or through any number of I/O ports. Each of these access methods has unlimited ways of designing the interface to the socket. Your system may be using one of the PCMCIA-controller chips or even custom discrete logic for the interface circuitry on its socket adapter.

In some situations, an OEM may even have several different computer products, each with different socket adapter hardware. Without a standardized software interface, the overabundance of possibilities makes it impossible to write just one flash file system. The ideal situation would be to take the exact same flash file system software and have it operate across the entire product line. This chapter discusses Socket Services, an integral part of a system's BIOS, that makes this possible. In other words, it provides the interface between the common flash file system and the specifics of a host adapter's implementation. Socket Services manages everything from voltage control for Vpp to selecting the memory offset within the flash memory array.

Card Services, on the other hand, resides on the *other* side of the interface. It dynamically allocates host system resources for the installed PC card. For example, before installing a flash memory card, the system does not need to keep its memory space available for the socket adapter. Upon detecting a flash memory card installation, the flash file system asks Card Services for allocation of a percentage of the host's memory map. If available, Card Services uses Socket Services to enable a window at the designated address.

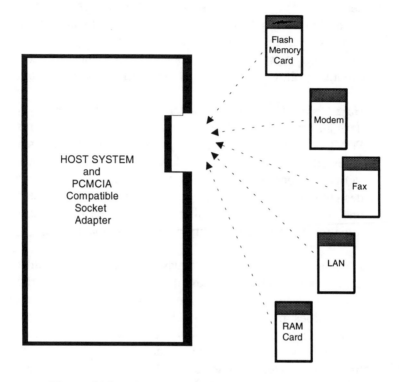

Figure 10.2: Many Types of PCMCIA-Compatible Cards can Operate in the Same Socket

3.   *Flash Memory Cards* - For the moment, assume that we could have one flash file system format and a standard host system interface. This would take care of the software glue-logic issues discussed in the two preceding paragraphs. But, how would we handle different flash memory cards? Cards from Intel, AMD, Toshiba, Mitsubishi, and Epson (to name but a few) all have slightly different internal register structures, and even entirely different flash memory components within them (Figure 10.2)

with different command interfaces, software algorithms, etc. What about the RAM cards, ROM cards, fax cards and modem cards that all fit into the same socket? A specification must be in place that allows recognition of the plethora of different cards. This chapter discusses the PCMCIA Card Information Structure (CIS) that provides this capability. After determining the flash memory card type, the correct flash memory algorithms must be employed. We will also describe the Memory Technology Driver (MTD), or flash card drivers, that serve this purpose.

THE PCMCIA-EXCA RELATIONSHIP

PCMCIA is represented by a consortium of companies that include computer OEMs, PC Card vendors, BIOS vendors and socket manufacturers. Originally, PCMCIA had several basic goals:

- Define the mechanical dimensions of the PC Card[77]
- Define the characteristics of the 68-pin electrical interface
- Define the elements of the Card Information Structure

A need soon became apparent for some sort of software interface for PC Card sockets. This led to the development and inclusion of Socket Services. It also became evident that the PCMCIA specification did not provide any system-level implementation details. So, a PCMCIA-compatible computer today guarantees only that a PCMCIA-compatible card can mechanically fit in the socket. Figure 10.3 represents PCMCIA as a general, three-dimensional specification covering processors, system architectures, and operating systems. This situation may not represent a problem for computer systems based on proprietary or closed architectures. But in the widespread PC market, standardization is critical. The 'Exchangeable Card Architecture' (ExCA) specification resolves these issues by providing implementation details of PCMCIA 2.0 for PC platforms[78]. ExCA was originated by Intel, but several groups have been pushing to incorporate it directly into PCMCIA[79]. In brief,

---

[77]The Appendix contains the measurements of Type I, Type II and Type III.
[78]To date, there have not been any analogous standards in place for other architectures.
[79]It will probably even have a different name.

ExCA compliance guarantees a minimum set of host system hardware and software interfaces that card, system, and software designers can rely on for basic compatibility (Figure 10.4 and Table 10.1).

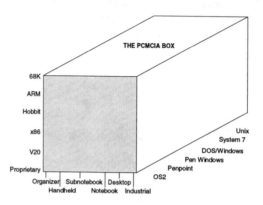

Figure 10.3: PCMCIA Provides a General, Three-Dimensional Specification Covering Processors, System Architectures, and Operating Systems

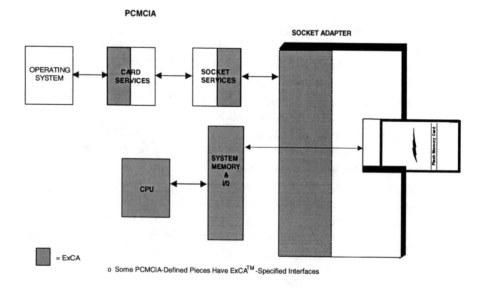

Figure 10.4: ExCA Provides a Specific Implementation of PCMCIA

PCMCIA	ExCA
* Card and Socket Mechanical Form Factors * Card and Socket Electrical Signals * Card Metaformat (i.e. CIS) * Generic Card and Socket Services	* Socket Hardware Specific to the PC Architecture (IRQs, Memory Windows, I/O Ports) * Socket Services Specific to the PC BIOS * Card Services Specific to DOS/Windows

Table 10.1: PCMCIA and ExCA Relationship

FLASH FILE SYSTEM MODELS

The Original Flash File System Model

The simplest but least flexible system model to accommodate is the "one-computer, one flash memory card type" design. In this model, the monolithic file system contains all essential pieces. In another approach, depicted in Figure 10.5, this single piece could be split into two pieces: the core file system and a low-level driver that interfaces to the hardware[80]. Regardless, running either of these in a different computer system or even using a different type of flash memory card requires modifications to the file system software. This model best fits in an embedded application where the manufacturer has complete control of the operating environment - the flash memory cards and the system don't change.

Modularizing the Flash File System Model

At the other extreme (of the Monolithic Flash File System Model), a flash file system can be split into several functional pieces. Using Microsoft's Flash File System as an example, you can see that a complete implementation actually consists of five modules (Figure 10.6).

1. *MS-FLASH.SYS* - The installable file system and redirector. As described in Chapter 9, this piece manages the media and translates commands between the operating system and the file system.

---

[80]This was the original model of Microsoft's Flash File System.

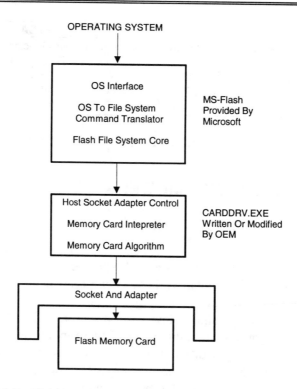

Figure 10.5: The Non-Modular Flash File System Lacked Flexibility

2.   *CARDDRV.EXE* - A memory card client device driver that interfaces to the flash file system. Originally, this piece had to be written by the OEM[81]. However, if your design implements the complete PCMCIA software model, CARDDRV.EXE can be obtained, along with Socket Services and Card Services from most major BIOS vendors (see Appendix for a list).

3.   *Card Services* - Provides five functional categories: Client Services, Resource Management, Client Utilities, Bulk Memory Services, and Advanced Client Services. It allows a system to maintain a virtual socket that can be dynamically reconfigured to work with memory cards and I/O cards.

---

[81]Sample CARDDRV.EXE source code is included in Microsoft's Flash File System OEM Adaptation Kit.

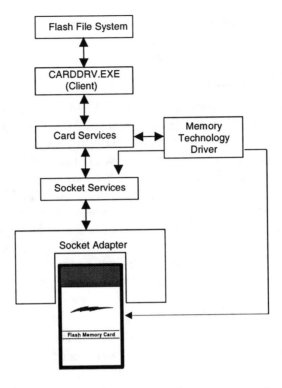

Figure 10.6: Complete and Flexible Implementation of a Flash File System Consists of Five Modules

4.　　*Memory Technology Driver (MTD)* - Handles all flash memory program/erase algorithms and specific functions associated with each flash memory card.

5.　　*Socket Services* - Provides a standardized interface to the socket hardware. The following sections on Socket Services aim to accommodate the writer as well as the user.

Although we've painted a rather "flash memory-centric" (and Intel microprocessor architecture-centric) picture, some of these modules can be expanded to include support for the other types of IC cards (collectively referred to as PC Cards). In particular, Socket Services (unofficially abbreviated S²) and Card Services are integral to the

PCMCIA 2.01 specification that supports memory and I/O cards. So from this point on, we'll expand this discussion, whenever appropriate, to include PCMCIA-compatible cards in general.

What's Really Necessary?

The exact nature of the software pieces described earlier may or may not coincide with the software model required for your hardware or operating system environment. Other flash file systems may take a simpler approach from a construction standpoint (although all have begun adapting to the PCMCIA model), but they lack the flexibility of the totally modularized model. The pieces of the software hierarchy that you decide to implement depend on the degree of flexibility required in your design. At the very least, Socket Services should be implemented to isolate the flash file system from the system's hardware. Additionally, you should consider some form of distinct upgradeable memory card driver to be able to handle future generations of flash memory cards.

SOCKET SERVICES

The concept of a S^2 first appeared within the PCMCIA specification with version 1.0 (August, 1991) and was intended for Real Mode applications only. During the development of Card Services, it became obvious that S^2 must have its applications program interface (API) modified to accommodate protected mode applications as well, leading to the next release, Version 2.0 (November, 1992). Some of the other differences between the two versions include:

- The socket base changed from 1 to 0.

- In version 1.0, a client's request for a buffer (e.g,. Window Characteristics Table) was handled by S^2 passing back a pointer to a location within itself. To accommodate the protected mode, an S^2 implementation now passes back the buffer contents in a client supplied buffer.

- The status change interrupt used to go to S^2, which then had to perform a callback to the appropriate client. This approach doesn't work in protected mode, so now the status change interrupt goes directly to the client of S^2 (e.g., Card Services) This allows the client to take the interrupt in either real or protected mode without having to shift back and forth.

Defining the Adapter Hardware

Before beginning a software-oriented discussion on the hardware-dependent S^2 software, it may be helpful for you to review some of the basic hardware design concepts from Chapter 8. While reviewing, think about how to use software to manipulate the hardware that controls and monitors a socket adapter's functions. In particular, the examples in the following discussion on S^2 will be based on Intel's 82365SL (PC Card Interface Controller, PCIC) because, at this time, it represents the most popular type of PC Card interface controller[82] and provides the compatibility reference for most other controllers now available. Even more important is this device's capability to handle most of the functions that you'll probably ever need for interfacing to a PC Card. From the concepts presented here, you should be able to extract enough understanding to write a S^2 for any socket adapter implementation in any operating system environment.

The PCIC's control and status functions are software-accessible using an indirect indexing scheme through two built-in I/O addresses. These I/O addresses allow read/write access to the PCIC's index and data registers. By default, the index and data registers are accessed at I/O addresses 3E0H and 3E1H. In order to read or write to the registers within the PCIC, the index register must first be written with a valid index (Figure 10.7). This is analogous to picking the right key for unlocking a door. This indexing method makes it possible to use only two system I/O addresses to access up to 64 individual data registers per socket, within the PCIC. While going through the following discussion, refer to the complete list of registers in the Appendix. Let's take a quick look at an example of reading the PCIC's Interface Status Register (located at index 0H and 40H for socket A and B, respectively).

---

[82]Vadem's VG-465, Cirrus Logic's CL-PD6710, and Databook's DB86082 have similar functionality. See the Appendix for more details.

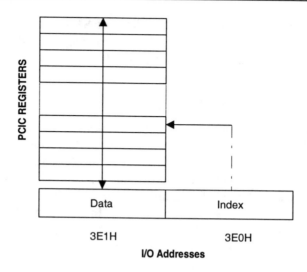

*Figure 10.7: Use an Index and Data Register Combination to Access
the PCIC's Internal Registers*

Reading Socket A's (or B's) Interface Status Register	
MOV AL, INTERFACE_STATUS	; The Interface Status Register has an offset of 1.
MOV DX, INDEX_REG	; The Index Register is I/O port 3E0H.
ADD AL, Base	; The base of socket A is 0; for B it is 40H.
OUT DX, AL	; Sets up the access.
MOV DX, DATA_REG	; The Data Register is I/O port 3E1H.
IN AL, DX	; Read from Interface Status Register.

Accessing Socket Services

The S^2 specification embodied in PCMCIA provides a list of hardware-
dependent functions that control the various pieces of a host system's
socket and associated adapter. The specification views each of its
functions as a black box. It gives explicit details of the parameters that
go in and out of the functions, but what actually happens within the
function itself depends entirely on the socket and adapter hardware
implementation (Figure 10.8). This approach is analogous to the
relationship between device drivers in the BIOS and the applications that
use them. For example, to utilize the disk drive functions provided by
the BIOS's Interrupt 13H, one only needs to know the specified registers

and parameters that must be passed within them. An application that takes advantage of any of these low-level functions (BIOS and S^2 alike)[83] can be assured of software and hardware compatibility, minimizing or eliminating the possibility of violating system integrity. Using any of these hardware-dependent functions also eliminates the need for the same code to be separately incorporated within each application that uses the socket adapter.

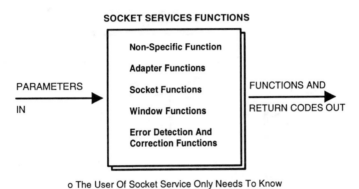

SOCKET SERVICES FUNCTIONS

o The User Of Socket Service Only Needs To Know
What Goes In And What Comes Out.

Figure 10.8: The Functions of Socket Services Act Like a Black-Box Where Parameters Go In and Out

As defined by PCMCIA, S^2 functions can be written for any processor or operating system environment. From a generic standpoint, use a format that resembles a C language function call to request the functions:

status = Function (arg1, arg2 ...)

The ExCA version (or PC implementation) of S^2 applies specifically to the Intel microprocessor platform. To be explicit, a real mode client will access the S^2 functions through INT 1AH, shared by the PC's Time-of-Day services (Figure 10.9)[84]. Standard access methods do not exist for other types of platforms and operating systems. The OEM must invent an interface that seems appropriate for a specific platform. This should

---

[83]Actually, most Socket Services will eventually be integrated into the system's BIOS.
[84]The Get/SetSSAddr function sets up protected mode access to S^2.

not be an issue in proprietary systems because compatibility will probably not be a concern and the OEM can essentially use any convenient method.

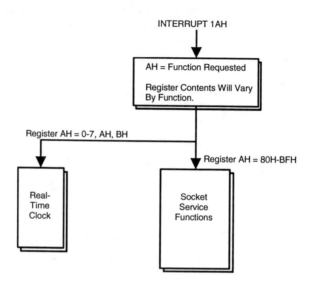

Figure 10.9: An Application Uses Interrupt 1AH to Access Socket Services or the PC's Real-Time Clock

Installing Socket Services

In a PC, S^2 may be loaded as an installable device driver or from the system's BIOS. If installing through CONFIG.SYS, it chains into the INT 1AH requests ahead of the Time-of-Day Clock, as shown in Figure 10.10 (refer to *Get/SetPriorHandler*). Loading S^2 in this manner allows some of the otherwise hard-coded values (such as the number of sockets supported and a window's base address) to be varied by using command line parameters (i.e., Device·= /parameter). This especially has value during code development for testing the same S^2 in different systems to debug any machine-specific idiosyncrasies. Incorporating S^2 directly into the BIOS, or installing it during ROM scan, allows its functions to be used during system initialization. This is particularly important if the socket adapter must be initialized in order to access a PC card containing boot information.

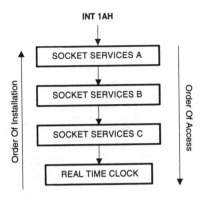

Figure 10.10: Multiple Socket Services can be Chained Together and Accessed Through the Common Entry Point of INT 1AH

THE SOCKET SERVICES FUNCTIONS

The original S² specification contained within PCMCIA supported eight functional categories. As mentioned earlier, the ExCA version of S² is almost identical to that found in the PCMCIA specification. The most notable exception is that ExCA removed the functional group for error detection and correction because it was felt that this capability would be most suitably performed within the PC Card, transparent to the system interface. Table 10.2 lists all the functions supported by PCMCIA and ExCA[85]. The table lists the functions required by the ExCA specification with the corresponding hex values that get placed into the [AH] register when calling a particular S² function[86]. For a PC implementation, all parameters and error codes get passed to and from the functions using Intel processor registers to avoid using system memory. Alternatively, for a generic implementation (e.g. using a non-Intel processor), memory variables (or CPU registers) could serve the same purpose.

---

[85] Functions not required by ExCA may optionally be supported to obtain the additional capabilities.

[86] Note that specific function values cannot be given for a PCMCIA implementation (non-ExCA) because the specification only defines a generic calling convention.

	FUNCTION	QUICK DESCRIPTION	ExCA VALUE
Non-Specific Functions	GetAdapterCount	Returns number of adapters	80H
	Reserved		81H
	Reserved		82H
	GetSSInfo	Returns compliance for S^2 implementation supporting specified adapter	83H
Adapter Functions	InquireAdapter	Returns adapter-specific information	84H
	GetAdapter	Returns adapter's configuration	85H
	SetAdapter	Sets adapter's current configuration	86H
Window Functions	InquireWindow	Returns information for window on adapter	87H
	GetWindow	Returns window's configuration	88H
	SetWindow	Sets window's configuration	89H
	GetPage	Returns page's configuration within a memory window	8AH
	SetPage	Sets a page's configuration within a memory window	8BH
Socket Functions	InquireSocket	Returns information about socket, such as status change interrupt masking	8CH
	GetSocket	Returns socket's configuration	8DH
	SetSocket	Sets socket's configuration	8EH
Card Functions	GetStatus	Returns status of PC Card and socket	8FH
	ResetSocket	Resets PC Card	90H
	Reserved by PCMCIA		91H-9CH
Vendor Specific Functions	GetVendorInfo	Returns S^2 vendor's information	9DH
	VendorSpecific	For proprietary functions	AEH
Protect-Mode and Low-Level Access	Get/SetPriorHandler	Replaces or obtains real-mode entry point for prior INT 1Ah handler	9FH
	Get/SetSSAddr	Returns entry point to S^2 and number of additional data segments required for specified mode	A0H
	GetAccessOffsets	Returns array of offsets for low-level, adapter-specific, optimized PC Card access routines	A1H
	AcknowledgeInterrupt	Acknowledge status change interrupt and identify socket causing interrupt	9EH
Error Detection and Correction Functions	GetEDC	Returns configuration of EDC generator	NA
	InquireEDC	Returns capabilities of EDC generator	NA
	PauseEDC	Pauses EDC generation	NA
	ReadEDC	Reads EDC value computed by EDC generator	NA
	ResumeEDC	Resumes EDC generation on a paused EDC generator	NA
	SetEDC	Sets configuration of EDC generator	NA
	StartEDC	Starts previously configured EDC generator	NA
	StopEDC	Stops EDC generation on a configured and computing EDC generator	NA

Table 10.2: Socket Services Functions

Non-Specific Functions

GetAdapterCount

During the installation of a client (e.g., flash file system), that client must determine the number of adapters and sockets available to it. A system may have multiple adapters, each with multiple sockets. To obtain this information, a client makes a call to *GetAdapterCount*. If successful, this function returns the total number of socket adapters within the system and verifies the existence of a functional S^2. ROM BIOS INT 1AH handlers normally return with [CF] = 1 if S^2 is absent[87]. In many cases, the adapter count will be a fixed number for a specific system implementation. This allows the adapter count to be a hard coded number within the S^2 function. Sometimes, however, an adapter may be installed as an after-market add-in to an ISA slot. This special case can be handled in one of two ways:

1. With S^2 built into the BIOS, *GetAdapterCount* must perform an I/O port scan in search of a signature on the add-in adapter board. Obviously, this implies that the adapter has to support this special I/O port feature. For example, a ROM, PLD, or PAL can be integrated into a board such that reading from a few consecutive I/O port addresses will retrieve a sequence of values representing the signature[88]. The adapter board designer must also ensure that the signature matches the value encoded into the S^2 function's search (Figure 10.11).

2. More flexibility can also be obtained by adding in the S^2 as an after-market product and installing it as a device driver via CONFIG.SYS (as opposed to being built into the BIOS). This allows the use of a command-line parameter that can be configured according to the number of adapters installed.

---

[87]This was one of the reasons INT 1AH was chosen.
[88]A PLD or PAL can also be used for the board's logic.

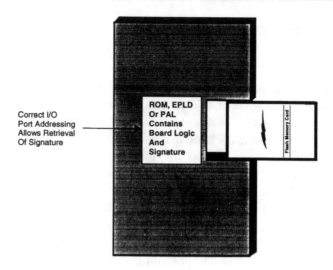

Correct I/O
Port Addressing
Allows Retrieval
Of Signature

*Figure 10.11: Reading a Signature from the Adapter Board to Identify
Its Presence*

GetAdapterCount

Entry setup for the PC version of the GetAdapterCount function:

[AH] = GET_ADAPTER_COUNT (ExCA calling value = 80H)
[CX] = 0, ensures CX doesn't contain 'SS' before making the call

After exiting from GetAdapterCount:

If [CF] = 1, function was unsuccessful
Else if
[CX] = 'SS', load ASCII 'SS' (5353h) to indicate the presence of a valid S^2
Then
[AL] = Number of Adapters Supported (0-255)

Refer to *GetSSInfo* for determining the adapter count where multiple
socket services supporting multiple adapters exist within a system.

GetSSInfo

The S^2 specification states that a particular system may support multiple S^2 implementations. Actually, this situation has a high likelihood in a system with multiple adapters, each with differing hardware characteristics. An example of this would be found in a system that contains both a resident flash array (or RFA) and flash memory cards. Removability dipicts the most obvious difference between a memory card and an RFA. This difference, among others (including how it interfaces into the system memory map), requires different adapter support and, therefore, a different S^2 to support it. Hiding behind the guise of S^2, a flash file system doesn't really care whether it's accessing flash memory in the form of an RFA or a flash memory card (Figure 10.12).

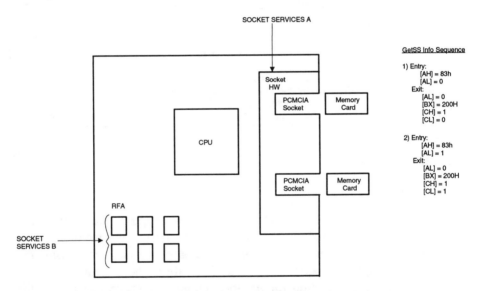

Figure 10.12: Socket Services Isolates the Differences between a Removable Memory Card and Permanently Resident Flash Array

The *GetSSInfo* function allows the client to match an adapter with a valid S^2. Each *GetSSInfo* call returns the base adapter number and the number of adapters supported by the implementation. The next S^2 implementation starts with the next adapter number (not supported by the previous implementation). Using Figure 10.12 as an example, the *GetAdapterCount* function indicates the presence of two adapters[89]. A client in this system would have to call the *GetSSInfo* function two times, once for each adapter. Just by knowing the adapter count, how would you know the number of S^2 implementations? The parameters for this function provide the number of adapters supported by a particular S^2 implementation and the first adapter it supports. This information allows the determination of the first and last adapter supported by a particular implementation. As in the example, if the two adapters were distinctly different, two S^2 implementations may be required.

GetSSInfo

Entry setup for the PC version of the GetSSInfo function:
        [AH] = GET_SS_INFO (ExCA calling value = 83H)
        [AL] = Adapter number

After exiting from GetSSInfo:
        If [CF] = 1, then [AH] = BAD_ADAPTER
        Else
    [AL] = 0, to insure backwards compatibility with Release 1.0
    [BX] = 200H, binary coded value (BCD) for Release 2.00
    [CH] = Number of adapters supported by this S^2
    [CL] = First adapter supported by this S^2 implementation in base 0 format

---

Adapter Functions

InquireAdapter

Once a client verifies the presence of S^2 and supported adapters (using *GetAdapterCount* and *GetSSInfo*), that client must determine the number of sockets and windows associated with a particular adapter by using the *InquireAdapter* function. In practice, after the client asks the *InquireAdapter* function for the total number of sockets, it passes the returned information back to MS-Flash, which in turn passes this information back to DOS. When a flash file system installs (or any block device driver, for that matter), it asks DOS to reserve drive letters for it. In this case, each socket represents one or more potential drives

---

[89]After initializing all S^2 implementations, the adapter count reflects the total number of adapters in the system.

requiring a drive letter (refer to card partitioning with the PCMCIA Data Organization Layer in the CIS section).

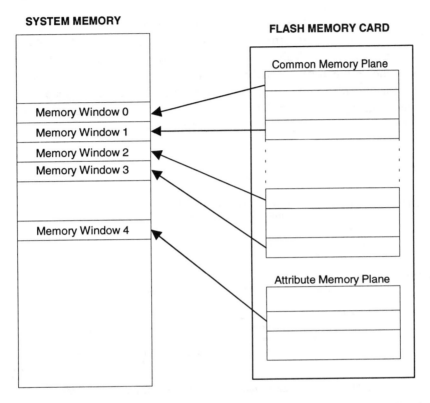

Figure 10.13: Five Memory-Mapped Windows for Flash Memory Card Access in an ExCA System

InquireAdapter also returns the number of system windows available to map these sockets. An ExCA-compliant system must support seven windows for each socket - five for memory mapping and two for I/O mapping. The five memory-mapped windows allow for support of a memory card's Attribute Memory Plane (one window) and a paging structure (four windows) similar to that required by the LIM-EMS specification (Figure 10.13). The two I/O windows allow one to be used for an address register and the other for the data register (much the same as the interface to the PCIC).

InquireAdapter returns information, in tabular form, that describes certain adapter characteristics (such as interrupt handling capabilities for status changes) and socket power characteristics (such as V_{CC} and V_{PP} voltage levels). The Adapter Characteristics and Power Management Table contains this information. A specific Adapter Characteristics and Power Management Table exists for each adapter in the system. Table 10.3 shows the format and Figure 10.14 provides an example. Notice that the *InquireAdapter* function only returns the adapter's capabilities - it has nothing to do with determining an adapter's current configuration (refer to the *GetAdapter* and *GetSocket* functions).

InquireAdapter

Entry setup for the PC version of the InquireAdapter function:

[AH] = INQUIRE_ADAPTER (ExCA calling value = 84H)
[AL] = Adapter number
[ES]:[(E)DI] = Pointer to client supplied buffer for storing the Adapter
Characteristics and Power Management Tables.

After exiting from InquireAdapter:

If [CF] = 1, then [AH] = BAD_ADAPTER
Else

[BH] = Number of windows possibly decoded into the system memory map.
NOTE: Must be 5 times the number of sockets for ExCA-compliance.
[BL] = Number of sockets (0-255)
[CX] = Number of error detection and correction generators available on the
adapter. These are not required for ExCA compliance and can be set
to zero.
[ES]:[DI] = Unchanged pointer. Buffer now contains table listed below.

Offset	DESCRIPTION
00H	Length of client supplied buffer in bytes, excluding first two words.
02H	Length of data filled by S^2, excluding first two words. If the data length supplied by S^2 exceeds the client-provided space, the S^2 supplied data will be truncated. While the Adapter Characteristics Table has a fixed length, the Power Management Table length can vary.
ADAPTER CHARACTERISTICS	
00H	Adapter capabilities. Flags indicating whether certain characteristics are controlled at the adapter or socket level (zero indicates control at the socket level). 　　Bit 0: Indicators (e.g., LEDs) for write-protect, card lock, battery status, busy status, and XIP status 　　Bit 1: Power-level control for V_{CC} and V_{PP}. If power control is available only at the adapter level, the client does not have control at the socket level, even through the use of *SetSocket*. For example, enabling V_{PP} at one socket will simultaneously enable V_{PP} at other sockets on the same adapter. 　　Bit 2: Determines if data bus width can be set separately for each window. A 1 indicates that all windows on the adapter must have the same width. Note: For ExCA-compliance, these bits must be zero (i.e., functioning at the socket level).
02H	Steerable IRQ levels for Status Change Interrupt. Each bit corresponds to an IRQ level from 0-15 (where Bit 0 = IRQ_0, Bit 1 = IRQ_1, and so on). NOTE: For ExCA compliance, at least one interrupt level must be specified. See discussion in Chapter 8 for more details on Interrupt Steering.
04H	Additional steerable IRQ levels for status change interrupt for NMI (Bit 0), I/O Check (Bit 1), and Bus Error (Bit 2).
06H	IRQ levels inverting status change where each bit corresponds to an IRQ level from 0-15 (where Bit 0 = IRQ_0, Bit 1 = IRQ_1, and so on).
08H	Additional IRQ levels inverting status change for NMI (Bit 0), I/O Check (Bit 1), and Bus Error (Bit 2).
0AH	IRQ levels not inverting status change where each bit corresponds to an IRQ level from 0-15 (where Bit 0 = IRQ_0, Bit 1 = IRQ_1, and so on).
0CH	Additional IRQ levels not inverting status change for NMI (Bit 0), I/O Check (Bit 1), and Bus Error (Bit 2).
POWER MANAGEMENT	
00H	Number of power entries to follow, where n = number of entries.
02H	Power entry: Bits 0-7 = Binary value representing a DC voltage level in tenth of a volt increments to a maximum of 25.5 volts. A power level of zero indicates a no connect or grounded. For example, 5.0 Volts = (50 × 0.1 Volts) corresponds to a value of 32H. Bits 8-12 = Reserved and equal to zero. Bit 13-15 = V_{pp2}, V_{pp1} and V_{cc} indicators, respectively, where set = available.
(2n)H	Additional supply & voltage entries (as indicated by number of power entries).

Table 10.3: Adapter Characteristics and Power Management

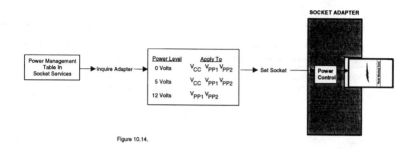

Figure 10.14.

Figure 10.14: InquireAdapter Returns Information Describing the Adapter's Capabilities, such as the Power Characteristics

By convention, all sockets on an adapter have the same power level capabilities. A power entry in the Power Management Table only indicates the possible voltage settings on a socket's power pins - it does not imply the validity of these voltage combinations. For example, V_{CC} may be set to zero and V_{PP} to 12 volts, but this is probably not a valid combination. The S^2 client has the responsibility of ensuring the validity of a particular combination of power levels for the PC card when using the *SetSocket* function.

Take a look at a specific example of an Adapter Characteristics and Power Management Table (Table 10.4) to use for reference and help clarify the definitions.

SetAdapter

The *SetAdapter* function handles an adapter's power management and controls the status change interrupt routing (i.e., card detect and ready/busy). Many systems being built with PCMCIA sockets have implemented some form of power management scheme. At the hardware level, the system's adapter capabilities determine the varying degrees of possible power management. This does not reflect power management capabilities of the PC card itself. Some socket interface controllers provide automatic power savings mechanisms. For example, the PCIC automatically enters into a low power state after disabling memory and I/O windows, and when sockets become empty. Likewise, Cirrus Logic's CL-PD6720, automatically enters a low power mode during periods of inactivity. Additionally, PCMCIA socket interface controllers have software programmable modes of power conservation, such as suspend mode.

Offset	Value	Description
00H	0016H	Client supplies 22-byte buffer.
02H	0016H	S^2 filled buffer with 22 data bytes.
00H	0000H	Indicates adapter capability control at the socket level. By restricting the use of capabilities to be at either the adapter or the socket level, a client does not have to provide two types of controlling routines.
02H	E053H	Status changes may be routed to IRQ levels 0, 1, 4, 6, 13, 14, and 15 as an active high signal. This provides a high degree of flexibility in selecting an interrupt level.
04H	0000H	No additional IRQ levels
06H	0000H	Status changes are not available on any level as an active low signal
08H	0000H	No additional IRQ levels
0AH	0000H	No additional IRQ levels
0CH	0000H	No additional IRQ levels
00H	0003H	Number of power entries = 3
02H	E000H	V_{CC}, V_{PP1} and V_{PP2} available as 'No-Connects'
04H	E032H	V_{CC}, V_{PP1} and V_{PP2} available at 5.0 Volts
06H	6078H	V_{PP1} and V_{PP2} available at 12.0 Volts

Table 10.4: Example Adapter Characteristics and Power Management

---

SetAdapter

Entry setup for the PC version of the SetAdapter function:
        [AH] = SET_ADAPTER (ExCA calling value = 86H)
        [AL] = Adapter_number
        [DH] = Adapter Control
                Bit 0 = Reduce Adapter Power Consumption ('1' = true)
                Bit 1 = Preserve Adapter State ('1' = true)
                Other bits are reserved and must equal 0.
        [DI] = Status Change Interrupt
                Bits 0-4 = IRQ level, (0 - 15 = IRQ 0-15, 16 = NMI, 17 = I/O Chk, 18 = Bus Error)
                Bit 6 = Enable Inverter (0 = disable, 1 = enable)
                Bit 7 = Enable Status Change Interrupts
                Other bits are reserved and must be 0.
After exiting from SetAdapter:
        If [CF] = 1, then [AH] = BAD_ADAPTER, BAD_ATTRIBUTE, BAD_IRQ

Two control bits have been defined to handle the power conservation capability:

1.   REDUCE ADAPTER POWER CONSUMPTION
      (Adapter_State_Powerdown) - Setting this bit indicates that the adapter should attempt to enter a power conservation mode. Again, this depends on the adapter's capabilities. If the adapter lacks this capability, the function can either ignore the request or return a BAD_ATTRIBUTE error. When resetting the adapter hardware, or before using the adapter, reset this bit to restore full power.

      In addition to being able to control power to the socket, the PCIC itself can be powered down using its Global Control Register (Figure 10.15). After setting the Power-Down bit and disabling all memory windows (see *SetWindow*) with an inactive chip select signal, this device enters its lowest power mode.

      NOTE: ExCA does not require this and the next field (Preserve Adapter State).

2.   PRESERVE ADAPTER STATE *(Adapter_State_Maintain)* - Setting this bit indicates that, before the adapter enters its power conservation mode, the adapter hardware should maintain all adapter and socket configuration information. Devices such as the PCIC provide this capability. Clearing this bit indicates that the client will handle configuration information. This functionality may support different levels of power conservation. For example, the adapter hardware may be able to enter the lowest power state if it does not have to maintain the configuration information (i.e., this requires keeping some circuitry powered-up). On the other hand, an adapter may be unable to support the maintenance of the configuration information. In this case, a request to enter the power conservation mode, in conjunction with a request for the adapter to maintain configuration information, will probably be ignored (or reported back as a bad attribute) by the S^2 function.

Alternatively, the S^2 function, if requested to maintain configuration information, may store it in a RAM data area. This should be avoided, if possible, to minimize the system RAM usage.

NOTE: Adapter_State_Powerdown must be set for this control bit to be valid.

82365SL GLOBAL CONTROL REGISTER

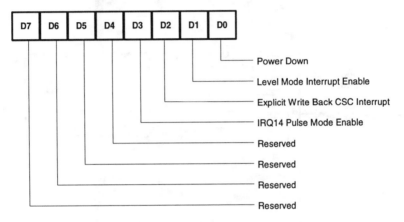

Figure 10.15: The Global Control Register Powers Down the PCIC

SetAdapter also sets up the status change interrupt routing. PCMCIA does not require a system to implement a status change interrupt (but ExCA does), so in some cases, it may not do any good to try and configure this interrupt. Your application will determine the adapter hardware's capability to support the status change interrupt by using the *InquireAdapter* function (Figure 10.16 points out the difference between an adapter interrupt and a socket interrupt). After determining that a system doesn't support status change interrupts, the S^2 could simply ignore any such requests and report back with a success status. On the other hand, reporting back as a failure will keep the client from waiting for an event that will never happen due to the lack of an interrupt signal (i.e., card detect change).

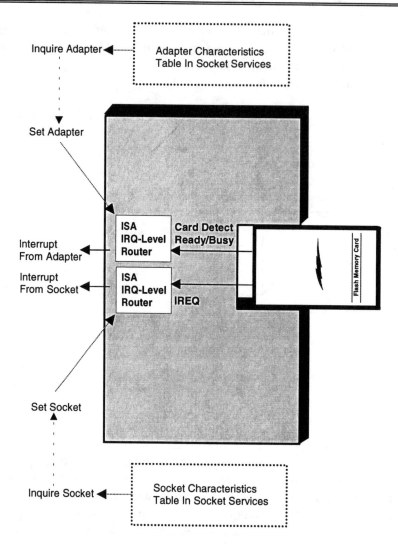

*Figure 10.16: Distinguishing Between an Adapter Interrupt and a
Socket Interrupt*

Using the example Adapter Characteristics Table (Table 10.4), we see
that for the imaginary system this table pertains to, it supports status
change interrupts that may be routed to IRQ 0, 1, 4, 6, 13, 14, and 15.
On adapters that do not have programmable status change level logic,

the desired interrupt setup must match the actual hardware or S^2 will fail the request. A request will also fail if your application tries to set up a specific IRQ level not supported by the adapter.

Three fields have been defined in the *SetAdapter* function to support the programmable status change interrupt:

1.   *IRQ_LEVEL* - Use the five bits in this field to represent, as a binary value, the routing of the status change interrupt.

2.   *ENABLE_INVERTER* - The status change interrupt is active high after setting this bit (referred to as IRQ_HIGH by PCMCIA). Clearing the bit inverts the interrupt.

3.   *ENABLE_SC_INTERRUPTS* - After setting this bit, an unmasked status change event causes the adapter to generate a hardware interrupt at the level specified by IRQ_Level. Perform the masking at the socket level using the *SetSocket* function (Figure 10.17).

The PCIC and compatible devices control the IRQ level and enabling of status change interrupts using the Card Status Change Interrupt Configuration Register (Figure 10.18). Table 10.5 shows how to set the appropriate bits in this register according to the desired interrupt routing (not including reserved bit combinations). The Level Mode Interrupt Enable bit in the Global Control Register configures the active state of the interrupt (Figure 10.15).

IRQ BIT 3	IRQ BIT 2	IRQ BIT 1	IRQ BIT 0	INTERRUPT REQUEST LEVEL
0	0	0	0	No Interrupts
0	0	1	1	IRQ3 Selected
0	1	0	0	IRQ4 Selected
0	1	0	1	IRQ5 Selected
0	1	1	1	IRQ7 Selected
1	0	0	1	IRQ9 Selected
1	0	1	0	IRQ10 Selected
1	0	1	1	IRQ11 Selected
1	1	0	0	IRQ12 Selected
1	1	1	0	IRQ14 Selected
1	1	1	1	IRQ15 Selected

Table 10.5: Card Status Change Interrupt Steering

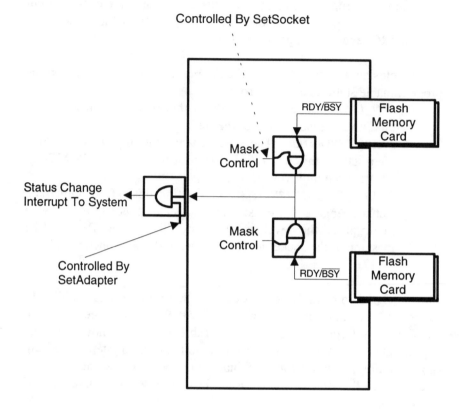

Figure 10.17: Mask Status Change Interrupts at the Socket Level,
Enabling Them at the Adapter Level

NOTE: Before using the *SetAdapter* function, use *GetAdapter* to determine previous configurations. This allows the client to perform a read-modify-write when changing the adapter's configurations.

GetAdapter

For system integrity, an application should determine the adapter's current configuration before making any alterations. Unlike

InquireAdapter (returning the adapter's capabilities) *GetAdapter* returns the adapter's current configuration. This function's parameters mirror those of the *SetAdapter* function.

82365SL CARD STATUS CHANGE INTERRUPT CONFIGURATION REGISTER (READ/WRITE)

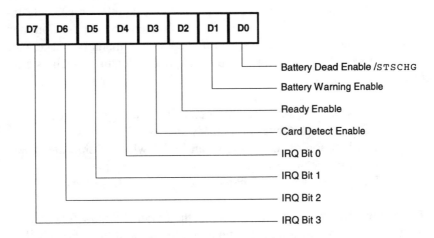

Figure 10.18: Writing a One to Bits 0-3 Enables the Corresponding Status Change to Generate an Interrupt

GetAdapter

Entry setup for the PC version of the GetAdapter function:
    [AH] = GET_ADAPTER (ExCA calling value = 85H)
    [AL] = Adapter number
 	
After exiting from GetAdapter:
    If [CF] = 1, then [AH] = BAD_ADAPTER
    Else
    [DH] = Adapter State (Same bit map as SetAdapter)
    [DI] = Status Change Interrupt Routing (Same bit map as SetAdapter)

Window Functions

InquireWindow

Any access to a PC Card must be through some window into the host system memory or I/O space. Windows allow direct access to Attribute Memory, Common Memory, or I/O ports. For example, an eXecute-In-Place (XIP) application requires the flash memory card's Common Memory to be mapped directly into the system memory space (see Figure 10.35). These windows have some generic features, such as size, location and their associated sockets:

- The window's size typically ranges from a single address for an I/O port to 64 Kbytes of memory space.
- The location of the window can be anywhere within the access space of the host system.
- Each window may be shared amongst multiple sockets.

To narrow down the possible variations, the *InquireWindow* function has been designed to return information about the capabilities of a specified window on an adapter.

InquireWindow

Entry setup for the PC version of the ExCA InquireWindow function:
    [AH] = INQUIRE_WINDOW (ExCA calling value = 87H)
    [AL] = Adapter number
    [BH] = Window number (use InquireAdapter to obtain the total number of windows)
    [ES]:[(E)DI] = Pointer to client-supplied buffer for storing Window Characteristics Table.

After exiting from InquireWindow:
    If [CF] = 1, then [AH] = BAD_ADAPTER, BAD_WINDOW
    Else
    [BL] = Window Capabilities (1 = true)
        Bit 0 = Common memory plane may be mapped into host system memory space
        Bit 1 = Attribute memory plane may be mapped into host system memory space
        Bit 2 = I/O ports on card may be mapped into host system I/O space
        Bit 7 = Window uses PC Card's WAIT signal to generate additional wait states
    [CX] = Assignable Socket Bit Map
    [ES]:[(E)DI] = Pointer to buffer containing the Window Characteristics Table

Windows support memory and/or I/O. After determining a window's capabilities (Common Memory, Attribute Memory, or I/O), the S^2 client can determine all the mapping characteristics of that window by interpreting the appropriate Window Characteristics Table returned in the buffer. To this effect, the Window Characteristics Table may be for memory or I/O. The tables are similar, with the exception that I/O windows omit the memory-specific parameters. When a window supports both memory and I/O, the I/O Characteristics Table will always immediately follow the Memory Characteristics Table within the buffer.

When using PCIC-compatible controllers, a window's capability can be determined within this function by using the interface type bits (Table 10.6) from the Identification and Revision Register (Figure 10.19). Since the PCIC supports both memory and I/O, these bits will read back as "10". Although all PCIC-compatible controllers support both memory and I/O, this register was incorporated into the device to provide a defacto standard for PCMCIA controllers.

Bit Values (bits 6 and 7)	Interface Type
00	I/O only
01	Memory only
10	Memory and I/O
11	Reserved

Table 10.6: Interface Identification for PCIC-Compatible Controllers

- The "assignable socket bit map" means that each bit corresponds to a socket number on the adapter that can be mapped into the specified window. For example, Bit 0 corresponds to Socket 0, Bit 1 corresponds to Socket 1, etc. To simplify matters, the bit map can be FFFFH for a window that supports all sockets on an adapter.
- Depending on the adapter's design, a window may be assignable to more than one socket or dedicated to a particular socket.
- The window can only be assigned to one socket at a time (i.e., multiple sockets must time-share).
- The size of the assignable socket bit map field limits the number of sockets that a window may support. In the parameter settings

shown above, the [CX] register limits the number of sockets to 16.

82365SL IDENTIFICATION AND REVISION REGISTER (READ ONLY)

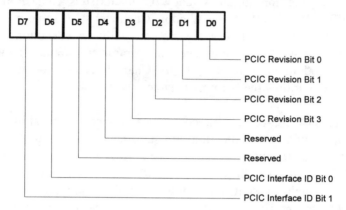

Figure 10.19: Determine the Interface Type from the Identification and Revision Register in PCIC-Compatible Controllers

---

Definitions of a Window

You may be wondering how a specific system window can support both memory and I/O capabilities. This is a good time to look more closely at the definition of a window. Actually, the concept of a window has two meanings:

1. A window provides a method for connecting an area of a host system's memory or I/O port space to a PC Card's memory or I/O space. When the system sends out an address that corresponds to the area designated for the window, the decoding hardware selects the PC Card, which then becomes accessible to the system. Aside from requiring different CPU instructions, the I/O and memory read/write signals represent a significant difference between the two types of windows.

2. A window also defines a label used by S^2 for configuring the socket adapter's hardware. S^2 views a window as an object that it can control. Therefore, a client can request S^2 to configure a window for memory or I/O.

The definitions above may lead you to believe that S^2 can reconfigure a window for memory or I/O. However, an adapter will probably not be built to change its decoding signals to switch between memory and I/O accesses to the PC Card; this would require complex decoding circuitry. For this reason, you will very rarely find a Memory and I/O Window Characteristics Table associated with the same window.

Offset	DESCRIPTION	
00H	Length of client supplied buffer in bytes, excluding first two words.	
02H	Length of data filled by S^2, excluding first two words. If the data length supplied by S^2 exceeds the space provided by client, the S^2 supplied data will be truncated.	
	MEMORY WINDOW CHARACTERISTICS	
00H	Memory Window Capabilities (1 = true)	
	Bit 0	Programmable Base Address (NOTE: Must be true for ExCA compliance)
	Bit 1	Programmable Window Size (NOTE: Must be true for ExCA compliance)
	Bit 2	Window Disable/Enable Supported (NOTE: Must be true for ExCA compliance)
	Bit 3	Eight-Bit Data Bus Supported
	Bit 4	Sixteen-Bit Data Bus Supported
	Bit 5	Base Address Alignment On Size Boundary
	Bit 6	Power of Two Size Granularity
	Bit 7	Card Offset Alignment on Size Boundary
	Bit 8	Paging Hardware Available
	Bit 9	Paging Hardware Shared
	Bit 10	Page Disable/Enable Supported
	Bit 11	Software Write-Protect Available
	Other bits are reserved and equal to zero	
02H	Minimum Address/First Byte (4Kbyte blocks)	
04H	Maximum Address/Last Byte (4Kbyte blocks)	
06H	Minimum Window Size (4Kbyte blocks)	
08H	Maximum Window Size (4Kbyte blocks)	
0AH	Required Window Size Granularity (4Kbyte blocks)	
0CH	Required Base Address Alignment (4Kbyte blocks)	
0EH	Required Card Offset Alignment (4Kbyte blocks)	
10H	Slowest Access Speed Supported	
11H	Fastest Access Speed Supported	

Table 10.7: Memory Window Characteristics

Memory Window Capabilities (Figure 10.20)

Programmable Base Address (WC_BASE, Bit 0)

When this bit equals one, it indicates that the window's base address is programmable within the range specified by the minimum and maximum address fields (see offsets 02H and 04H in the Memory Window Characteristics Table). The flexibility of a programmable base address comes in handy when the computer user attempts to use add-in boards that require access to the host's memory.

A zero in this bit indicates a fixed window base address in the system's memory space at the address specified by the minimum address field (invalidating the maximum address field). Many closed systems hardwire their windows at a specific address because the need for flexibility does not exist. For example, an embedded system with all of its functionality built-in at assembly time will not need to accommodate future add-in modifications. A system like this can tolerate a non-changing window base address. This also simplifies the client software.

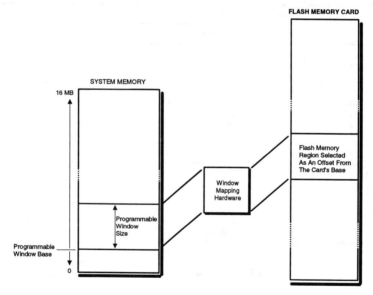

Figure 10.20: As the Memory Window Chacteristics Table Indicates, the Base Address and Size may be Programmable

Programmable Window Size (WC_SIZE, Bit 1)

Similar to the programmable base address, a one in this bit indicates a programmable window size within the range specified by the minimum and maximum window size fields (see offsets 06H and 08H in the Memory Window Characteristics Table). This flexibility can be important in certain situations, depending on the amount of system memory available. In other words, different run-time applications consume varying amounts of system memory. When running an application that consumes a small amount of system memory, the system can afford to provide a larger window size, or vice versa.

When this bit equals zero, the window has a fixed size. This may be desirable in some systems, as it simplifies the client software that manipulates memory card offsets.

Window Disable/Enable Supported (WC_WENABLE, Bit 2)

When this bit equals one, the window may be disabled and enabled without having to reprogram its characteristics. Interface controller chips such as the PCIC support this capability by maintaining register contents. Specifically, disabling and enabling the windows has no affect on the corresponding memory and I/O registers in the PCIC. Power management software may take advantage of this capability, using the *SetAdapter* function.

When this bit equals zero, the adapter does not automatically maintain the window characteristics. This responsibility passes to the client requesting the window disabling. To do this, the client uses the *GetWindow* function to retrieve the current configuration, that can be restored after re-enabling the window.

Eight and Sixteen Bit Data Bus Supported (WC_8BIT and WC_16BIT, Bits 3 and 4)

When either or both of these bits equal one, this window supports the corresponding data bus size(s). PCMCIA defines the data-bus size on a

PC Card to be 8 or 16 bits to accomodate either type of system. This flexibility has the most usefulness in a system where the system incorporates the socket adapter as an add-in board. This allows the same board to be used in an 8 or 16-bit slot. Otherwise, if the socket adapter is fixed on the system's mother board, the bus size can also be fixed in accordance with the bus size of the CPU.

The Adapter Characteristics Table obtained using the *InquireAdapter* function contains information that indicates whether the adapter can set the data bus width separately for each window. The S^2 client must interpret this information before trying to adjust a window's data bus size.

Base Address Alignment on Size Boundary (WC_BALIGN, Bit 5)

When this bit equals one, the window's base address must be programmed to some multiple of the window's size within the specified valid range. This helps simplify the adapter's decoding circuitry, because it minimizes the number of address lines that must be decoded. ExCA requires the system base address boundary alignment to be at any 4Kbyte segment.

When this bit equals zero, the window's base address may be programmed at any address (meeting the constraints imposed by the Required Base Address Alignment field) within the specified valid range. Although this provides higher flexibility, it complicates the decoding circuitry.

Power of Two Size Granularity (WC_POW2, Bit 6)

When this bit equals one (and the window size is programmable), window size must be a power of two of the required window size granularity. For example, a required window size granularity of 4 kbytes has possible window sizes (between a 4 kbyte minimum and 64 kbyte maximum size) of 4, 8, 16, 32 and 64 kbytes. Similar to the description earlier (Base Address Alignment on Size Boundary), the lower the flexibility, the simpler will be the decoding circuitry.

When this bit equals zero (and the window size is programmable), window size can be any multiple of the required window size granularity. For example, with a required window size granularity of 4 kbytes and a specified window size range from 4 kbytes to 64 kbytes, the window sizes can be any of the sixteen multiples of 4 kbytes contained within that range.

Card Offset Alignment on Size Boundary (WC_CALIGN, Bit 7)

When this bit equals one, the PC Card offsets must be specified to the *SetPage* function in increments of the window's size. For example, a 4 kbyte window size requires the PC Card offsets to be on 4 kbyte boundaries. For hardware decoding, as well as from a software perspective, this makes the most sense. When this bit equals zero, PC Card offsets can be specified without relation to the window's size.

Paging Hardware Available (WC_PAVAIL, Bit 8)

When this bit equals one, the windowing hardware can divide the window into multiple pages, for memory space only. A zero indicates that the window must be treated as a single page. According to the PCMCIA specification, a window can only be sub-divided into 16 kbyte pages (Figure 10.21). If the software implemented (i.e., flash file system) requires multiple pages, it is generally easier to use multiple windows because of decoding hardware simplification and the flexibility of a window's size and location (within the bounds of the Memory Window Characteristics Table). Typically, system designers have implemented windows without pages.

Paging Hardware Shared (WC_PSHARED, Bit 9)

Windows may share paging hardware when this bit equals one. Pay attention when attempting to use the paging hardware for a window because it may already be in use by another window. A client can determine the availability of the paging hardware via the *SetWindow* function, checking for a successful return status. Trying to use already-busy paging hardware should return an error. This bit will be zero in a system with dedicated window paging hardware.

Page Disable/Enable Supported (WC_PENABLE, Bit 10)

When this bit equals one, the page may be disabled and enabled without having to reprogram its characteristics. When WC_PENABLE equals zero, the adapter hardware does not automatically maintain page characteristics and this responsibility passes to the client requesting the page disabling. To do this, the client uses the *GetPage* function to retrieve the current configuration, which can be restored after re-enabling the page.

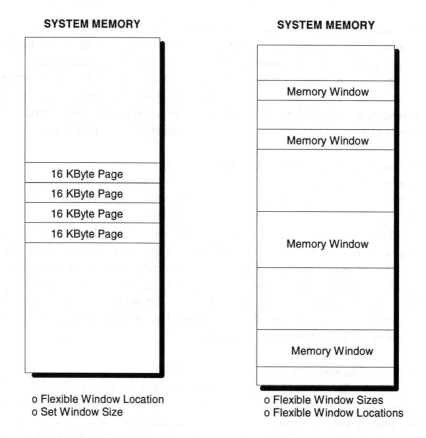

Figure 10.21: Contrasting Windows Divided into Pages and Multiple Windows

Software Write-Protect Available (WC_WP, Bit 11)

When this bit equals one, the window has software-controlled write protect capability; preventing writes to the PC Card. The hardware that controls this can do so by blocking the $\overline{\text{WE}}$ signal whenever it detects a system write to the address range corresponding to the window. Use

SetPage to invoke this capability, available with the PCIC and compatible devices (Card Memory Offset Address High Byte Register, Figure 10.27).

When this bit equals zero, the window may not be software write-protected. Alternatively, you can enable write protection by using a PC Card's write protect switch. Intel's Series 2 Flash Memory Cards also provide a Write Protection Register that allows write protection of certain areas of the flash memory array.

Minimum and Maximum Address (FirstByte and LastByte)

These fields represent the first and last addressable bytes (respectively) for this window in the system memory space. Values depend on the adapter's decoding capabilities and components occupying other parts of the memory space. These fields can be defined in terms of 4 kbyte units. This allows a word to accommodate up to 256 Mbytes. Some non-ExCA systems have windows with non-programmable base addresses (refer to Programmable Base Address bit). Therefore, the minimum address value added to the maximum window size also determines the maximum address, or LastByte (Figure 10.22).

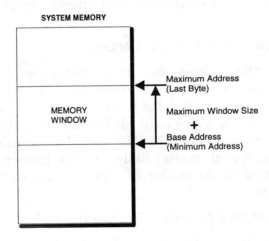

Figure 10.22: Minimum and Maximum Memory Window Address

The last byte of the window (base address + window size - one) may not exceed the value in the maximum address field. Some non-ExCA systems have windows with non-programmable base addresses (i.e., fixed). This situation invalidates the "Maximum address/Last byte" field.

Minimum and Maximum Window Size (MinSize and MaxSize)

These fields represent the range of sizes allowable for a window within the system memory map. They can be defined in terms of 4 kbyte units. This allows a word to accommodate up to 256 Mbytes. Expressing the maximum window size as zero indicates the largest window size value that may be represented by the "SIZE data type plus one". For example, a 16-bit SIZE data type supports a maximum of 65535 (0FFFFH). Adding 1 to this generates a zero, defined as 65536 (64 kbytes). The size programmed with the *SetWindow* function must also meet the requirements described by the following fields:

- Power-of-two size granularity
- The minimum address plus the window size, minus one, must not exceed the maximum address

These two fields will be equal with a fixed window size (i.e., WC_SIZE = 0)

Required Window Size Granularity (ReqGran)

This field gives the minimum units for expressing window size due to hardware constraints, and can be expressed as 4 kbyte units. For example, a one indicates that the window size can be expressed in multiples of 4 kbytes. With a fixed window size (WC_SIZE = 0), this field will be the same as the MinSize and MaxSize fields. Systems designed with special paging hardware will have window size restrictions based on the number of address lines generated by the paging hardware.

Required Base Address Alignment (ReqBase)

When the Base Address Alignment on Size Boundary (WC_BALIGN) bit equals zero, this field describes any alignment boundary requirement for programming the window's base address with *SetWindow*. Expressed in 4 kbyte units, a value of one indicates that the window's base address can be placed on any 4 kbyte boundary.

If WC_BALIGN equals one, the base address is some multiple of the window's size specified within the valid range (see WC_BALIGN above). In this situation, the ReqBase field is undefined. Figure 10.23 exemplifies this situation.

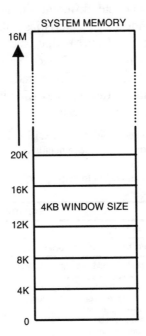

Figure 10.23: Example Showing Potential Base Address for a 4 Kbyte Window that Must Reside on a Multiple of the Window's Size

Required Card Offset Alignment (ReqOffset)

When the WC_CALIGN bit equals zero, this field describes any alignment boundary requirement for programming the PC Card offset address with *SetPage*. For example, in an implementation using units of 4 kbyte blocks, a one in this field indicates the card offset could be placed on any 4 kbyte boundary.

If WC_CALIGN equals one, PC Card offsets must be specified in increments of the window's size (see WC_CALIGN above). In this situation, the ReqOffset field is undefined.

Fastest and Slowest Access Speed Supported

Flash cards (and memory cards, in general) exist in a variety of configurations and access speeds. Some socket hardware adapters may be reconfigured to accomodate different timing requirements. These fields in the Memory Window Characteristics Table express the range of access speeds (slowest to fastest) that the socket hardware can accomodate. These fields match the Device Speed Code and Extended Device Speed Codes of the Device Information Tuple defined in the PCMCIA PC Card Standard Release 2.0 (Section 5.2.7.1.3). The bit-mapped fields are expressed as follows:

Bits 0-2   = Device speed code, if mantissa is zero
            = Speed exponent, if speed mantissa is non-zero
Bits 3-6   = Speed mantissa
Bit 7   = Reserved and equal to zero

OFFSET	VALUE	DESCRIPTION
00H	12H	Client-supplies 18-byte buffer
02H	12H	Length of data filled by S^2 is 18 bytes.
00H	089FH	Programmable base address and window size Window disable/enable supported Eight and sixteen-bit data bus supported Base address alignment on size boundary Power of two size granularity Card offset alignment on size boundary No paging hardware capability Software write-protect available
02H	00C0H	Minimum base address equals C0000H
04H	00DFH	Maximum base address DF000h (4Kbytes less than E0000H)
06H	0001H	Minimum window size equals 4Kbytes
08H	0010H	Maximum window size equals 64Kbytes
0AH	0001H	Required window size granularity expressed in 4Kbyte units
0CH	0001H	Window can be aligned on any 4Kbyte boundary
0EH	0001H	Card Offset Alignment on any 4Kbyte boundary
10H	01H	Slowest access speed equals 250 nanoseconds
11H	04H	Fastest access speed equals 100 nanoseconds

Table 10.8: Example Memory Window Characteristics

Offset	DESCRIPTION
00H	I/O window capabilities (1 = true) Bit 0: Programmable base address Bit 1: Programmable window size Bit 2: Window disable/enable supported Bit 3: Eight-bit data bus supported Bit 4: Sixteen-bit data bus supported Bit 5: Requires base address alignment on size boundary Bit 6: Power of 2 size granularity Bit 7: INPACK supported Other bits are reserved and equal to zero
02H	Minimum base address/First byte (Bytes)
04H	Maximum base address/Last byte (Bytes)
06H	Minimum window size (Bytes)
08H	Maximum window size (Bytes)
0AH	Required window size granularity (Bytes)
0CH	Number of address lines decoded by the socket hardware

Table 10.9: I/O Window Characteristics

Fields In The I/O Window Characteristics Table

As mentioned earlier, most fields in the I/O and Memory Window Characteristics Tables are the same, with a few exceptions:

- The I/O fields associated with addresses are expressed in bytes rather than 4 kbyte blocks.
- Addresses reference the I/O space rather than memory space.

I/O Window Capabilities

The descriptions in the Memory Window Characteristics Table apply for all I/O windows characteristics, with the following exceptions:

INPACK (WC_INPACK)
EISA-LIKE I/O MAPPING (WC_EISA)
EISA ADDRESS ENABLES (WC_CENABLE)

Number of Address Lines Decoded by Socket Hardware (AddrLines)

Despite the fact that systems containing processors like an Intel CPU have the potential to access up to 64 kbyte I/O addresses, many systems do not decode all address lines. For example, an ISA platform only decodes 10 address lines allowing accesses up to 1 kbyte, and any access above 1 kbyte will be aliased to an address within the first 1 kbyte.

SetWindow

When using the *SetWindow* function to change a window's configuration, be sure to match the desired configuration with the allowable configuration obtained from the appropriate window characteristics table supplied by *InquireWindow*. Viewed another way, the client should use the *InquireWindow* function to determine if the window had characteristics suitable for its application.

SetWindow

Entry setup for the PC version of the SetWindow function:
        [AH] = SET_WINDOW (ExCA calling value = 89H)
        [AL] = Adapter number
        [BH] = Window number
        [BL] = Socket number
        [CX] = Window Size (Bytes for I/O windows, 4Kbyte units for memory windows)
        [DH] = Window state
                Bit 0   Window type (WS_IO), 1 = I/O window, 0 = memory window
                Bit 1   Enable Window (WS_ENABLED), 1 = enable, 0 = disable
                Bit 2   Data path width (WS_16BIT), 1 = 16-bit, 0 = 8-bit
                Bit 3   Paged (WS_PAGED), 1 = divide into 16 Kbyte pages, 0 = single page or I/O mapping type (WS_EISA), 1 = EISA I/O mapping, 0 = ISA I/O mapping
                Bit 5   1= EISA common I/O areas configured to generate card enables, 0 = ignore accesses to I/O ports in EISA common I/O areas
                Other bits are reserved and equal to zero
        [DL] = Requested access speed (refer to InquireWindow function)
        [DI] = Window base address (bytes for I/O, 4 Kbyte units for memory)

After exiting from SetWindow:
        If [CF] = 1, then [AH] = BAD_ADAPTER, BAD_ATTRIBUTE, BAD_SIZE, BAD_SPEED, BAD_WAIT, BAD_BASE, BAD_PAGE, BAD_SOCKET, BAD_TYPE, BAD_WINDOW

Window Size

The *SetWindow* function allows a client to set up the specified window's size within the system's memory or I/O space. An application should typically request as large a window as possible to achieve the highest performance. For example, a flash file system will generally request a window size up to 64 kbytes. This will save having to frequently update the flash card's offset.

If the *SetWindow* function returns with a BAD_SIZE error, you should first check the Programmable Window Size field in the corresponding window characteristics table. You may be trying to program a fixed size window. However, if your system has a programmable window size, check the legality of the desired value. Determine the legal values from a combination of the Power of Two Size Granularity, the Minimum and Maximum Window Size, and the Required Window Size Granularity fields.

Refer to the Window Base Address field for specific details on using the PCIC to set up Window Size.

WINDOW STATE

Window Type

From the *InquireWindow* function, a client can determine whether a window supports memory (Common or Attribute), I/O or both. Since this book specifically discusses flash memory, assume that all windows discussed here support memory. When programming devices like the PCIC, selecting a memory window type allows the *SetWindow* function to configure the memory window registers (as opposed to the I/O window registers).

Enable Window

Before enabling the window, set up the proper configuration, including the window's start and stop addresses and the card's offset. Assuming that the client has done this, enabling the window from a hardware standpoint consists of turning on the appropriate decoder signal(s). This allows matching addresses to generate the card select signals. The PCIC makes this operation simple with the Address Window Enable Register

(Figure 10.24). This register contains five memory window enable bits - one for each window.

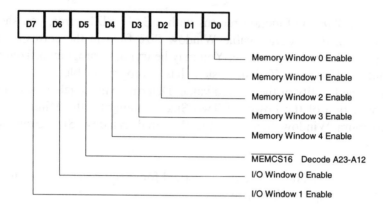

Figure 10.24: *Use this Register to Enable and Disable Memory and I/O*
Windows

Data Path Size

What are the advantages of a flexible data bus size? For a socket adapter built into a system's motherboard, you would assume that the bus size could be fixed according to the data path of the processor. However, the ability to control the data path size plays a significant role in four situations:

1.   The first and probably most important situation pertains to the use of I/O cards. In particular, modem and fax cards that transfer data in bytes (rather than words) require an 8-bit data path. Memory cards have a 16-bit interface, and although data could be transferred in bytes, the transfer should be done in words, if possible, for highest data bandwidth.

2.   The second situation pertains to a PC Card's Attribute memory plane, which PCMCIA defines to be valid only at even-byte locations. So, although you can access the Attribute memory plane in words, the odd byte will return invalid data in this case.

3. The third and least apparent situation has to do with after-market socket adapters add-ins. To add flexibility to the adapter, it can be designed to plug into an 8 or 16-bit system ISA slot.

4. When using the ISA-bus to interface between the CPU and a flash memory card, beware that the socket adapter cannot use the memory COMMAND signal lines (i.e., $\overline{\text{MEMR}}$ and $\overline{\text{MEMW}}$) to qualify a 16-bit access. It blindly decodes the LA_{17-23} signal lines and activates $\overline{\text{MEMCS16}}$ if required. As a result, the entire 128 kbyte block selected by LA_{17-23} must be the same data width. Therefore, the flexible data bus size allows more convenient memory mapping.

I/O Mapping Type

This value only has validity for I/O windows. It has applicability for ATA flash drives.

REQUESTED ACCESS SPEED

The format of this parameter corresponds to the Fastest and Slowest Access Speed Supported fields obtained through the *InquireWindow* function. A system may not support every possible speed requested, even if it falls within the legal limits. If a client requests an unsupported speed, S^2 defaults to using the next slower supported speed. For example, a client may request an access time of 130 nanoseconds. If the hardware only supports 120 and 150 nanoseconds, 150 ns will be selected.

The PCIC controls this function using the Wait-State select bits of a System Memory Address Mapping Stop High Byte Register (Figure 10.25). These bits control the number of additional wait states for a 16-bit access to the system memory window. When the client reads the Card Information Structure (CIS), it can determine the speed of the flash memory card and, therefore, the number of wait states needed.

SYSTEM MEMORY ADDRESS 0 MAPPING STOP LOW BYTE REGISTER (READ/WRITE)

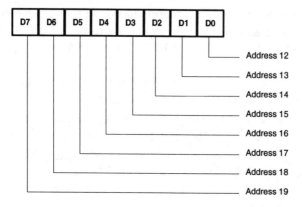

SYSTEM MEMORY ADDRESS 0 MAPPING STOP HIGH BYTE REGISTER (READ/WRITE)

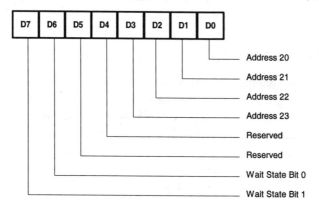

Figure 10.25: These PCIC Registers Control the Access Speed and Determine the Stop Address of the Corresponding Memory Window

WINDOW BASE ADDRESS

When setting the window base address, the client must consider the window's maximum address and size. Referring to the *InquireWindow* function, the last byte of the window (base address + window size - 1) may not exceed the value in the maximum address field.

Using the PCIC or compatible devices, a client sets up a system's memory window address with four registers (there are actually five sets of these four registers, one for each window):

1. *System Memory Address Mapping Start Low and High Byte Registers* (Figure 10.26)- These registers set up the base address of the window. The address bits in the low register start at 12, automatically placing the window's base address on 4 kbyte boundaries. Loading these registers within the *SetWindow* function is simplified because the base address (and all other memory-related addresses) get passed to the function in 4 kbyte units already. This means that the S^2 function can load the value as it appears in the input parameters. Therefore, the calling client must manipulate the start address. For example, a desired base address of D0000H would be changed to D0H by the client. It would then use D0H as the value to pass in with the [DI] register.

2. *System Memory Address Mapping Stop Low and High Byte Registers* (Figure 10.25) - These registers indirectly specify the window's size. Since the address bits begin at 12, the smallest window size will be 4 kbytes. The process for loading these registers follows the same protocol as the System Memory Address Mapping Start Low and High Byte Registers.

NOTE: Before using the *SetWindow* function to change the current window configuration, it may be useful to first call upon the *GetWindow* function to ensure that you don't overwrite an existing setup. The *GetWindow* and *SetWindow* functions assist this comparison by having directly-mapped input and output parameters.

GetWindow

In general, good coding practice warrants the use of the *GetWindow* function to check a window's current configuration before attempting to make any changes. The only time when this should not be necessary is during system initialization. In this case, the initializing code can proceed directly to the *SetWindow* function. Regardless of which function you use first, these two functions have directly mapped parameters. Therefore, for full parameter details, refer to the *SetWindow* function.

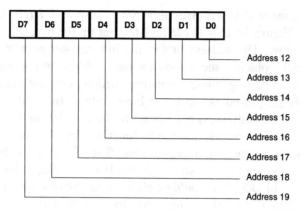

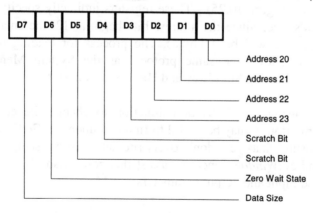

Figure 10.26: These PCIC Registers Set Up the Base Address of the System Memory Window

---

GetWindow

Entry setup for the PC version of the GetWindow function:
        [AH] = GET_WINDOW (ExCA calling value = 88H)
        [AL] = Adapter number
        [BH] = Window number

After exiting from GetWindow:
        If [CF] = 1, then [AH] = error code (BAD_ADAPTER, BAD_WINDOW)
        Else
        [BL] = Socket number assigned to this window
        [CX] = Window size (bytes for I/O windows, 4 Kbyte units for memory windows)
        [DH] = Window state
                Same bit map as SetWindow
        [DL] = Access speed (refer to InquireWindow function)
        [DI] = Window base address (bytes for I/O, 4 Kbyte units for memory)

Besides determining a window's configuration, a client may also use this function to determine if a window has been previously assigned to a socket. One by one, the client may call the *GetWindow* function with a different window number until locating an available window (obtain the total number of windows using *InquireAdapter*). A socket number of zero in the [BL] register indicates that the window has not been assigned to a socket. After locating an unused window, the client can now proceed to the *SetWindow* function and configure that window for its own use.

SetPage

This function, only applicable to memory windows, configures the specified page, or offset, in the flash memory card according to the input parameters. As discussed in the *InquireWindow* function, a window can consist of one or more pages (but it usually doesn't). Typically, once a client requests S^2 to set up a window, that window stays fixed (for example, from D0000H to DFFFFH). On the other hand, a page within the flash memory card (not to be confused with a page in system memory) must have its offset continuously updated in order to access different regions (Figure 10.20).

```
                              SetPage

Entry setup for the PC version of the SetPage function:
          [AH] = SET_PAGE (ExCA calling value = 8BH)
          [AL] = Adapter number
          [BH] = Window number
          [BL] = Page number
          [DX] = Page control
                    Bit 0     Memory Plane Select (PS_ATTRIBUTE), 1 = Attribute, 0 =
                              Common
                    Bit 1     Enable Page (PS_ENABLED)
                    Bit 2     Write protect page (PS_WP), 1 = write protect, 0 = no write
                              protect
          [DI] = Memory card offset (4 Kbyte units)

After exiting from SetPage:
          If [CF] = 1, then [AH] = BAD_ADAPTER, BAD_ATTRIBUTES, BAD_OFFSET,
              BAD_PAGE, BAD_WINDOW)
```

Memory Plane Select

This bit controls the manipulation of the $\overline{\text{REG}}$ pin (Register select of the PC Card's interface) that selects between the Attribute or Common memory planes. The window capabilities of the *InquireWindow* function indicates whether this capability exists.

The PCIC and compatible devices handle this function with the Card Memory Offset Address High Byte Register (Figure 10.27).

Enable Page

For a window with a single page, this function performs the same function as the Enable Window of the *SetWindow* function. However, if a window consists of several pages, this function must be able to selectively control the enabling and disabling of individual pages.

Write Protect Page

Write protecting a page can be a matter of blocking the write enable signal whenever the system generates an address within that page. If a window contains multiple pages, each page must have this capability independent of the others. When a client attempts to use this software write protection mechanism but the capability doesn't exist, a BAD_ATTRIBUTES error will be reported upon returning from this function. To avoid this error, analyze the appropriate Memory Window Characteristics (returned by *InquireWindow*) first.

CARD MEMORY OFFSET ADDRESS 0 LOW BYTE REGISTER (READ/WRITE)

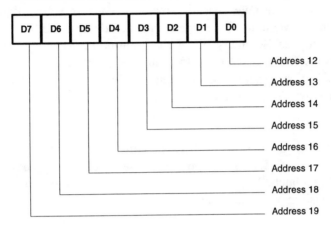

CARD MEMORY OFFSET ADDRESS 0 HIGH BYTE REGISTER (READ/WRITE)

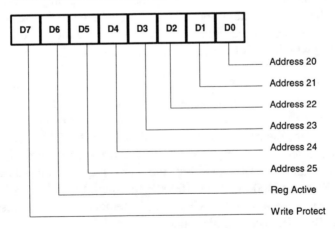

Figure 10.27: These PCIC Registers Set Up the Flash Memory Card's Offset, Enables Write Protection, and Selects the Memory Plane

The PCIC and compatible devices handle this function with the Card Memory Offset Address High Byte Register (Figure 10.27).

Memory Card Offset

First, and foremost, note that the memory card offset is typically expressed in 4 kbyte units. Second, a client should check the Card Offset Alignment on Size Boundary bit of the appropriate Memory Window Characteristics Table. If set, the offset must be specified as a multiple of the size of the associated host's window. For example, a 64 kbyte window size would allow memory card offsets of 0, 64 kbytes, 128 kbytes, etc.

In a simple hardware design that uses a paging mechanism to access the flash memory card, setting up the card offset could simply consist of programming a latch. The value loaded into the latch represents a region within the flash memory card's array.

The PCIC uses two registers to set up the flash memory card's offset (it actually has five sets of these two registers per socket, one for each of the five windows) - The Card Memory Offset Address Low and High Byte Registers (Figure 10.27). The address bits, starting at 12, allow offsets to be on any 4 kbyte boundary within the card. These registers contain the value to be added to the host's memory address for determining which part of the card will be accessible.

As shown in Figure 10.28, when the host system generates an address within its window, that address must be translated to allow access to the various regions within the flash memory card. As an example, assume a 64 kbyte system memory window located at D0000H. The client wants to access the second 64 kbytes of flash memory on the card. The host outputs the address D0000H, but the card requires an address of 10000H. Subtract D0000H from 10000H to obtain the value (F40000H) that must be plugged into the PCIC's Card Memory Offset Address Low and High Byte Registers. This value can also be expressed as the 2's-complement of the difference between the system memory start address and the start address on the flash memory card.

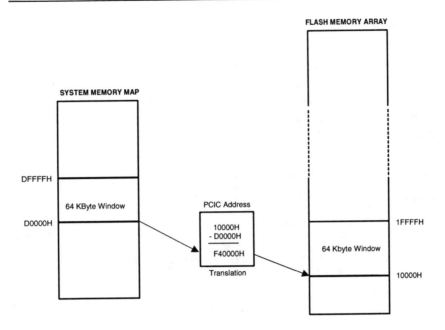

Figure 10.28: Translating System Addresses to Access Various Regions within the Flash Memory Card

GetPage

This function returns a specific page's current configuration within a specific memory window. Refer to the *SetPage* function for parameter explanations.

GetPage

Entry setup for the PC version of the GetPage function:
        [AH] = GET_PAGE (ExCA calling value = 8AH)
        [AL] = Adapter number
        [BH] = Window number
        [BL] = Page number
 	
After exiting from GetPage:
        If [CF] = 1, then [AH] = error code (BAD_ADAPTER, BAD_PAGE,
                BAD_WINDOW)
        Else
        [DX] = Page state (Same bit map as SetPage)
        [DI] = Memory card offset (4Kbyte units)

Socket Functions

InquireSocket

The characteristics obtained by the *InquireAdapter* function primarily describe the available power levels and the adapter's physical connection to the ISA bus' ten interrupt request lines. A separate socket characteristics table describes a PC card's physical connection capabilities (through the IREQ signal[90]) to one of these interrupt request lines.

```
                           InquireSocket
Entry setup for the PC version of the InquireSocket function:
        [AH] = INQUIRE_SOCKET (ExCA calling value = 8CH)
        [AL] = Adapter number
        [BL] = Socket number, this function must be called once for each socket that the
               application plans on using
        [ES]:[(E)DI] = Pointer to client supplied buffer for storing the socket
               characteristics table.

After exiting from InquireSocket:
        If [CF] = 1, then [AH] = BAD_ADAPTER, BAD_SOCKET
        Else
        [BH] = Bit map of status change interrupt capabilities (SC_INT_CAPS, set to 1 =
               true)
               Bit 0     Write Protect Change
               Bit 1     Card Lock Change
               Bit 2     Ejection Request
               Bit 3     Insertion Request
               Bit 4     Battery Dead Change
               Bit 5     Battery Warning Change
               Bit 6     Ready Change
               Bit 7     Card Detect Change
        [DH] = Bit map of status change reporting capabilities (SC_RPT_CAPS, set to 1
               = true)
               Same as status change interrupt capabilities
        [DL] = Bit map of control and indicator capabilities (CTL_IND_CAPS , set to 1 =
               true)
               Bit 0     Write Protect Status (Indicator)
               Bit 1     Card Lock Status (Indicator)
               Bit 2     Motorized Card Ejection (Control)
               Bit 3     Motorized Card Insertion (Control)
               Bit 4     Card Lock (Control)
               Bit 5     Battery Status (Indicator)
               Bit 6     Busy Status (Indicator)
               Bit 7     Execute-in-Place (XIP) Status (Indicator)
        [ES]:[(E)DI] = Unchanged buffer pointer.
```

---

[90]This pin functions as a Ready/Busy signal for memory cards and as IREQ for I/O cards.

Figure 10.16 pictorially describes the difference between the two types of interrupt connections. Before the client begins to initialize the adapter and socket hardware, the *InquireSocket* function must be called to obtain the Socket Characteristic Table. Similar to the *InquireAdapter* function, *InquireSocket* only returns the capabilities of the sockets. It has nothing to do with determining a socket's current configuration (refer to the *GetSocket* function).

- *STATUS CHANGE INTERRUPT CAPABILITIES* - Identifies items that can cause a status change interrupt (bit set). To trigger a status change interrupt on a socket, the corresponding value in the status change interrupt mask of *SetSocket* must be set, and status change interrupts must be enabled.

- *STATUS CHANGE REPORTING CAPABILITIES* - Identifies items that the installed socket hardware can report. These may not necessarily have an interrupt generating capability, but their status may be obtained through the *GetSocket* and *GetStatus* functions. Some clients (and some systems) do not utilize interrupts for status change notification. Instead, the client software performs periodic polling to check status. For example, the system's time-of-day clock, updated every 55 milliseconds, can be used to provide the time period.

- *CONTROL AND INDICATOR CAPABILITIES* - Identifies items which can be <u>controlled</u> or represented by <u>indicators</u> on the hardware. For example, an LED may be used to indicate the setting of the write protect switch or a flash memory card's ready/busy status. An indicator for ready/busy status is highly recommended. This will notify the system user when the flash memory card is busy and minimize the chance of inadvertant card removal during an operation.

The Socket Characteristics Table and Adapter Characteristics Table are identical with two exceptions:

1.   Sockets use the PC card's IREQ line versus the adapter's status change interrupt.

2.   A field describing the interface type supported (e.g., memory only or I/O and memory) replaces the adapter capabilities field.

SOCKET CHARACTERISTICS TABLE[91]	
00H	Socket interface type supported where: Bit 0 = Memory only Bit 1 = I/O and memory Note: A system can be PCMCIA compatible but not support an I/O interface. This means that a person purchasing a PCMCIA-compatible system has no guarantee of its capabilities. On the other hand, an ExCA-compliant system must support both interfaces.
02H	Steerable IRQ levels where each bit corresponds to an IRQ level from 0 to 15 (where Bit 0 = IRQ_0, Bit 1 = IRQ_1, and so on). See discussion in Chapter 8 for more details on Interrupt Steering.
04H	Additional steerable IRQ levels for NMI (Bit 0), I/O Check (Bit 1), and Bus Error (Bit 2).
06H	IRQ levels inverting IREQ line, where each bit corresponds to an IRQ level from 0 to 15 (where Bit 0 = IRQ_0, Bit 1 = IRQ_1, and so on).
08H	Additional IRQ levels inverting IREQ line for NMI (Bit 0), I/O Check (Bit 1), and Bus Error (Bit 2).
0AH	IRQ levels not inverting IREQ line, where each bit corresponds to an IRQ level from 0 to 15 (where Bit 0 = IRQ_0, Bit 1 = IRQ_1, and so on).
0CH	Additional IRQ levels not inverting IREQ line for NMI (Bit 0), I/O Check (Bit 1), and Bus Error (Bit 2).

SetSocket

The *SetSocket* function controls a range of operations, from status change interrupt masking to setting V_{CC} and V_{PP} voltage levels.

---

[91] Although not shown here, the first two words of this table provide the size of the client-provided buffer and the length of the data that Socket Services returns.

```
                              SetSocket

Entry setup for the PC version of the SetSocket function:
        [AH] = SET_SOCKET (8EH)
        [AL] = Adapter number
        [BL] = Socket number
        [BH] = Status Change Interrupt Enable Mask (0 = mask, 1 = enable; same bit
               map as InquireSocket)
        [CH] = V_CC level (lower nibble)
        [CL] = V_PP1 level (upper nibble), V_PP2 level (lower nibble)
        [DH] = Socket State Control (1 = reset state; same bit map as InquireSocket)
        [DL] = Controls and Indicators (1 = on; same bit map as Inquire Socket)
        [DI] = IRQ Steering and Interface Type Control
               Bits 0-4: Values 0-15 = IRQ 0-15, 16 = NMI, 17 = I/O Check, 18 = Bus
                         Error
               Bit 5: Enable IREQ inverter (1 = enabled)
               Bit 7: Enable IREQ steering (1 = enabled)
               Bit 8: Memory only interface (This interface invalidates IREQ-related
                      bits)
               Bit 9: I/O and Memory interface

After exiting from SetSocket:
        If [CF] = 1, then [AH] = BAD_ADAPTER, BAD_ATTRIBUTE, BAD_INDICATOR,
               BAD_IRQ, BAD_SOCKET, BAD_VCC, BAD_VPP
```

- *STATUS CHANGE INTERRUPT MASK ENABLE* - This mask determines which status change can cause an interrupt. It only has effect if the specific interrupt is supported, as indicated by the status change interrupt capabilities (obtained from the *InquireSocket* function), and if status change interrupts have been enabled by *SetAdapter*. Although interrupts get generated at the adapter level (which explains why the *SetAdapter* function enables the status change interrupts), this mask provides the capability to mask interrupts at the socket level (Figure 10.17).

Bits in the Card Status Change Interrupt Configuration Register of the PCIC, defined as interrupt enabling bits, provide the masking for the *SetSocket* function (Figure 10.18). For example, bit 2, the Ready Enable bit, controls the appropriate mask by enabling or disabling the specific interrupt.

- V_{CC} *AND* V_{PP} *LEVELS* - This field specifies an index into the array of power entries in the Power Management Table returned by *InquireAdapter*. Individual values are specified for V_{CC}, V_{PP1} and V_{PP2}. The *SetSocket* function takes the input parameters, looks into the table and sets the sockets accordingly (Figure 10.14). This function must ensure that the specified voltages make sense. For example, setting V_{CC} to 0V and V_{PP} to 12V should be defined as an invalid combination.

To demonstrate setting V_{CC} to 5 volts and V_{PP1}/V_{PP2} to 12 volts, refer to the example Power Management Table (Table 10.4) and the entry setup for *SetSocket* listed above. From the table, "2" indexes V_{CC} at 5 volts and "3" indexes V_{PP} at 12 volts. Therefore, the [CH] and [CL] registers would be loaded with 02H and 33H, respectively, before calling *SetSocket*.

Use a V_{PP} power switch (discussed in Chapters 6 and 8) to accommodate the voltage capabilities depicted in the Power Management Table (Table 10.3). The switch must decode the inputs to activate the desired voltage level. The PCIC provides each socket with 5 power control pins for controlling V_{CC}, V_{PP2} and V_{PP1}. The Power Control and RESETDRV Register shown in Figure 10.29 controls these pins. PC Card Power Enable (Bit 4) acts as a global socket power control. Clearing this bit disables all power to the socket, including V_{CC}, V_{PP2} and V_{PP1}. Setting this bit puts 5 volts on V_{CC} and enables V_{PP1} and V_{PP2} according to bits 0 through 3. Table 10.10 describes the relationship between the register's bit settings and the state of the V_{PP1} control pins. A similar relationship exists for V_{PP2}. You can decide, for your specifications, how to decode these output signals to the voltage switch.

POWER AND RESETDRV CONTROL REGISTER (READ/WRITE)

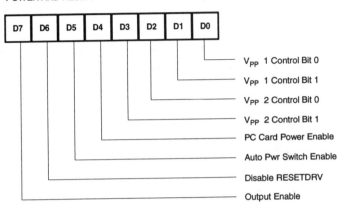

Figure 10.29: This PCIC Register, Power Control and RESETDRV, Controls a Socket's Voltage Levels

Bit 4	Bit 1	Bit 0	V_{PP1}_EN1	V_{PP1}_EN0
1	0	0	0	0
1	0	1	0	1
1	1	0	1	0
1	1	1	0	0
0	X	X	0	0

Table 10.10: Controlling V_{PP} Enable Signals with the PCIC's Power Control Register

- SOCKET STATE CONTROL - This field resets latched values representing state changes (after setting the corresponding bit) experienced by the socket hardware. It must allow selective state changes, and requires a one to have an effect. In other words, writing a zero to any bit must have no effect. This field only supports the capabilities obtained from *InquireSocket*.

In the PCIC, the Card Status Change Register contains the status of the sources for the card status change interrupts (Figure

10.30). Clearing select status bits in the PCIC requires a two step process:

1.   Set the "Explicit Write Back Card Status Change Acknowledge" bit in the Global Control Register (Figure 10.15). This bit unlocks access to the individual bits of the Card Status Change Register.

2.   Write a 1 to the appropriate bit in the Card Status Change Register. This performs the same function as acknowledging a specific interrupt. Once acknowledged, the corresponding bit in the CSCR reads back as zero.

CARD STATUS CHANGE REGISTER (READ ONLY)

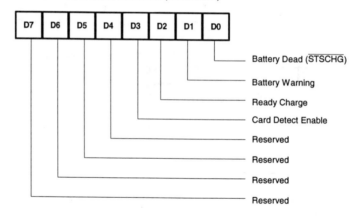

Figure 10.30: The Card Status Change Register Reports on the Source of the Status Change

•   *CONTROL AND INDICATORS* - This field turns indicators and other mechanisms on or off, if supported (one = on, zero = off). The *InquireSocket* function identifies the supported capabilities. Ignore requests to control unsupported capabilities. Switches supporting control capabilities can be built into the system as an

I/O port (Figure 10.31), or the indicators can be taken directly from the PC Card's interface[92].

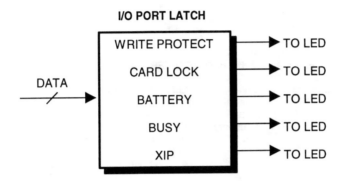

I/O PORT LATCH

Figure 10.31: Use an I/O Port to Control the Socket's Indicators

- *IREQ_LEVEL* - This field controls the steering of the interrupt request level for the PC Card, only valid for I/O cards.

- *ENABLE_INVERTER* (referred to as IRQ_HIGH by PCMCIA) - Set this flag to have an active high signal on the PC Card's IREQ signal. Reset this flag to invert the interrupt. It is only valid for I/O cards.

- *ENABLE_STATUS_CHANGE_INTERRUPTS* - After setting this flag, an unmasked IREQ event will cause the socket to generate a hardware interrupt at the level specified by IRQ_Level.

GetSocket

For system integrity, an application should use *GetSocket* to determine a socket's current configuration (unlike *InquireSocket*, which returns the socket's capabilities) before making alterations with *SetSocket*. The parameters of this function directly map into the *SetSocket* function.

---

[92]Use something like a latched buffer or an 8255.

GetSocket

Entry setup for the PC version of the GetSocket function:
        [AH] = GET_SOCKET (ExCA calling value = 8DH)
        [AL] = Adapter number
        [BL] = Socket number

After exiting from GetSocket:
        If [CF] = 1, then [AH] = BAD_ADAPTER, BAD_SOCKET
        Else
        [BH] = Status Change Interrupt Enable Mask (0 = masked, 1 = enabled; same
                bit map as SetSocket)
        [CH] = V_{CC} level (lower nibble)
        [CL] = V_{PP1} level (upper nibble), V_{PP2} level (lower nibble)
        [DH] = Socket State (1 = state change experienced; same bit map as SetSocket)
        [DL] = Control and Indicator State (1 = on; same bit map as SetSocket)
        [DI] = IRQ Steering and Interface Type State (same bit map as SetSocket)

Card Functions

GetStatus

Q: What's the first thing you need to do before using a flash memory card?

A: Determine if it's in the socket.

Card presence represents one of the most important responsibilities of the *GetStatus* function. During system power up, the socket hardware should be initialized. The events that occur during socket and adapter initialization vary from system to system. From a hardware perspective, initialization means anything from turning on the socket's power to setting up interrupts to enabling address windows. The degree of initialization depends on whether or not a socket contains a PC card when the system initializes.

On the other hand, when removing or inserting a card, the interrupt handler should call the *GetStatus* function and verify the cause of the status change interrupt. Earlier when we explained the indexing mechanism of the PCIC, the example code demonstrated access to the Interface Status Register (Figure 10.32). As shown below for a PC implementation, the *GetStatus* function returns the information obtained from the Interface Status Register in the [BH] register.

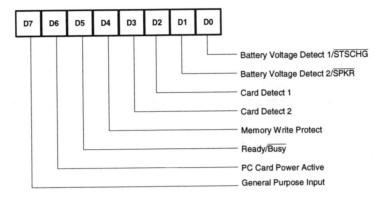

82365SL INTERFACE STATUS REGISTER

- Battery Voltage Detect 1/$\overline{STSCHG}$
- Battery Voltage Detect 2/$\overline{SPKR}$
- Card Detect 1
- Card Detect 2
- Memory Write Protect
- Ready/$\overline{Busy}$
- PC Card Power Active
- General Purpose Input

Figure 10.32: Read the Interface Status Register with the GetStatus Function to Determine the Presence of a Card

---

GetStatus

Entry setup for the PC version of the GetStatus function:
  [AH] = GET_STATUS (ExCA calling value = 8FH)
  [AL] = Adapter number
  [BL] = Socket number, this function must be called once for each socket in system.

After exiting from GetStatus:
  If [CF] = 1, then [AH] = BAD_ADAPTER, BAD_SOCKET
  Else
  [BH] = Current card state (1 = true)
      Bit 0: Write Protected, reflects the card's write protect switch via the WP output
      Bit 1: Card Locked into socket
      Bit 2: Ejection Request, this monitors a socket's eject button
      Bit 3: Insertion Request
      Bit 4: Reflects the output of BVD_1 and BVD_2 (1 = buy new batteries, but not if the card is flash memory!)
      Bit 5: Battery Low
      Bit 6: Card Ready, reflects the output of the Ready/Busy pin (1 = card ready)
      Bit 7: Card Detected, reflects the AND-ed value of the CD_1 and CD_2 pins
  [DH] = Socket state (Same function as GetSocket)
  [DL] = Control and indicator state (Same function as GetSocket)

ResetSocket

In general, the reset function enables the user to place a card into a power-on default state (or more appropriately, return from an unknown state). *ResetSocket*, as well as *GetStatus*, can be called after card detection as the first step in card installation. Many PC cards, especially I/O cards, have registers that occasionally need to be reset. For example, Intel's Series 2 Flash Memory Cards contain several registers (known as Component Management Registers) that can be reset.

PCMCIA defines two ways of resetting a PC card:

1.   *SOFT RESET* - Toggle the Reset bit in the PCMCIA-defined Configuration Option Register. A client using the card handles this operation, not S^2.

2.   *HARDWARE RESET* - Use *ResetSocket* to invoke a hardware reset through the PC card's RESET pin. *ResetSocket* must complete an entire RESET pulse, from reset state and back to the non-reset state, ensuring the observance of the minimum reset pulse width. In a PCIC implementation, *ResetSocket* controls the PC Card's Reset pin using the PC Card RESET bit (bit 6) of the Interrupt and General Control Register (Figure 10.33). Clearing this bit activates the RESET signal to the PC card. This signal remains active until setting this bit. After returning from *ResetSocket*, some cards may require an additional time delay after reset before being accessed. The client must account for this. For example, the resetting of Intel's Series 2 Flash Memory Card temporarily forces all the devices into a deep sleep mode. After being woken up (coming out of reset), a 600 nanosecond delay must be met before accessing a flash memory component within the card.

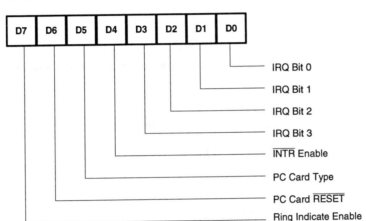

INTERRUPT AND GENERAL CONTROL REGISTER (READ/WRITE)

| D7 | D6 | D5 | D4 | D3 | D2 | D1 | D0 |

- IRQ Bit 0
- IRQ Bit 1
- IRQ Bit 2
- IRQ Bit 3
- $\overline{\text{INTR}}$ Enable
- PC Card Type
- PC Card $\overline{\text{RESET}}$
- Ring Indicate Enable

Figure 10.33: Writing to this PCIC Register Activates the PC Card's Reset State

---

ResetSocket

Entry setup for the PC version of the ResetSocket function:
        [AH] = RESET_SOCKET (ExCA calling value = 90h)
        [AL] = Adapter number
        [BL] = Socket number

After exiting from ResetSocket:
        If [CF] = 1, then [AH] = BAD_ADAPTER, BAD_SOCKET, NO_CARD

Vendor Specific Functions

GetVendorInfo

This function returns ASCIIZ information about the vendor implementing S^2 for the specified adapter. During initialization, this information could be displayed on the screen.

GetVendorInfo

Entry setup for the PC version of the GetVendorInfo function:
        [AH] = GET_VENDOR_INFO (ExCA calling value = 9DH)
        [AL] = Adapter number
        [BL] = Type (0 = ASCIIZ string describing implementor, other values not defined
                yet)
        [ES]:[(E)DI] = Pointer to client supplied buffer for ASCIIZ string

After exiting from GetVendorInfo:
        If [CF] = 1 then [AH] = BAD_ADAPTER, BAD_FUNCTION
        Else
        [DX] = Vendor's Release Number (BCD-encoded)
        [ES]:[(E)DI] = Unchanged pointer, buffer now contains ASCIIZ string.

Vendor's Release Number

A few simple rules about this field:

1.　　The vendor must update this value with each new release.
2.　　The initial release, represented as Release 1.0, uses the value 0100H (returned in [DX]).
3.　　Subsequent releases should update this value according to the vendor's customary procedures.
4.　　The vendor should reset this value to 0100H when releasing a new version that maintains compliance with a new PCMCIA S^2 specification.
5.　　The combination of the compliance level returned by the *GetSSInfo* function and the vendor's release number of each S^2 must be unique.

For general implementations, the information provided by the ASCIIZ string can be anything you want, as long as it fits in the buffer. When the client passes the buffer to S^2, the first word indicates the buffer size. When S^2 returns the buffer, the second word tells the client how many bytes were passed back in the buffer. An ExCA-compliant S^2 must have "ExCA Vx.xx" at the beginning of the ASCIIZ string[93].

---

[93]The x.xx refers to the ExCA-compliance level associated with this version of S^2

VendorSpecific

With this free-for-all you can do with it what you like. Add custom extensions. Hide secret test code. From the client perspective, check the *GetVendorInfo* function first to confirm the implementor and validate the availability of this function. On the other hand, if this function has no support, it should return an UNSUPPORTED_FUNCTION error code.

VendorSpecific

Entry setup for the PC version of the 'What_Ever_You_Want_To_Call_It' function:
    [AH] = VENDOR_SPECIFIC (ExCA calling value = AEH)
    [AL] = Adapter number
    All other registers are vendor specific.

After exiting from 'What_Ever_You_Want_To_Call_It':
    If [CF] = 1 then [AH] = BAD_ADAPTER, UNSUPPORTED_FUNCTION, or
            anything you want
    Else
    The rest is left for you.

Protected Mode and Low-Level Access Functions

Get/SetPriorHandler

Some systems, as exemplified in the discussion on *GetSSInfo*, require more than one S² implementation. The access points to each S² implementation must be chained together using the *Get/SetPriorHandler* (GSPHandler) function to locate the links.

Get/SetPriorHandler

Entry setup for the PC version of the Get/SetPriorHandler function:
    [AH] = GET_PRIOR_HANDLER (ExCA calling value = 9FH)
    [AL] = Adapter number
    [BL] = Mode (0 = Get, 1 = Set)
    If [BL] = 1
    [CX]:[DX] = Pointer to handler

After exiting from Get/SetPriorHandler:
    If [CF] = 1 then [AH] = BAD_ADAPTER, UNSUPPORTED_FUNCTION
    Else
    [CX]:[DX] = Pointer to handler

The GSPHandler has several purposes:

1.   Adding a new implementation (as in the case of an add-in socket adapter) to a system that already has one installed. When adding a new one, use the *Get* mode to get the prior handler's address for the new one to use. When using the INT 1AH calling method, the adapter number specified in the call determines the S^2 implementation that handles the call. Each implementation passes the call down to the next S^2 implementation in the chain, until the call reaches the implementation that handles the specified adapter.

2.   Hooking a new implementation ahead of, or superceding, a prior one. This requires both a *Get* and *Set* mode.

Regardless of the purpose, the *GSPHandler* function only needs to be called once for each S^2 implementation. The *GetSSInfo* function returns information that ties a specific implementation to the adapter(s) it supports. As an example, assume that one S^2 implementation supports adapter numbers 0-3 and another S^2 implementation supports adapter number 4. So the *GSPHandler* can be called twice, first with a zero and second with a four.

Get/SetSSAddr

This pair of functions primarily sets up protected mode access into Socket Services. It also sets up the addresses for any data areas used by S^2. To avoid redundancy, the details of this function can be obtained in the PCMCIA specification.

GetAccessOffsets

Certain adapters, such as that used in some of Databook's card reader/writers[94], require a register-based approach and a basic command set to access a flash memory card (refer to Chapter 8). The *GetAccessOffsets* function allows the client using this type of adapter to obtain the code location for each of these basic commands, which for each S^2 will be specific for the associated adapter.

---

[94]See the appendix for a list of card reader/writers.

GetAccessOffsets

Entry setup for the PC version of the GetAccessOffsets function:
    [AH] = GET_ACCESS_OFFSETS (A1H)
    [AL] = Adapter number
    [BH] = Processor Mode Offset
    [CX] = Number of offsets that fit in buffer
    [ES]:[(E)DI] = Pointer to the buffer for storing the offsets

After exiting from GetAccessOffsets:
    If [CF] = 1, then [AH] = BAD_ADAPTER, BAD_FUNCTION, BAD_MODE
    Else
    [DX] = Number of Offsets supported by this S^2
    [ES]:[(E)DI] = Pointer to the buffer of offsets

AcknowledgeInterrupt

When a PC Card's status changes (card removal/insertion and ready/busy changes, for example), the client utilizing S^2 may require notification. During the initialization of a flash file system, it can install a status change interrupt handler that can be accessed through the host's interrupt mechanism. The status change associated with removing the flash memory card results in the generation of a system interrupt. This, in turn, invokes the flash file system's status change interrupt handler, which then figures out what caused the interrupt (*GetStatus* function). In this case, a card removal caused the interrupt. So ultimately, the card removal event results in telling the flash file system that it no longer has a drive to support, at least until the next card status change event - card insertion. But that's another story.

In a simple, single-socket, single-adapter system, it's fairly easy to deduce where the card status change interrupt came from. In systems housing multiple sockets and multiple adapters, locating the cause of the interrupt may not be so obvious. Let's look at the following steps used to analyze how to process a card status change interrupt:

1.   Card status change generates interrupt through pre-configured interrupt level (refer to *SetAdapter* and Adapter Characteristics Table for capabilities)

2.   Client's interrupt handler calls *AcknowledgeInterrupt* function to find the interrupt-causing socket. As shown below,

AcknowledgeInterrupt returns a bit map representing the sockets that have experienced a status change.

3.   Within the *AcknowedgeInterrupt* function, the software resets the adapter hardware to allow it to generate another interrupt, should another status change occur. This may be as simple as clearing a latch. *AcknowledgeInterrupt* should also preserve the information related to the cause of the interrupt if the adapter hardware itself does not support this.

4.   Client prepares the host system's interrupt hardware for another interrupt. This may include sending End of Interrupt (EOI) commands to the Programmable Interrupt Controller (PIC) or re-enabling the PIC's interrupt mask register.

5.   Once the interrupt-generating socket has been detected, the client calls the *GetStatus* function to determine exactly what caused the interrupt. This information could have been stored by *AcknowledgeInterrupt* in a variable that *GetStatus* uses. In an adapter using the PCIC, this information can be found by reading the Interface Status Register (see the example in the "Defining the Adapter Hardware" section and Figure 10.32). How the client processes this information depends on what caused the status change in the first place, and the client's implementation.

AcknowledgeInterrupt

Entry setup for the PC version of the AcknowledgeInterrupt function:
　　　[AH] = ACKNOWLEDGE_INTERUPT (ExCA calling value = 9EH)
　　　[AL] = Adapter number

After exiting from AcknowledgeInterrupt:
　　　If [CF] = 1, then [AH] = BAD_ADAPTER
　　　Else
　　　[CX] = Socket Bit Map (Bit 0 = Socket 0, Bit 1 = Socket 1, etc.)

Some additional points need to be made when processing interrupts:

1. S^2 should minimize the amount of time interrupts are disabled. However, never enable interrupts during the *AcknowledgeInterrupt* function. This will avoid confusion during interrupt processing.

2.   Within some systems, adapters may share a status change interrupt. *AcknowledgeInterrupt* may be called for an adapter even if a status change has not occurred on the adapter specified in the input parameter. In this case, the bit map returns with all bits equal to zero.

Detecting Card Insertion

Let's add a little excitement and say that we've determined that a PC card is not present. How should we prepare for the big event - card insertion? A moment that every socket lives for! A system may use several methods for detecting card insertion:

•   Link into the system timer interrupt (this gets a call every 55 milliseconds in the PC) and periodically call the *GetStatus* function. This method eliminates the need to invoke hardware interrupts, which in turn reduces the complexity of the software and adapter hardware. Continuous polling consumes CPU bandwidth; the downside to this method. Also, other subsystems may be sharing the system timer interrupt, resulting in increased delays.

•   Enable the status change interrupt. This hardware dependent operation will be relying on, and simplified by, the use of S^2. In particular, the *SetSocket* and *SetAdapter* functions will be used.

Error Detection and Correction Functions

The functions within this category support error detection and correction (EDC) mechanisms on the socket adapter. Since the majority of EDC mechanisms are implemented within the flash memory card itself (such as a flash memory drive interfaced to the system using the PCMCIA-ATA specification), consider these functions to be optional and not a requirement of ExCA compliance. A discussion of the individual EDC functions can be found in the PCMCIA specification.

SOCKET SERVICE DESIGN CONSIDERATIONS AND BENEFITS

The original flash file systems can be viewed as a big "module", as they were written basically as one piece of code containing all functional categories. By including S^2 as part of your system's software solution, it removes the flash file system's (or client's) dependency on a hardware specific implementation.

S^2 can be obtained in two ways:

1.   Write your own - Use this approach for after-market installations of S^2 where it can be loaded as a TSR or through CONFIG.SYS. Also, if you write the BIOS for your systems, you have the ability to incorporate S^2 (which you can also write yourself) directly into the BIOS.

2.   The BIOS vendor - Alternatively, if you employ the services of a BIOS vendor, for an additional fee, S^2 (as well as the other PCMCIA-defined pieces of software) can be included with your system's BIOS[95].

The latter method of obtaining S^2 leads us to an important consideration - Would you like to use a customized or off-the-shelf version? The PC BIOS vendors listed in the Appendix current provide different versions of S^2 for a variety of hardware interfaces.

Whether you write your own S^2 or purchase it through third party vendors, ensure that the implementation uses minimal system RAM, especially when built into the BIOS. The S^2 specification has been written under this consideration and many of the PCMCIA interface controllers have been designed to accommodate this. These devices

---

[95]Card Services can be obtained in the same way.

accomplish this by using read/write registers that not only perform specific functions but also provide status information. In developing S^2 (it should also go without saying), code should also be compact and have optimized performance.

Testing Your Socket Services Implementation

When testing your S^2 implementation, you should check for the following characteristics[96]:

- The function calls do not fail unexpectedly.
- All register contents must be preserved, except [AH] and other registers used to pass back parameters from the function.
- Invalid requests must be handled properly.
- Functions must execute quickly and minimize the time interrupts are disabled.

THE CARD INFORMATION STRUCTURE

As quoted in the PCMCIA PC Card Standard Specification Release 2.0, "The PC Memory Card International Association was formed with the goal of promoting interchangeability of Integrated Circuit Cards among a variety of computer and other electronic products". The specification established by PCMCIA defined three sections:

1. The Card Physical, for the mechanical dimensions and tolerances for cards and connectors. This standard allows different package form factors,[97]
2. The Card Interface, for the electrical interface of the card, including signal and pinout definitions for both memory and I/O cards, and
3. The Card Software, addressing the organization of data on the card (unrelated to the file storage format). The card software Metaformat is divided into 5 levels:

---

[96]Calling each function with all possible valid input parameters and the worst-case values for invalid parameters.

[97]The Appendix contains the measurements for Type I, Type II and Type III cards.

1.   Physical Layer
2.   Basic Compatibility Layer
3.   Data Recording Format Layer
4.   Data Organization Layer, and
5.   System-Specific Layer.

These layers pertain to levels of compliance. The Card Information Structure (CIS) accommodates a requirement of the Basic Compatibility Layer. The CIS provides card-specific information to the host system such as the card size, types of components, speed, system resource requirements, etc. The open nature of the PCMCIA standard allows a card to comply at the Basic Compatibility Layer without being required to comply at any higher level. This allows a card to be used in a wide range of environments and, therefore, places a great deal of significance on the CIS[98].

Although it won't be discussed in detail here (because it currently lacks widespread usage), the ultimate goal of the Data Organization Layer makes it worth briefly mentioning. This standard allows a special card formatting utility to divide the flash memory card array into multiple functions, such as a boot record or XIP area (Figure 10.34 provides two examples of this partitioning capability).

Accessing the Card Information Structure

The memory card's address space is divided into an Attribute and Common Memory Plane selected via the $\overline{REG}$ pin. Common Memory handles direct-memory access read and write operations maintained in the array of flash memory components. The Attribute Memory Plane contains the CIS and PCMCIA-defined card configuration registers. It is generally contained within separate devices in the card (e.g., ASICs), but is only required to occupy a logically distinct address plane from Common Memory. The Register Select pin ($\overline{REG}$, pin 61) selects between the Common Memory Plane ($\overline{REG}$ = one) and the Attribute Memory Plane ($\overline{REG}$ = zero). Refer to Figure 10.35.

---

[98]It also means that cards may be formatted with different file data structures; this leads to incompatibilities when transferring these cards between systems.

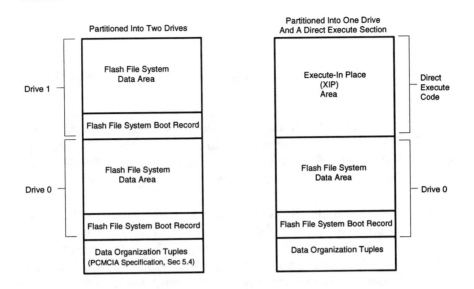

Figure 10.34: Flash Memory Card Partitioning Examples

FLASH MEMORY CARD PLANES

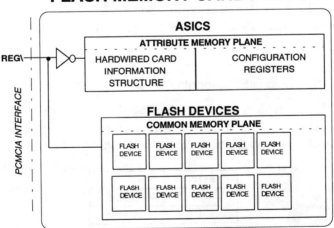

*Figure 10.35: Select between a Flash Memory Card's Common and
Attribute Memory Planes using the $\overline{REG}$ Signal*

The CIS may be stored in flash memory cards using three basic alternatives:

1.   No CIS. This card does not truly comply with PCMCIA 2.0 compatibility.

2.   A separate EEPROM device within the card, requires the card's user to program the correct and necessary tuples. This provides flexibility but requires more work on behalf of the developer building the card format utility.

3.   Hardwired by the card vendor into the card's ASICs. This approach removes the responsibility from the card's format utility. On the other hand, this approach has an element of risk involved due to potential errors and changing specifications. It also means that the format utility must use a portion of the Common Memory CIS if additional CIS information is desired.

PCMCIA requires the CIS in the Attribute Memory Plane to be located at even addresses; invalid data will be obtained when reading from an odd-byte location. A CIS jump to Common Memory may be provided, where additional CIS information can be stored in both even and odd bytes.

Tuples - The Basic CIS Elements

The CIS, a variable length chain (or linked-list), consists of data blocks called *tuples,* starting at address zero of the Attribute Memory Plane. Table 10.11 displays the basic format of the PCMCIA-defined tuple.

BYTES	
0	TPL_CODE
1	TPL_LINK
n	Bytes specific to this tuple

Table 10.11: Tuple Format

- Byte 0 of the tuple contains the *tuple code* (TPL_CODE), a tuple's unique identifier.

- Byte 1 (actually address 2) of each tuple contains a *tuple link* (TPL_LINK) to the next tuple in the *tuple list*. The TPL_LINK byte equals the number of bytes remaining in the tuple after the TPL_LINK (Figure 10.36). For example, if a tuple consists of a total of five bytes, byte 1 (TPL_LINK) would contain the value 03H; the total number of tuples (5) minus the first two bytes dedicated to the tuple code and tuple link.

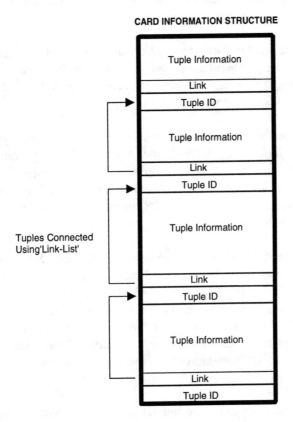

Figure 10.36: A Tuple is the Basic Data Structure in the CIS

Some basic rules of tuple design:

- In general, each byte in a tuple represents another piece of information. Different tuples, characterized by different tuple codes, may have different lengths.

- Each tuple has a maximum length of 256 bytes (limited by the size of the link field data size).

- The tuple code of 0FFH, anywhere within the tuple, marks the tuple's end. For example, if byte 5 has the value 0FFH, that byte is the last byte in the tuple.

- Some tuples have an end-of-tuple byte, and others do not. Typically, the variable length tuples will use an end-of-tuple byte. Therefore, CIS-parsing software must be able to handle tuples with and without end-of-tuple bytes.

- Tuple bytes may be further sub-divided into tuple byte fields or just *fields*. PCMCIA defines specific fields (a range of bits within a byte) for certain tuple bytes. For example, byte 0 of the Device ID tuple has three fields; Device Speed in bits 0 through 3, write protect switch (WPS) in bit 5, and Device Type Code in bits 4 through 7.

Note that the PCMCIA PC Card Standard 2.0 document uses the terms tuple, tuple byte, tuple list and field rather loosely. For example, *tuple* may refer to a single tuple, to the linked-list of tuples or to one of the bytes within a tuple. *Tuple chain* is synonymous with *tuple list*. Likewise, *field* may refer to one or more bits in a tuple byte, or it may refer to one of the bytes within a tuple. Because of these inconsistencies, pay attention to the context in which these terms are used.

Tuple Processing

PCMCIA makes several recommendations for software designers who write code that parses the CIS. (From the Microsoft Flash File System standpoint, the CARDDRV.EXE piece contains this code.) These recommendations must be used to prevent incompatibilities between systems:

- The first tuple starts at address 0 of the Attribute Memory Plane. This tuple must be the Device Information Tuple, Null Control Tuple, or End of List Tuple.

- PCMCIA recommends that an unknown tuple code be ignored. The first two bytes which include the tuple code and tuple link may be read. No other bytes should be read, since they may contain active registers that could be altered by reading them.

Tuple Descriptions

The PCMCIA specification has defined tuples that describe many different aspects of a PC card. Staying on track with the subject of this book, we will focus on the tuples that relate directly to flash memory cards. Table 10.12 lists the tuples that should be implemented in a flash memory card, as a bare minimum[99]:

TUPLE	TUPLE CODE	TUPLE ID
Device Information	CISTPL_DEVICE	01H
	CISTPL_DEVICE_A	17H
Level 1 Version/Product Information	CISTPL_VERS_1	15H
Configuration	CISTPL_CONF	1AH
Configuration Table Entry	CISTPL_CE	1BH
JEDEC Device ID	CISTPL_JEDEC_C	18H
	CISTPL_JEDEC_A	19H
Device Geometry Info	CISTPL_DEVICEGEO	1EH
	CISTPL_DEVICEGEO_A	1FH

Table 10.12: Minimum Tuple Requirements

---

[99]A minimum requirement of ExCA.

THE DEVICE INFORMATION TUPLE

A tuple code of 01H indicates that this tuple describes the components of the Common Memory address space. Most flash memory cards contain only one type of memory technology in Common Memory, and therefore only contain one Device Information Field. Some cards contain mixtures of memory technologies (e.g., RAM, ROM, FLASH). A PCMCIA card containing a mixture of memory technologies, such as RAM and FLASH, requires an equivalent number of Device Information Fields.

A tuple code of 17H pertains to Attribute Memory. Typically, flash memory card vendors use ROM or EEPROM to store the card's CIS in Attribute Memory. Cards that use EEPROMs have a bit more flexibility but usually ship blank. The OEM or card user then has the responsibility of programming the correct information into the CIS. However, it also means that the EEPROM can be used for something other than a CIS (as in the case of a proprietary application).

OFFSET	DESCRIPTION	VALUE
00H	TUPLE CODE = CISTPL_DEV	01H
02H	TPL_LINK	03H
04H	DEVICE ID = FLASH,150ns	53H
	DEVICE ID = FLASH,200ns	52H
06H	DEVICE SIZE = 4M	0EH
	DEVICE SIZE = 10M	26H
	DEVICE SIZE = 20M	4EH
08H	END OF DEVICE TUPLE	FFH

Table 10.13: Sample Device Information Tuple

Device ID (Table 10.14)

PCMCIA defines the device ID as the device type (Flash EPROM, UV EPROM, DRAM, etc.) and access time. According to Table 5-14 of the PCMCIA 2.01 specification, Flash EPROM has a device type of "5". The Device Speed Field depicts the device access time and the codes can be found in PCMCIA's Table 5-12. The specification also has provisions for an extended speed byte, usually equal to zero, indicating that it can be ignored. The extended speed field handles speed granularities (e.g., 135ns, 90ns, etc.) not explicitly listed in PCMCIA's Table 5-12.

The WPS bit within the Device ID byte indicates whether the card's mechanical write protect switch has an effect on the devices in the card. A zero value means that the write protect switch and WP signal indicate the 'writability' of the flash devices in the card. A value of one in this field indicates always-writable flash devices. In this case, a system can use the write protect capability (if available), determined by the Window Characteristics Table (InquireWindow of Socket Services).

Bit7	Bit6	Bit5	Bit4	Bit3	Bit2	Bit1	Bit0
Device Type Code				WPS	Device Speed		
Flash EPROM = 5				0 = Writable	DSPEED_200ns = 2H DSPEED_150ns = 3H		

Table 10.14: Sample Device ID Byte

Device Size (Table 10.15)

The Device Size byte (PCMCIA Table 5.15), consisting of an addressable unit field and a size code field, provides information to determine the card's size, or density. The size code merely provides a value that gets multiplied by the addressable unit. The address unit field, more appropriately named a "size-code multiplier", bears no relationship to the devices in the flash memory card. As an example, assume a size unit of 2MB (code value of 6). For a 20 Mbyte card, this unit would require an addressable unit, or multiplier of 10. The 5 bits corresponding to the "# of ADDRESS UNITS - 1" allow for a maximum card density of 64 Mbytes (2Mbytes × 32).

Bit7	Bit6	Bit5	Bit4	Bit3	Bit2	Bit1	Bit0
# of ADDRESS UNITS - 1					SIZE CODE		
4 Megabyte Card = (2-1) = 1 10 Megabyte Card = (5-1) = 4 20 Megabyte Card = (10-1) = 9					Code = 6 Indicates Unit Size Ranges From 2M to 64 Mbytes		

Table 10.15: Sample Device Size Byte

THE DEVICE GEOMETRY TUPLE

The Device Geometry Tuple (Table 10.16) provides information for flash file systems regarding the flash memory card's internal low-level formatting structure. Although this tuple can be implemented for randomly rewritable SRAM or EEPROM, the flash memory technology with its large-block erase functionality introduces additional needs for device information with respect to erase blocking and partitioning boundaries.

The DGTPL_BUS field indicates the *system bus width*, where the value (n) equals $2^{(n-1)}$ bytes. N = 2 for the standard PCMCIA-defined, 16-bit bus. This entry accommodates the possibility of wider-width cards in the future and/or allows file systems to use this tuple structure in non-PCMCIA memory card environments (e.g., resident flash memory arrays).

The DGTPL_EBS field indicates the *erase block size*, where the value of $2^{(n-1)}$ equals the address increments of DGTPL_BUS-wide accesses. For example, a value of 11H ($2^{(16)}$) represents a 64KWord address increment for the 16-bit wide card. This corresponds to the 64 kbyte erase blocks of Intel's 28F008SA devices within the Series 2 Card, paired to provide 64KWord erase blocks.

The DGTPL_RBS and DGTPL_WBS field indicate the *read block size* and *write block size*, respectively. The value of $2^{(n-1)}$ equals the address increments of DGTPL_BUS-wide accesses. For example, a value of 01H ($2^{(0)}$) represents 1 block address increment. In other words, any address within the entire card's memory array can be read or written without using special read or write modes such as paging. This is the typical situation (refer to Chapter 7 for more information on writing to devices and cards).

DGTPL_PART is a *special partitioning* information field based on physically distinct segments of the memory array(s), such that its contents cannot be affected by read/write/erase operations in adjacent partitions. This field indicates the number of *electrically-isolated partitions* within a device. As an example, a tuple value of 03H ($2^{(p-1)}$ or 4) yields the number of completely electrically isolated blocks.

In practice, apply this information when storing "permanent" code or data, such as that used for XIP software, boot code or special card formatting data (Figure 10.34). With some flash memory devices, repeated writes and erases of adjacent blocks may eventually disturb the "permanent" contents, unless fully electrically isolated from one another.

DGTPL_HWIL (FL_DEVICE_INTERLEAVE) is used where card architectures employ a multiple of $2^{(q-1)}$ times interleaving of the entire memory arrays or subsystems with the above characteristics. Non-interleaved cards have values of q = 1. The value q = 00H is not allowed.

The DGTPL_EBS, DGTPL_RBS, and DGTPL_WBS (address increment- or bus operation-based values) are multiplicative of the DGTPL_BUS entry (denoting bus width) to define the *non-interleaved* physical memory erase-, read-, and write-block sizes in bytes, respectively. The DGTPL_HWIL value for cards employing *hardware-interleaved* (i.e., banks of) memory arrays or subsystems (where DGTPL_HWIL _ 2) is multiplicative of the resulting non-interleaved erase-, read-, and write geometries. The product of these three geometry information layers yields the resulting <u>card-level</u> minimum physical block geometries.

OFFSET	DESCRIPTION	VALUE
00H	TUPLE CODE = CISTPL_DEVICEGEO	1EH
02H	TPL_LINK	06H
04H	DGTPL_BUS	02H
06H	DGTPL_EBS	11H
08H	DGTPL_RBS	01H
0AH	DGTPL_WBS	01H
0CH	DGTPL_PART	03H
0EH	FL_DEVICE_INTERLEAVE	01H

Table 10.16: Sample Device Geometry Tuple[100]

THE JEDEC IDENTIFIER TUPLE

Use the Jedec Identifier Tuple to determine the device type (JEDEC component ID and manufacturer ID) in the memory card. The devices within many flash memory cards also support an identifier read mode used to obtain the same information without using a CIS. However, if possible, use the CIS because it provides a more standardized method for determining device types in PCMCIA cards.

The JEDEC ID tuple is the only data CIS parsing software can use to determine the size of the flash memory devices within a card. This may present a problem, because cards containing unknown devices (i.e., present or future) will not be able to match-up with a value contained in the CIS parser's lookup table. Although this shouldn't be a problem in a read-only situation, it can be a problem with bulk and block erase flash when the physical device boundaries must be known for writes and erases. (Oops!) The flash card driver, described later in this chapter, represents one solution to this issue.

---

[100]The sample CIS uses the format for Intel's Series 2 Flash Memory Card

OFFSET	DESCRIPTION	VALUE
1AH	CISTPL_JEDEC	18H
1CH	TPL_LINK	02H
1EH	INTEL JEDEC ID	89H
20H	28F008SA JEDEC ID	A2H

Table 10.17: Sample JEDEC Identifier Table

THE CONFIGURATION TUPLE

The fields in this tuple describe the interfaces supported by the card and configurable registers within the card (Table 10.18). Most flash memory cards do not support this tuple because they generally consist of nothing more than an interface ASIC and a memory array[101]. The flash memory cards that do support this tuple include Intel's Series 2 cards and some flash memory cards using a PCMCIA-ATA interface.

The TPCC_SZ byte, referred to as the Size of Field Byte, consists of several bit fields, as shown below:

7	6	5	4	3	2	1	0
TPCC_RFSZ - Reserved for future use, must equal 0.		TPCC_RMSZ - Value indicates number of byte addresses used by TPCC_RMSK minus 1. Flash cards that support this function typically have a 0 in this field indicating only 1 byte is required by the presence mask.				TPCC_RASZ - Value indicates number of byte addresses used by TPCC_RADR minus 1.	

Table 10.18: Size of Field Byte

The TPCC_LAST byte contains the Configuration Index Number of the last configuration described in the Card Configuration Table. For example, a value of zero indicates the absence of a Card Configuration Table.

---

[101] I/O Cards are the predominant users of this field.

The Configuration Registers Base Address in REG Space (TPCC_RADR) field contains the base address of the card's PCMCIA-defined configuration registers. The length of this field can be from one to four bytes long and is determined from the two bits of the TPCC_RASZ field of the TPCC_SZ byte. The address is displayed from low order bits to high. As an example, a base address of 4000H would be displayed in the first and second bytes of TPCC_RADR as 00H and 40H, respectively.

The Configuration Register Presence Mask (TPCC_RMSK) tuple field contains a bit map corresponding to the presence (one) or absence (zero) of the Configuration Registers described in Section 4-15 of the PCMCIA 2.01 specification. As an example, a value of 3 (i.e., bits 0 and 1) indicates the presence of two registers, the Configuration Option Register and the Configuration and Status Register.

OFFSET	DESCRIPTION	VALUE
C6H	CISTPL_CONF	1AH
C8H	TPL_LINK	06H
CAH	TPCC_SZ	01H
CCH	TPCC_LAST	00H
CEH	TPCC_RADR	00H
D0H	TPCC_RADR	40H
D2H	TPCC_RMSK	03H
D4H	CISTPL_END	FFH

Table 10.19: Sample Configuration Table

THE CONFIGURATION-TABLE ENTRY TUPLE

This tuple supports miscellaneous (and sometimes unusual) card functions such as special timing and power requirements, system I/O and memory requirements and an interrupt structure. Currently, this field is not implemented in any flash memory cards but in the future it will support things such as dual voltage operation (3.3V and 5.0V) and special power requirements.

THE END-OF-LIST TUPLE

Simply stated, this tuple marks the end of a tuple chain and causes the most confusion because when system software encounters it, several actions can be taken:

- If a long-link tuple was encountered previously in the chain, continue processing at the location specified in the long-link tuple.

- If processing the CIS and neither a long-link nor a no-link tuple were seen in this chain, then continue processing as if a long-link tuple to address 0 of Common Memory space were encountered. This approach allows the interpretation of custom card information that may have been formatted into the card's Common Memory Plane (e.g., file system formatting, boot partition, etc.). For validation of the implied long-link tuple to Common Memory, the tuple chain in Common Memory must begin with a valid Link Target tuple. Encountering an invalid Link Target tuple signifies the assumed end of the CIS.

OFFSET	DESCRIPTION	VALUE
00H	CISTPL_END	FFH

Table 10.20: Sample End-of-List Tuple

CARD SERVICES

The subject of Card Services, like Socket Services, could actually encompass a whole book in and of itself. As a matter of fact, Card Services takes up almost 150 pages in the PCMCIA specification. The task of developing a complete Card Services implementation consumes more time and effort than is available for all but the largest manufacturers. Therefore, we recommend that if you plan on using Card Services, contact your favorite BIOS vendor and buy it[102]. However, for non-PC implementations, only proprietary Card Services solutions exist

---

[102]A list of BIOS vendors supporting Card Services can be found in the Appendix.

today and you must therefore write Card Services yourself (or hire a consultant).

What is Card Services?

Fundamentally, Card Services monitors the way in which PC cards and their applications utilize, and interface to, the host system. It primarily benefits systems where a variety of PC cards will continuously be swapped in and out of the same socket. The following example best portrays this situation:

A socket contains a flash memory card. The system has installed flash file system software. Furthermore, the flash memory card maps into a 64 kbyte window in the host's memory map. Now, remove the flash memory card and insert a fax card. The need for the 64 kbyte window goes away, but now the fax card requires some I/O ports. Simultaneously, the flash file system must be notified that it doesn't have a card anymore. However, the user loads up fax software that must be hooked up with the fax card. Card Services keeps track of all this activity and negotiates the available system resources to service them.

As shown in Figure 10.37, Card Services acts as the interface between clients (applications, device drivers) and PC Cards, sockets and system resources. PCMCIA describes this interface as a client/server model; Card Services is the server and the application programs, device drivers and utility programs represent the clients.

Card Services consists of five functional categories:

1.   *Client Services* provides support for client callback registration with Card Services to allow event notification, such as card removal or insertion.

2.   *Resource Management* maintains constant knowledge of the available system resources to allocate for the use of PC Cards. These resources include memory and I/O address space and interrupts.

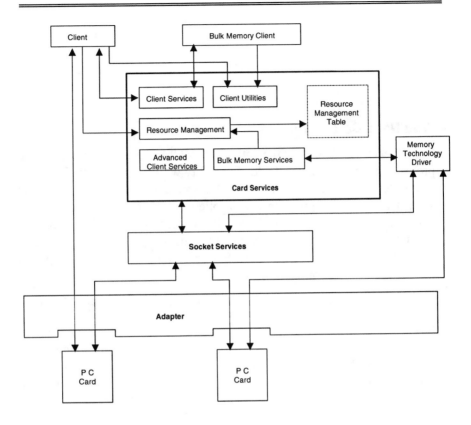

Figure 10.37: Card Services Interfaces between Clients (Applications, Device Drivers) and PC Cards, Sockets, and System Resources

3. *Client Utilities* primarily provide a common access to the Card Information Structure of PC cards. In other words, the Client Utilities contain code that a client may use to read tuples from a card. This eliminates redundant code within each of the clients.

4. *Bulk Memory Services* provides basic read/write/copy/erase functionality for RAM cards; it does not accommodate flash memory algorithms. It calls upon a special memory technology driver to handle flash memory cards.

5.   *Advanced Client Services* provides a miscellaneous set of functions for clients with special needs. An example is a special utility that uses this service to obtain direct access to socket services.

Do You Need Card Services?

Card Services, like all the other PCMCIA software components, promotes an open system. It adds flexibility while, at the same time, acts as a watchdog to ensure that PCMCIA-aware applications do not violate system resource integrity. In a controlled environment (i.e., embedded applications), flexibility may not be necessary and simplifies the restriction of what software and/or PC cards get plugged into a socket. These systems may not need Card Services and can avoid development costs and system resources used to load it.

FLASH CARD MEMORY TECHNOLOGY DRIVERS

From a read standpoint, most flash memory cards appear to function about the same as ROM cards! In other words, they don't require any special algorithms to read from them. But the fact is, all flash memory cards are not created equal, especially from a program and erase standpoint. Flash memory programming and erase algorithms can differ significantly, depending on the card manufacturer and the type of flash memory devices in the card (refer to Chapter 3).

At the beginning of this chapter, we described the first-generation monolithic flash file system model (Figure 10.5). In such a system, the low-level driver, (CARDDRV.EXE), contained all the code to interface the flash file system and the hardware (socket adapter, system memory and flash memory card). It even included the program and erase algorithms for the flash memory cards. After writing this monolithic piece of software and installing it in the computer system, the algorithms it contained dictated the specific flash memory cards it supported. An unsupported flash memory card could probably be read, but any attempts to program or erase it would probably end up failing, for one reason or another (due to differences in algorithms).

To include support for additional cards obviously required a code modification to incorporate the required software algorithms. This was never simple, except if the system hadn't shipped yet. But if the system containing this flash file system software was already in the field, how easy would it be to upgrade it to include the additional card support? This was one of the biggest limitations of the monolithic file system.

What if there was a way to hook the new flash memory card algorithms to the main body of code without any modifications? What if installing new flash card algorithms was as simple as inserting the new card into the socket? The flash card driver must take this approach to allow systems to function with new cards.

Why Support New Cards?

Face it, building in the ability to support additional flash memory cards requires a nontrivial amount of effort. What is the motivation? Some OEMs will build a computer and ship it with a certain level of flash memory card support (i.e., drivers that only support a limited number of vendor's cards). These same OEMs do not care about supporting other cards. However, new memory cards can provide higher performance, higher densities and increased functionality. This lack of obsolescence, in turn, may make a computer system more desirable to end users, which ultimately provides a competitive advantage. On the other hand, being able to support new cards, gives the OEM an opportunity to make more money by selling these cards on the after-market.

Flash Card Driver Functions

A flash card driver only contains code that deals specifically with the card's functionality. It has complete knowledge of the card's program and erase algorithms and any special control registers the card may contain. This driver knows what it takes to optimize, or fine-tune, any operations within the card. Fundamentally, a flash card driver manages four types of operations in association with a flash file system:

- *Read* - transfers specified bytes from the flash memory card to a system buffer
- *Write* - transfers specified bytes from a system buffer to the flash memory card

- *Copy* - transfers specified bytes from one location to another within the same flash memory card, as seen when doing block-to-block transfer during flash file system cleanup
- *Erase* - restores a block or chip to an erased state (i.e., all ones)

Interfacing to the Flash Card Driver

In a PCMCIA-compatible software implementation (Figure 10.6), Card Services provides the interface between the flash file system and the flash card driver (referred to as the Memory Technology Driver, or MTD). Any time the file system needs to perform one of the operations listed above, it makes its request to Card Services, which in turn calls the MTD. To fit this role of interfacing to Card Services, all MTDs must implement a standardized interface, as described in the PCMCIA specification.

A system using proprietary software may still utilize similar concepts for linking a flash card driver to the flash file system. This MTD can be written as a separate device driver that the flash file system software can call into for the basic read/write/copy/erase functions. Perhaps the new driver can be written in such a way as to overlay on top of the original driver it replaces (i.e., as a set of subroutines) during run time. A proprietary solution has the advantage of allowing the flash card driver interface to be tailored explicitly for the system. Whatever the interface, it should be clear that the flash card driver has to be a unique piece of code for each type of flash memory card.

Installing the Flash Card Drivers

The biggest challenge in MTD integration lies in determining how the new flash card driver gets loaded or installed into the system. Fundamentally, when a different flash memory card is distributed or sold by the computer OEM, the supporting driver must come along with it, somehow. How that driver gets loaded into the system and/or where it resides depends on the system's memory architecture, as depicted in Table 10.18.

Case	Hard Drive	Floppy Drive	Flash Disk	ROM Disk
1	No	No	No	Yes
2	No	No	Yes	No
3	Yes	External	Don't Care	Don't Care
4	Yes	Yes	Don't Care	Don't Care

Table 10.21: System Memory Architectures

Installing the new driver into the system can be accomplished in several ways, depending on the system's capabilities:

- Modem the new driver from a bulletin board - If the system doesn't have a built-in modem, the user has to buy a modem just to use a flash memory card. No way!

- Use a serial port and a link to a host computer (i.e., LapLink) - Again, not always the most convenient solution.

- Floppy disk - OEM must distribute this with each card, and the system must support floppy disks.

- Flash memory card - Except for the Case 4 system architecture (with a built-in floppy drive) the flash card driver on the card provides the most general solution. It can deliver the most convenient approach, especially when it has the ability to be automatically pulled off the card without user intervention. The mechanism to accomplish this could proceed as follows (Figure 10.37):

1. User inserts a new card which generates a card insertion event.

2. Software interprets the CIS to identify the card. Two possibilities exist:

SOCKET ADAPTER

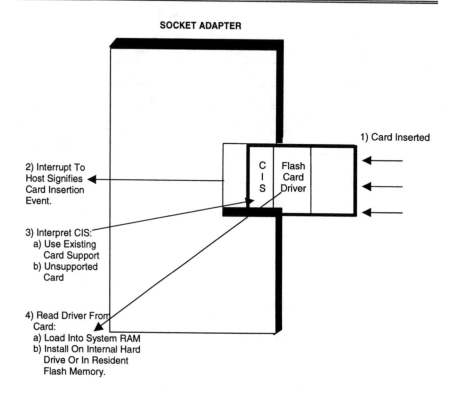

1) Card Inserted

2) Interrupt To Host Signifies Card Insertion Event.

C I S | Flash Card Driver

3) Interpret CIS:
a) Use Existing Card Support
b) Unsupported Card

4) Read Driver From Card:
a) Load Into System RAM
b) Install On Internal Hard Drive Or In Resident Flash Memory.

Figure 10.38: Installing a New Flash Card Driver

a. The software already in the system supports the card. Remember, there can be some flash memory card support integrated into the flash file system software.

b. An unrecognized card needs a new driver.

3.   A special loader utility reads the flash card driver from the flash memory card. Two possibilities exist:

a. A Case 1 system has no way to permanently store the new driver (i.e., ROM-based, no hard drive, etc.). The flash card driver must be pulled from the card and loaded into system RAM for execution each time it is inserted (a temporary installation).

b. System Cases 2-4 have more flexibility. The flash disk or hard disk in these systems can "permanently" store the flash card driver after pulling it off the card. A Case 4 system provides the easiest solution for installing the flash card driver. A floppy disk containing the driver can be shipped along with the new flash card. Install the floppy disk, copy the file to the hard drive and load it at run time along with the rest of the flash file system software. However, it may be just as convenient to leave the driver on the card and automatically pull it off each time.

SUMMARY

This chapter was written to provide you with insight and an appreciation for the software components that can be used in a system incorporating a PCMCIA socket. Actually, much of the PCMCIA software can even be used in a system that has resident, non-removable flash memory. Regardless, the components and their most important functions include:

- *Socket Services* - Software specific to the host adapter hardware, much like system BIOS.

- *Card Services* - Manages system resources, such as memory windows and I/O ports

- *Memory Technology Drivers* - Device drivers containing the flash memory program and erase algorithms, either resident in the system or on the card itself. They optimize the performance of the flash memory card.

- *Card Information Structure* - Data structures "permanently" stored in the flash memory card (and PC cards in general) that describe the features of the card.

At this point, you may also be making the decision whether to buy or build. The Appendix lists some of the sources for purchasing the software. If you decide to write your own, you must first decide what is needed. Don't limit yourself, decide this with a forward-looking attitude. Enjoy the challenge!

Appendix A: Flash Memory Component Vendors

The following list is a representative summary of flash memory component manufacturers. Due to the rapid change in product line items, it is best to contact these companies directly for product-specific information.

Advanced Micro Devices Inc.
Box 3453
Sunnyvale, CA   94088
(800) 222-9323
(408) 749-5703

Atmel Corp.
2125 O'Neil Dr.
San Jose, CA   95131
(408) 441-0311

Catalyst Semiconductors, Inc.
2231 Calle de Luna
Santa Clara, CA   95054
Tel: (408) 748-7700
Fax: (408) 980-8209

Fujitsu Microelectronics Inc.
IC Division
3545 N. First St.
San Jose, CA   95134
(800) 642-7616
(408) 954-0616

Hitachi America Ltd.
Semiconductor and IC Division
2000 Sierra Point Parkway
Brisbane, CA   94005
(800) 448-2244
(415) 589-8300

Intel Corp.
Literature Center
Box 7641
Mt. Prospect, IL   60056
(800) 548-4725

Mitsubishi Electronics of America
1050 E. Arques Ave.
Sunnyvale, CA   94086
(408) 730-5900

NEC Electronics Inc.
Box 7241
Mountain View, CA   94039
(415) 960-6000

Oki Semiconductor
785 N. Mary Ave.
Sunnyvale, CA   94086
(408) 720-1900

Samsung Semiconductor
3725 N. First Street
San Jose, CA   95134
(408) 954-7274

SGS-Thomson
1000 E. Bell Road
Phoenix, AZ   85022
(602) 867-6100

Texas Instruments Inc.
Box 172228
Denver, CO   80217
(800) 477-8924

Toshiba   America   Electronic Components Inc.
9775 Toledo Way
Irvine, CA   92718
(800) 879-4963
(714) 455-2000

Appendix B: Flash Memory Card/Drive Vendors

The following list is a representative summary of flash memory card and drive manufacturers. Due to the rapid change in product line items, it is best to contact these companies directly for product-specific information.

Advanced Micro Devices, Inc
P.O. Box 3453
Sunnyvale, CA 94088-3453
Tel: (408) 749-5981
Fax: (408) 749-3240

AMI ASIS Division
200 South Main St.
Pocatello, Idaho 83204
Tel: (208) 234-6661
Fax: (208) 234-6695

Atmel Corporation
2125 O'Nel Drive
San Jose, CA 95131
Tel: (408) 441-0311
Fax: (408) 436-4300

Catalyst Semiconductors, Inc.
2231 Calle de Luna
Santa Clara, CA   95054
Tel: (408) 748-7700
Fax: (408) 980-8209

Centennial
37 Manning Road
Billerica, MA 01821
Tel: (508) 670-0646
Fax: (508) 670-9025

Computer Modules, Inc.
2350 A Walsh Ave,
Santa Clara, CA 95051
Tel: (408) 496-1881
Fax: (408) 496-1886

Enhance Memory Products, Inc.
18720 Oxnard St. #102
Tarzana, CA 91356
Tel: (818) 343-3066
Fax: (818) 343-1436

Epson America, Inc.
20770 Madrona Ave.
Torrance, CA 90503
Tel: (310) 782-5341
Fax: (310) 782-5320

Epson Semiconductor GMBH
Riesstr. 15
W-8000 Munich 50, Germany
Tel: 49(89) 149703
Fax: 49(89) 149703-10

EXP Computer, Inc.
223 Michael Drive
Syosset, NY 11791
Tel: (516) 496-3703
Fax: (516) 496-2914

FDK America, Inc.
3099 N. First St.
San Jose, CA 95134
Tel: (408) 432-8331
Fax: (408) 435-7478

Fujitsu Microelectronics Inc.
IC Division
3545 N. First St.
San Jose, CA   95134
(800) 642-7616

Intel Corp.
Literature Center
Box 7641
Mt. Prospect, IL   60056
(800) 548-4725

MagicRAM, Inc.
1850 Beverly Blvd.
Los Angeles, CA 90057
Tel: (213) 413-9999
Fax: (213) 413-0828

Maxell Corp. of America
22-08 Route 208
Fair Lawn, NJ 07410
Tel: (201) 794-8382
Fax: (201) 794-3274

Mitsubishi Electronics America, Inc.
1050 East Arques Ave.
Sunnyvale, CA 94086
Tel: (408) 730-5900
Fax: (408) 732-9382

New Media Corp.
15375 Barranca B101
Irvine, CA 92718
Tel: (714) 453-0550
Fax: (714) 453-0114

Panasonic
P.O. Box 1511
Secaucus, NJ 07096
Tel: (201) 348-5266
Fax: (201) 392-4782

Pretec Electronics Corp.
39899 Balentine Dr. Suite 305
Newark, CA 94560
Tel: (510) 440-0535
Fax: (510) 440-0534

Psion PLC
Alexander House, 85 Frampton St.
London, NW8 8NQ England
Tel: 44(71) 262-5580
Fax: 44(71) 258-7340

Rohm Corp.
3034 Owen Dr.
Antioch, TN 37013
Tel: (615) 641-2020
Fax: (615) 641-2022

Silicon Storage Technology, Inc.
1208 Apollo Way
Suite 502
Sunnyvale, CA 94086
Tel: (408) 735-9110
Fax: (408) 735-9036

Smart Modular Technologies
45531 Northport Loop West
Fremont, CA 94538
Tel: (510) 623-1231
Fax: (510) 623-1434

Sundisk Corp.
3270 Jay Street
Santa Clara, CA 95054
Tel: (408) 562-0500
Fax: (408) 980-8607

Telecomputer, Inc.
15026 Moran Street
Westminster, CA 92683
Tel: (714) 894-8954
Fax: (714) 891-8364

Toshiba America Electronic Cmpts, Inc.
9775 Toledo Way
Irvine, CA 92718
Tel: (714) 455-2292
Fax: (714) 859-3963

Appendix C: Flash Memory Component and Card Programmers

The following list is a representative summary of flash memory component and card programmer manufacturers. Contact them directly for information on their products.

Advantest Corp.
2880 San Tomas Expy. #105
Santa Clara, CA 95051
(408) 970-9922

Advin Systems Inc.
1050-L E. Duane Avenue
Sunnyvale, CA   94086
(408) 243-7000
(800) 627-2456
(Components)

Aval Data Corp.
Information System Division
Shinyuri-21 Bldg.
1-2-2 Mampukuji, Asao-ku
Kawasaki-City, Kanagawa 215
Japan
011-81-44-952-1322

B&C Microsystems, Inc.
750 North Pastoria Ave.
Sunnyvale, CA 94086
Tel: (408) 730-5511
Fax: (408) 730-5521
(Cards)

BP Microsystems, Inc.
10681 Haddington #190
Houston, TX   77043
(713) 461-9430
(800) 225-2102
(Components)

Bytek Corp.
543 NW 77th Street
Boca Raton, FL   33487
(407) 994-3520
(800) 523-1565
(Components)

Data I/O Corporation
10525 Willows Road NE
Redmond, WA   98073
(206) 881-6444
(800) 247-5700
(Components and cards)

Elan Systems, Inc.
365-700 Woodview Ave.
Morgan Hill, CA 95037
Tel: (800) 541-ELAN
Fax: (408) 778-2597
(Components and cards)

Logical Devices, Inc.
692 S. Military Trail
Deerfield Beach, FL   33442
(305) 428-6868
(800) 331-7766
(Components)

Minato Electronics Inc.
4105, Minami Yamada-cho
Kohoku-ku, Yokohama
Kanagawa 223
Japan
011-81-45-591-5611

Minato Electronics Inc.
3628 Madison Ave. #5
North Highlands, CA 95660
(916) 348-6066

Needham's Electronics
4539 Orange Grove Ave.
Sacramento, CA   95841
(916) 924-8037
(Components and cards)

SMS Mikrocomputer Systeme GmbH
Im Grund 15
D-7988 Wangen
Germany
011-49-7-522-5018
(Components and cards)

SMS North America, Inc.
16522 NE 135th Pl.
Redmond, WA 98052
(800) 722-4122
(Components and cards)

Sunrise Electronics, Inc.
524 South Vermont Avenue
Glendora, CA   91740
(818) 914-1926
(Components)

Stag Microsystems, Inc.
1600 Wyatt Drive, Suite 3
Santa Clara, CA   94054
(408) 988-1118
(800) 227-8836
(Components and cards)

System General Corp.
3F, #1 Alley 8, Lane 45
Bao Shing Rd., Shin Dian
Taipei, Taiwan
Republic of China
011-886-2-917-3005
(Components and cards)

System General Corp.
510 S. Park Victoria Drive
Milpitas, CA   95035
(408) 263-6667
(800) 967-4776
(Components and cards)

Tribal Microsystems Inc.
44388 S. Grimmer Blvd.
Fremont, CA   94538
(510) 623-8859
(Components)

Xeltek
757 N. Pastoria Ave.
Sunnyvale, CA   94086
(408) 524-1929
(Components)

Appendix D: Component and Card Socket and Adapter Vendors

The following list is a representative summary of flash memory component socket, component socket adapter and card connector manufacturers. Contact them directly for information on their products.

Component Socket Vendors

AMP, Inc.
P.O. Box 3608
Harrisburg, PA   17105-3608
Tel: (800) 526-5105
Fax: (717) 986-7605

Augat Inc.
P.O. Box 2510
Attleboro Falls, MA   02763
Tel: (508) 699-7646
Fax: (508) 699-0678

Burndy Corp.
51 Richards Avenue
Norwalk, CT   06856
Tel: (203) 838-4444
Fax: (203) 852-8629

Methode Electronics, Inc.
7444 W. Wilson Ave.
Chicago, IL   60656
Tel: (708) 867-9600
Fax: (708) 867-9130

Samtec Inc.
810 Progress Boulevard
P.O. Box 1147
New Albany, IN   47151-1147
Tel: (812) 944-6733
Fax   (812) 948-5047

Texas Instruments Corp.
34 Forest Street, Mail Station 14-01
Attleboro, Mass   02073
Tel: (508) 699-5216

Yamaichi Electronics
1420 Koll Circle, Suite B
San Jose, CA   95112
Tel: (408) 452-0797

Component Socket Adapter Vendors

Emulation Technology, Inc.
2344 Walsh Avenue, Building F
Santa Clara, CA   95051
Tel: (408) 982-0660

California Integration Coordinators, Inc.
656 Main Street
Placerville, CA   95667
Tel: (916) 626-6168

Card Connector Vendors

AMP, Inc.
P.O. Box 3608
Harrisburg, PA   17105-3608
Tel: (800) 526-5105
Fax: (717) 986-7605

Amphenol
22952 Alcalde Drive
Suite 110
Laguna Hills, Ca. 92653
Tel: (714) 855-4454
Fax: (714) 855-9115

Berg Electronics
825 Old Trail Road
Etters, PA   17319-1769
Tel: (800) 237-2374

DDK
47873 Freemont Boulevard
Freemont, Ca. 94538
Tel: (415) 226-0400
Fax: (415) 226-0494

ELCO USA
Huntingdon Industrial Park
Huntingdon, PA 16652
Tel: (814) 643-0700
Fax: (814) 643-0426

Foxconn International
930 West Maude Avenue
Sunnyvale, Ca. 94086
Tel: (408) 749-1228
Fax: (408) 749-1266

Fujitsu Microelectronics, Inc.
3545 N. 1st St.
San Jose, CA 95134-1804
Tel: (800) 642-7616
Fax: (408) 428-0640

ITT Cannon
1851 E. Deere Ave.
Santa Ana, CA   92705
Tel: (714) 757-8337
Fax: (714) 757-8470

JAE Electronics
142 Technology Drive
Suite 100
Irvine, Ca. 9271
Tel: (800) 523-7278
Fax: (714) 753-2699

Maxell Corp. of America
22-08 Route 208
Fair Lawn, NJ 07410
Tel: (201) 794-8382
Fax: (201) 794-3274

Methode Electronics, Inc.
7444 W. Wilson Ave.
Chicago, IL   60656
Tel: (708) 867-9600
Fax: (708) 867-9130

Molex Inc.
2222 Wellington Court
Lisle, IL 60532
Tel: (708) 527-4522
Fax: (708) 969-1352

Pan International Inc.
9477 Archibald Ave.
Rancho Cucamonga, CA 91730
Tel: (909) 945-1365
Fax: (909) 989-9935

Stocko Connectors
P.O. Box 187
Carlstadt, New Jersey 07072
Tel: (201) 933-4452
Fax: (201) 933-4522

TelTec, Inc.
7890 12th Avenue South
Minneapolis, MN 55425
Tel: (612) 854-9177
Fax: (612) 854-8601

Appendix E: 12V Converters

The following list is a representative summary of flash memory 12V program/erase voltage converter manufacturers. Contact them directly for information on their products.

Linear Technology Corporation
1630 McCarthy Blvd.
Milpitas, CA 95035-7487
Tel: (408) 432-1900
Fax: (408) 432-0507

In Europe (U.K.):
111 Windmill Road
Sunbury
Middlesex TW16 7EF
U.K.
Tel: (44)(932) 765688
Fax: (44)(932) 781936

In Asia (Japan):
4F Ichihashi Bldg
1-8-4 Kudankita Chiyoda-ku
Tokyo 102 Japan
Tel: (81)(03) 32377891
Fax: (81)(03) 32378010

Maxim Integrated Products
120 San Gabriel Drive
Sunnyvale, CA 94086
Tel: (408) 737-7600
Fax: (408) 737-7194

In Europe (U.K.):
Maxim Integrated Products (UK), Ltd.
Tel: (44)(734) 845255

In Asia (Japan):
Maxim Japan Co., Ltd.
Tel: 81(03) 32326141

MicroLinear Corp.
2092 Concourse Drive
San Jose, CA   95131
Tel: (408) 433-5200
Fax: (408) 432-0295

Motorola Semiconductor Inc.
616 West 24th Street
Tempe, AZ 85282
Tel: (800) 521-6274

In Europe (U.K.):
Tel: (44)(296) 395252

In Asia (Japan):
Tel: (81)(3) 4403311

National Semiconductor Inc.
2900 Semiconductor Drive
P.O. Box 58090
Santa Clara, CA 95052
Tel: (408) 721-5000

In Europe:
National Semiconductor (UK) Ltd.
The Maple, Kembrey Park
Swindon, Wiltshire SN26UT
U.K.
Tel: (07-93) 614141
Fax: (07-93) 697522

In Asia:
National Semiconductor Japan Ltd
Sanseido Bldg. 5F
4-15 Nishi Shinjuku
Shinjuku-ku
Tokyo 160 Japan
Tel: (81)(3) 2997001
Fax: (81)(3) 2997000

Newport Components/Intl Power
International Power Sources
200 Butterfield Drive
Ashland, MA 01721
Tel: (508) 8817434
Fax: (508) 8798669

In Europe:
Newport Components
4 Tanners Drive
Blakelands North
Milton Keynes MK14 5NA
Tel: (0908) 615232
Fax: (0908) 617545

Power Trends, Inc.
1101 N. Raddant Road
Batavia, IL 60510
Tel: (708) 406-0900
Fax: (708) 406-0901

Shindengen Electric Co. LTD.
2649 Townsgate Road #200
Westlake Village, CA 91361
Tel: (800) 634-3654
Fax: (805) 373-3710

In Europe:
Shindengen Magnaquest U.K. Ltd.
Unit 13, River Road,
Barking Business Park,
33 River Road, Barking,
Essex 1G11 ODA
Tel: (44)(81) 5918703
Fax: (44)(81) 5918792

In Asia:
2-1,2-Chome Ohtemachi
Chiyoda-ku
Tokyo 100
Japan
Tel: (81)(3) 2794431
Fax: (81)(3) 2796478

Valor Electronics, Inc.
9715 Business Park Avenue
San Diego, CA   92131-1642
Tel: (619) 537-2500
Fax: (619) 537-2525

Xentek Inc.
760 Shadowridge Drive
Vista, CA 92083
Tel: (619) 727-0940
Fax: (619) 727-8926

In Europe (Germany):
Xentek, Inc.
C/O Taiyo Yuden GMBH.
Obermaierstrasse 10,
D-8500 Nurnberg 10
Federal Republic of Germany
Tel: (49)(911) 3508400
Fax: (49)(911) 3508460

In Asia (Japan):
Xentek, Inc,
C/O Taiyo Yuden., Ltd.
6-16-20, Ueno, Taito-ku
Tokyo 110
Japan
Tel: (81)(3) 38376547
Fax: (81)(3) 38354752

Appendix F: Flash Memory Card Readers and Writers

The following is a representative list of flash memory card reader/writers and vendors. The table is the result of a survey and should serve mainly as a guide for product features and capabilities. Contact the vendors directly for up to date information on their products.

Adtron Corp.
3050 South Country Club Dr.
Suite 24
Mesa, AZ 85210
Tel: (602) 926-9324
Fax: (602) 926-9359

Altec Computer Systeme GMBH
Vahrenwalder Str 20517
3000 Hannover, Germany
Tel: 49(577) 63088-36
Fax: 49(577) 63088-49

Computer Modules, Inc.
2350 A Walsh Ave,
Santa Clara, CA 95051
Tel: (408) 496-1881
Fax: (408) 496-1886

Data I/O Corp
10525 Willows Rd. NE.
Redmond, WA 98052
Tel: (206) 867-6886
Fax: (206) 881-6856

Databook Inc.
Tower Bldg. Terrace Hill
Ithaca, NY 14850
Tel: (607) 277-4817
Fax: (607) 273-8803

DIP Systems Ltd.
32 Frederick Sanger Rd.
Surrey Research Park
Guildford
Surrey GU2 5XN, UK
Tel: 44(0) 483-301555
Fax: 44(0) 483-301434

Elan Systems, Inc.
365-700 Woodview Ave.
Morgan Hill, CA 95037
Tel: (408) 778-7267
Fax: (408) 778-2597

FDK America, Inc.
3099 N. First St.
San Jose, CA 95134
Tel: (408) 456-7975

Greystone Peripherals, Inc.
130-A Knowles Dr.
Los Gatos, CA 95030
Tel: (408) 866-4739
Fax: (408) 866-8328

MSD3
365 Woodview Ave, #700
Morgan Hill, CA 95037
Tel: (408) 778-7267

Rhombus Technology, LTD.
The Common, Cranleigh
Surrey, GU6 8LU, UK
Tel: 44(483) 277916

SCM Microsystems
Fraunhoferstr. 11A
D-8033, Martinsried, Germany
Tel: 49(89) 8598702
Fax: 49(89) 8595806

Stag Microsystems, Inc.
1600 Wyatt Dr.
Santa Clara, CA 95054
Tel: (408) 988-1118
Fax: (408) 988-1232

Vendor/Model	PCMC Releas	ExCA Compati	Type of Inter Chip	File System Support		Hex/Binary Programming			
				Flash Optimiz	Disk Emulat	Binary Image Generat	Binary Image Copyin	Data Edito	PCMC Tuple Editor
ADTRON SDD-R-PCC	2.0	No	Xilinx	No	Yes	Yes	Yes	Yes	No
ADTRON SDD-L-PCC	2.0	No	Xilinx	No	Yes	Yes	Yes	Yes	No
ADTRON SDD-B-PCC	2.0	No	Xilinx	No	Yes	Yes	Yes	Yes	No
ADTRON SDD-P-PCC	2.0	Yes	Cirrus Logic 3120	No	Yes	Yes	Yes	Yes	No
ADTRON SDD-C-PCC	2.0	Yes	Cirrus Logic 3120	No	Yes	Yes	Yes	Yes	No
Altec MCD3-IDE	1.0	No	Intel PLD 5C180	No	Yes	Yes	Yes	Yes	Yes
Altec MCD3-P	1.0	No	Intel PLD 5C180	No	Yes	Yes	Yes	Yes	Yes
Altec MCD3-S	1.0	No	Intel PLD 5C180	No	Yes	Yes	Yes	Yes	Yes
Data I/O Cardpro	2.0	No	Xilinx	Yes	Yes	Yes	Yes	No	No
Databook TMB-200-03	2.0	No	Prop. Logic	Yes	Yes	Yes	Yes	No	No
Databook TMD-550	2.0	No	MB86301	Yes	Yes	Yes	Yes	No	No
Databook TM-140	2.0	Note 1	DB86082	Yes	Yes	Yes	Yes	No	No
Elan J101	2.0/2.01	Yes	i82365SL	No	Yes	Yes	Yes	Yes	Yes
Elan J102	2.0/2.01	Yes	i82365SL	No	Yes	Yes	Yes	Yes	Yes
MSD3 ICCP	2.0/2.01	Yes	DB86082	No	Yes	Yes	Yes	Yes	Yes
MSD3 ICPV	2.0/2.01	Yes	DB86082	No	Yes	Yes	Yes	Yes	Yes
MSD3 SCSI	2.0/2.01	No	Proprietary	No	Yes	Yes	Yes	Yes	Yes
SCMMCD2	1.0	No	Proprietary	No	Yes	Yes	Yes	Yes	No
SCMMCD2-B	1.0	No	Proprietary	No	Yes	Yes	Yes	Yes	No
SCMMCD2-BFD	1.0	No	Proprietary	No	Yes	Yes	Yes	Yes	No
SCMMCD2-IDE	1.0	No	Proprietary	No	Yes	Yes	Yes	Yes	No
SCMEMCD-P	1.0	No	Proprietary	No	Yes	Yes	Yes	Yes	No
SCMEMCD-SR	1.0	No	Proprietary	No	Yes	Yes	Yes	Yes	No
SCMMCD-F	2.0	Yes	i82365SL	No	Yes	Yes	Yes	Yes	No
SCMMCD-FD	2.0	Yes	i82365SL	No	Yes	Yes	Yes	Yes	No
SCMMCD-S	2.0	Yes	i82365SL	No	Yes	Yes	Yes	Yes	No
SCMMCD-SD	2.0	Yes	i82365SL	No	Yes	Yes	Yes	Yes	No
SCMMCD-V	2.0	Yes	Vadem VG465	No	Yes	Yes	Yes	Yes	No

Vendor/Model	Number of Sockets	External Interface	Internal Interface	Error Detection/ Correction Method	User Indication		System Detection		Hot Insertion Removal	Boot Capability
					Write Protect	Card Busy	Card Detect	Card Change		
ADTRON SDD-R-PCC	1	Serial		16-Bit CRC Transfer	Yes	Yes	Yes	Yes	Yes	w/ext. BIOS
ADTRON SDD-L-PCC	1	Parallel		16-Bit CRC Transfer	Yes	Yes	Yes	Yes	Yes	w/ext. BIOS
ADTRON SDD-B-PCC	1		8-bit ISA	16-Bit CRC Transfer	Yes	Yes	Yes	Yes	Yes	w/ext. BIOS
ADTRON SDD-P-PCC	1		PC-104	16-Bit CRC Transfer	Yes	Yes	Yes	Yes	Yes	w/ext. BIOS
ADTRON SDD-C-PCC	2		16-bit ISA	16-Bit CRC Transfer	Yes	Yes	Yes	Yes	Yes	w/ext. BIOS
Altec MCD3-IDE	1		IDE	Altec's Pre-Image	S/W	Yes	Yes	Yes	Yes	No
Altec MCD3-P	1	Parallel		Altec's Pre-Image	S/W	Yes	Yes	Yes	Yes	No
Altec MCD3-S	1	Serial		Altec's Pre-Image	S/W	Yes	Yes	Yes	Yes	No
Data I/O Cardpro	1	Parallel		None	No	Yes	Yes	Yes	Yes	No
Databook TMB-200-03	1		8-bit ISA	SW CRC & Checksum	Yes	Yes	Yes	Yes	Yes	No
Databook TMD-550	1	Parallel		HW CRC & Checksum	Yes	Yes	Yes	Yes	Yes	No
Databook TMI-140	2		16-bit ISA	HW CRC & Checksum	Yes	Yes	Yes	Yes	Yes	Yes
Elan J101	1		8/16-bit ISA	Software CRC	No	Yes	Yes	Yes	Yes	No
Elan J102	1		8/16-bit ISA	Software CRC	No	Yes	Yes	Yes	Yes	No
MSD3 ICOP	2		16-bit ISA	HW CRC & Checksum	Yes	Yes	Yes	Yes	Yes	No
MSD3 ICFV	2		16-bit ISA	HW CRC & Checksum	Yes	Yes	Yes	Yes	Yes	No
MSD3 SCSI	2		8/16-bit ISA	HW CRC	Yes	Yes	Yes	Yes	Yes	Yes
SCM MCD2	1		8/16-bit ISA	n/a	Yes	Yes	No	No	No	No
SCM MCD2-B	1		8/16-bit ISA	n/a	Yes	Yes	No	No	No	Yes
SCM MCD2-BFD	2		8/16-bit ISA	n/a	Yes	Yes	No	No	No	Yes
SCM MCD2-IDE	1		8/16-bit ISA	n/a	Yes	Yes	No	No	No	No
SCM EMCD-P	1	Parallel		n/a	Yes	Yes	No	No	No	No
SCM EMCD-SR	1	Serial		n/a	Yes	Yes	No	No	No	No
SCM MMCD-F	2		16-bit ISA	n/a	Yes	Yes	Yes	Yes	Yes	No
SCM MMCD-FD	2		16-bit ISA	n/a	Yes	Yes	Yes	Yes	Yes	Yes
SCM MMCD-S	3		16-bit ISA	n/a	Yes	Yes	Yes	Yes	Yes	No
SCM MMCD-SD	3		16-bit ISA	n/a	Yes	Yes	Yes	Yes	Yes	Yes
SCM MMCD-V	1		16-bit ISA	n/a	Yes	Yes	Yes	Yes	Yes	Yes

Appendix G: Flash File Systems

The following list is a representative summary of flash memory file system vendors. Contact them directly for information on their products.

Datalight
307 N. Olympic
Suite 201
Arlington, WA 98223
Tel: (800) 221-6630
(Disk Emulator)

M-Systems
200 Broadhollow Rd., Suite 207
Melville, NY 11747
Tel: (516) 424-5100
(Disk Emulator)

Microsoft Corp.
One Microsoft Way
Redmond, WA 98052-6399
Tel: 206-936-3109
(Flash Optimized File System)

Saville Associates
4425 Esta Lane
Soquel, CA 95073
Tel: (408) 479-7199
(Flash Optimized File System)

SCM Microsystem
Fraunhoferstr. 11A
82 152 Martinsried, Germany
Tel: 49-89-859-8702
Fax: 49-89-859-5806
(Disk Emulator)

Appendix H: PCMCIA and Software Vendors

The following list is a representative summary of PCMCIA software vendors. Contact them directly for information on their products.

Award Software Inc.
130 Knowles Drive
Los Gatos, CA 95030
Tel: (408) 370-7979
Fax: Tel: (408) 370-3399

DIP Research Ltd.
2 Frederick Sanger Rd.
Surrey Research Park
Guildford, Surrey, Gu2 5XN,
England UK
Tel: 44-04-8330-1555
Fax   44-04-8330-1434

PCMCIA
10309 E. Duane Ave.
Sunnyvale, CA 94086
Tel: (408) 720-0107

Phoenix Technologies Ltd.
40 Airport Pkwy.
San Jose, CA 95110
Tel: (408) 452-6833
Fax: (408) 452-1985

SystemSoft Corp.
313 Speen Street
Natick, MA 01760
Tel: (508) 651-0088
Fax: (508) 651-8188

Vadem
1885 Lundy Avenue, #201
San Jose, CA 95131
Tel: (408) 943-9301
Fax: (408) 943-9735

Ventura Micro, Inc.
200 South A Street
Suite 208
Oxnard, CA 93030-5717
Tel: (408) 476-1910
Fax: (408) 476-4563

Appendix I: PCMCIA Compliance Testing Facilities

Ingram
1600 E. St. Andrew Place
Santa Ana, CA 92799
Tel: (714) 566-1000

Synova Systems
1977 Otoble Ave., Suite B-207
San Jose, CA 95131
Tel: (408) 428-0310
Fax: (408) 436-0379
(This company develops tools for
PCMCIA products)

Veritest Inc.
3420 Ocean Park Blvd.
Suite 2030
Santa Monica, CA 90405
Tel: (310) 450-0062
Fax: (310) 399-1760

Appendix J: PCMCIA Card Types

(With approximate card dimensions)

	LENGTH (mm)	WIDTH (mm)	HEIGHT (mm)
TYPE 1	85.6	54.0	3.3
TYPE 2	85.6	54.0	5.0
TYPE3	85.6	54.0	10.5

Appendix K: PCMCIA Controller Register Functions and Vendors

The following tables demonstrate the compatibility between three leading PCMCIA-Interface controller chips and provide a summarized format that will help in your programming efforts. Consult the corresponding data sheets for more information.

Registers Supported by Intel's 82365SL, Cirrus Logic's CL-PD67XX and Vadem's VG-465		
REGISTER NAME and CATEGORY	FUNCTION	SOCKET OFFSET (A/B)
GENERAL SETUP REGISTERS		
Identification and Revision	Determines type of PC cards supported and identifies PCIC version.	00H/40H
Interface Status	Provides current status of PC card interface signals	01H/41H
Power and Resetdrv Control	Controls the PC card power and resetting of the PCIC registers	02H/42H
Card Status Change	Contains the status of the sources for the card status change interrupts	04H/44H
Address Window Enable	Controls enabling of memory and I/O mapping windows to PC card memory or I/O space	06H/46H
INTERRUPT REGISTERS		
Interrupt and General Control	Controls the interrupt steering for the PC card I/O interrupt as well as general control of the PCIC	03H/43H
Card Status Change Interrupt Configuration	Controls interrupt steering of the card status change interrupt and card status change interrupt enables	05H/45H

I/O REGISTERS		
I/O Control	Contains the I/O configuration for I/O windows 0 and 1 based upon information read from the card's CIS	07H/47H
I/O Addr. 0 Start Low Byte	Low order address bits indicating start address of I/O address window 0	08H/48H
I/O Addr. 0 Start High Byte	High order address bits indicating start address of I/O address window 0	09H/49H
I/O Addr. 0 Stop Low Byte	Low order address bits indicating stop address of I/O address window 0	0AH/4AH
I/O Addr. 0 Stop High Byte	High order address bits indicating stop address of I/O address window 0	0BH/4BH
I/O Addr. 1 Start Low Byte	Low order address bits indicating start address of I/O address window 1	0CH/4CH
I/O Addr. 1 Start High Byte	High order address bits indicating start address of I/O address window 1	0DH/4DH
I/O Addr. 1 Stop Low Byte	Low order address bits indicating stop address of I/O address window 1	0EH/4EH
I/O Addr. 1 Stop High Byte	High order address bits indicating stop address of I/O address window 1	0FH/4FH
MEMORY REGISTERS		
System Memory Addr. 0 Mapping Start Low Byte	Low order address bits indicating start address of corresponding system memory address mapping window	10H/50H
System Memory Addr. 0 Mapping Start High Byte	High order address bits indicating start address of corresponding system memory address mapping window	11H/51H
System Memory Addr. 0 Mapping Stop Low Byte	Low order address bits indicating stop address of corresponding system memory address mapping window	12H/52H
System Memory Addr. 0 Mapping Stop High Byte	High order address bits indicating stop address of corresponding system memory address mapping window	13H/53H
Card Memory Offset Addr. 0 Low Byte	Low order address bits added to system address bits A19-A12 to generate memory address for PC card	14H/54H
Card Memory Offset Addr. 0 High Byte	High order address bits added to system address bits A23-A20 to generate memory address for PC card	15H/55H
System Memory Addr. 1 Mapping Start Low Byte	Low order address bits indicating start address of corresponding system memory address mapping window	18H/58H
System Memory Addr. 1 Mapping Start High Byte	High order address bits indicating start address of corresponding system memory address mapping window	19H/59H
System Memory Addr. 1 Mapping Stop Low Byte	Low order address bits indicating stop address of corresponding system memory address mapping window	1AH/5AH

System Memory Addr. 1 Mapping Stop High Byte	High order address bits indicating stop address of corresponding system memory address mapping window	1BH/5BH
Card Memory Offset Addr. 1 Low Byte	Low order address bits added to system address bits A19-A12 to generate memory address for PC card	1CH/5CH
Card Memory Offset Addr. 1 High Byte	High order address bits added to system address bits A23-A20 to generate memory address for PC card	1DH/5DH
System Memory Addr. 2 Mapping Start Low Byte	Low order address bits indicating start address of corresponding system memory address mapping window	20H/60H
System Memory Addr. 2 Mapping Start High Byte	High order address bits indicating start address of corresponding system memory address mapping window	21H/61H
System Memory Addr. 2 Mapping Stop Low Byte	Low order address bits indicating stop address of corresponding system memory address mapping window	22H/62H
System Memory Addr. 2 Mapping Stop High Byte	High order address bits indicating stop address of corresponding system memory address mapping window	23H/63H
Card Memory Offset Addr. 2 Low Byte	Low order address bits added to system address bits A19-A12 to generate memory address for PC card	24H/64H
Card Memory Offset Addr. 2 High Byte	High order address bits added to system address bits A23-A20 to generate memory address for PC card	25H/65H
System Memory Addr. 3 Mapping Start Low Byte	Low order address bits indicating start address of corresponding system memory address mapping window	28H/68H
System Memory Addr. 3 Mapping Start High Byte	High order address bits indicating start address of corresponding system memory address mapping window	29H/69H
System Memory Addr. 3 Mapping Stop Low Byte	Low order address bits indicating stop address of corresponding system memory address mapping window	2AH/6AH
System Memory Addr. 3 Mapping Stop High Byte	High order address bits indicating stop address of corresponding system memory address mapping window	2BH/6BH
Card Memory Offset Addr. 3 Low Byte	Low order address bits added to system address bits A19-A12 to generate memory address for PC card	2CH/6CH
Card Memory Offset Addr. 3 High Byte	High order address bits added to system address bits A23-A20 to generate memory address for PC card	2DH/6DH
System Memory Addr. 4 Mapping Start Low Byte	Low order address bits indicating start address of corresponding system memory address mapping window	30H/70H
System Memory Addr. 4 Mapping Start High Byte	High order address bits indicating start address of corresponding system memory address mapping window	31H/71H

System Memory Addr. 4 Mapping Stop Low Byte	Low order address bits indicating stop address of corresponding system memory address mapping window	32H/72H
System Memory Addr. 4 Mapping Stop High Byte	High order address bits indicating stop address of corresponding system memory address mapping window	33H/73H
Card Memory Offset Addr. 4 Low Byte	Low order address bits added to system address bits A19-A12 to generate memory address for PC card	34H/74H
Card Memory Offset Addr. 4 High Byte	High order address bits added to system address bits A23-A20 to generate memory address for PC card	35H/75H

Additional Registers Supported by Çirrus Logic's CL-PD67XX		
REGISTER NAME and CATEGORY	FUNCTION	SOCKET OFFSET
EXTENSION REGISTERS		
Misc Control 1	V_{CC} control and status, IRQ function, speaker enable	16H
FIFO Control	Controls FIFO operation and reports FIFO status	17H
Misc Control 2	Controls clock freq, controls LED, IRQ15 control	1EH
Chip Information	Identifies controller revision and identification	1FH
ATA Control	ATA mode select, speaker or LED input select	26H
TIMING REGISTERS		
Setup Timing 0	Controls setup timing for addresses and control signals before asserting read or write signals	3AH
Command Timing 0	Indicates length of read or write control signals	3BH
Recovery TIming 0	Indicates amount of hold time given to card for addresses and control before deasserting read or write signals	3CH
Setup Timing 1	Controls setup timing for addresses and control signals before asserting read or write signals	3DH
Command Timing 1	Indicates length of read or write control signals	3EH
Recovery TIming 1	Indicates amount of hold time given to card for addresses and control before deasserting read or write signals	3FH

Additional Registers Supported by Vadem's VG-465		
REGISTER NAME and CATEGORY	**FUNCTION**	**SOCKET OFFSET**
Control	Controls compatibility, enables INPACK, selects IREQ level, enables PCMCIA interface, controls memory timing	38H
Timer	Controls activity timer	39H
Mouse	Enables mouse interface, mouse I/O ports and interrupt levels	3AH
GPIO Configuration	Controls 3 GPIO lines	3BH
Programmable Chip Select	Selects base address for programmable chip select output.	3CH/3DH
Programmable Chip Select Configuration	Controls the programmable chip select functions	3EH
ATA	Sets up configuration for ATA drive.	3FH

The following list is a representative summary of the manufacturers of PCMCIA-interface controller chips. Due to the rapid change in product line items, it is best to contact these companies directly for product-specific information.

Cirrus Logic, Inc.
3100 W. Warren Ave,
Fremont, CA 94538
Tel: (510) 623-8300

Databook Inc.
Tower Bldg. Terrace Hill
Ithaca, NY 14850
Tel: (607) 277-4817
Fax: (607) 273-8803

Intel Corp.
Literature Center
Box 7641
Mt. Prospect, IL   60056
(800) 548-4725

Texas Instruments Inc.
Box 172228
Denver, CO   80217
(800) 477-8924

Vadem
1885 Lundy Ave., #210
San Jose, CA 95131
Tel: (408) 943-9301

Appendix L: INT 21H Standard Disk-Related Functions

The functions listed below are mainly for pointing out the flexibility of a flash file system using the redirector interface that operates through the INT21H functions.

Function Number	Function Name	Usage
3CH	Create Handle	Creates file for subsequent I/O; erases existing file, if any
3DH	Open Handle	Readies file for I/O; assigns handle number
3EH	Close Handle	Closes handle; frees handle pointer
3FH	Read Handle	Reads from file at current pointer location
40H	Write Handle	Writes to file at current pointer location
41H	Delete Handle	Deletes file
42H	Move File Pointer	Moves location of pointer in file
43H	Get/Set File Attributes	Changes or retrieves attribute byte for file
45H	Duplicate File Handle	Assigns additional handle number to existing handle
46H	Force Duplicate File Handle	Forces existing handle to refer to file that has a different handle
56H	Rename File	Renames file
57H	Get/Set File Date/Time	Changes or retrieves last update time and date associated with file
5AH	Create Temporary File	Creates file with unique name for subsequent I/O
5BH	Create New File	Creates file for subsequent I/O only if it does not already exist
67H	Set Handle Count	Allows the specification of more than 20 handles
68H	Commit File	Insures file is written to disk

Appendix M: Sample Flash File System Benchmarking Code

```
/********************************************************
         Program:        Snip
*********************************************************/
#include <stdio.h>
#include <alloc.h>
#include <stdlib.h>

long                    time_start=0;
long                    time_finish=0;
long            far *the_time;
long                    i_ctr;
long                    repeat;
float long              total_time;

FILE                    *log;                   // logfile structure

void main(void)

        {
        void start_time(void);
        void stop_time(void);

        char            *c_buff;                // temporary input buffer

        c_buff          =       (char *)malloc(15);// and allocate memory

        the_time=       (long far *)0x046C;     // read BIOS timer chip

        system("cls");
```

```
        printf("\nThis program copies files from one drive to another. Timing is
                kept in c:log.out.");
        printf("\nThis may take some time...");
        printf("\nJust hit ctrl-C to stop me anytime.\n");
        printf("\nHow many times to go through the run?.\n");
        gets(c_buff);

        repeat=atol(c_buff);                    // convert input string to
                                                // a number


        if ((log=fopen("c:\\log.out","a+"))==NULL) // open log file and
                                                         // exit on errors
                {
                printf("\nBad log file");
                exit(0);
                }

        fprintf(log,"\n\n*** Recorded Times ***");

        for (i_ctr=0; i_ctr < repeat; i_ctr++)
                {
                start_time();
                system("copy file0.dat e:");
                system("copy file1.dat e:");            //Or use
                system("copy e:\\file0.dat");           //any system
                system("copy e:\\file0.dat");           //commands
                system("copy e:\\file0.dat");           //you want
                system("copy e:\\file0.dat");           //to plug
                system("copy file2.dat e:");            //in here.
                system("copy file3.dat e:");
                stop_time();
                }
                fclose(log);                            // close file on exit
        }

void start_time(void)
        {
        time_start=*the_time;
        }
```

```
void stop_time(void)
    {
    time_finish=*the_time;
    if ((time_finish-time_start)>0)
            {
            total_time = float((time_finish-time_start)/18.2);
            fprintf(log,"\n%ld)Time = %.4lf seconds.", i_ctr, total_time);
            printf("\n%ld)Total Time = %.4lf seconds.\n", i_ctr,
            total_time);
            }
    }
```

Index

You are welcome to send us comments or questions concerning this or
other Annabooks products, or to request a catalog of our
products and seminars.

Annabooks
11848 Bernardo Center Drive, Suite 110
San Diego, CA 92128

616-673-0870

1-800-462-1042

616-673-1432 FAX